Leviathans

Leviathans represents a path-breaking effort to look a. ....ational corporations in the round, emphasizing especially their scope, history, development, culture and social implications, and governance problems. Following the first chapter, a primer on MNCs, the book consists of eight chapters devoted to a variety of aspects, including global elites. The overall perspective is provided by the New Global History initiative described in the Introduction. This approach compels us to recognize that the MNCs are not merely economic entities but part of a complex interplay of factors. In turn, our study of MNCs forces us to rethink our views on the globalization process.

Alfred D. Chandler, Jr., is Isidor Straus Professor of Business History Emeritus at Harvard Business School. He is internationally renowned as one of the most promient and influential contemporary business historians. His major works, *Strategy and Structure* (1962), *The Visible Hand* (1977), and *Scale and Scope* (1990), have won many awards, including the Pulitzer and Bancroft prizes. He is also coeditor with Franco Amatori and Takashi Hikino of *Big Business and the Wealth of Nations* (Cambridge 1997).

Bruce Mazlish is Professor of History Emeritus at the Massachusetts Institute of Technology. His publications include *The Uncertain Sciences* (1998), *The Fourth Discontinuity: The Co-Evolution of Humans and Machines* (1993), *A New Science: The Breakdown of Connections and the Birth of Sociology* (1989), and *Conceptualizing Global History* (1993), which he coedited with Ralph Buultjens. He has also written numerous articles on globalization.

Chandler's major books *Strategy and Structure* (1962), *The Visible Hand* (1997), and *Scale and Scope* (1990) all received the Newcomen book award in Business History. In addition, the *Visible Hand* was awarded the Pulitzer and Bancroft prizes, and *Scale and Scope* received two awards. With coauthor Steve Salisbury, he wrote *Pierre S. Du Pont and the Making of the Modern Corporation* (1970), and with coeditors he published other works, including *Managerial Hierarchies* (1980), *The Coming of Managerial Capitalism* (1985), *Big Business and the Wealth of Nations* (1997), and *A Nation Transformed by Information* (2000).

Mazlish's publications include *The Uncertain Sciences* (1998); *The Fourth Discontinuity: The Co-Evolution of Humans and Machines* (1993), which was awarded the National University Press Book Prize of 1994; *A New Science: The Breakdown of Connections and the Birth of Sociology* (1989); and *Conceptualizing Global History*, which he coedited with Ralph Buultjens (1993). In addition, he has written numerous articles on globalization.

Leviathans

MULTINATIONAL CORPORATIONS AND THE NEW GLOBAL HISTORY

Edited by

ALFRED D. CHANDLER, JR.

Harvard University

BRUCE MAZLISH

Massachusetts Institute of Technology

CAMBRIDGE UNIVERSITY PRESS
Cambridge, New York, Melbourne, Madrid, Cape Town, Singapore, São Paulo

Cambridge University Press
32 Avenue of the Americas, New York, NY 10013-2473, USA
www.cambridge.org
Information on this title: www.cambridge.org/9780571840613

© Cambridge University Press 2005

First published 2005
Reprinted 2006

Printed in the United States of America

A catalog record for this publication is available from the British Library.

Library of Congress Cataloging in Publication Data

Leviathans : multinational corporations and the new global history / edited by
Alfred D. Chandler, Jr., Bruce Mazlish.
p.   cm.
Includes bibliographical references and index.
ISBN 0-521-84061-9 (hbk.) – ISBN 0-521-54993-0 (pbk.)
1. International business enterprises.   2. Globalization–Economic aspects.
I. Chandler, Alfred Dupont.   II. Mazlish, Bruce, 1923–
HD2755.5.L484   2004
338.8′8 – dc22   2004048881

ISBN-13 978-0-521-84061-3 hardback
ISBN-10 0-521-84061-9 hardback

ISBN-13 978-0-521-54993-6 paperback
ISBN-10 0-521-54993-0 paperback

Contents

List of Figures and Tables

Acknowledgments

Bringing a book of this kind to publication is a major task involving many hands. We can only acknowledge a few by name here but wish to thank as well all those who remain unnamed. The book itself, *Leviathans*, is a product of the Mapping the Multinational Corporations project, which, in turn, is part of the New Global History (NGH) initiative, whose other product was *Global Inc. An Historical Atlas of the Multinational Corporations* (New Press, 2003). Although each work is free-standing, *Leviathans* serves as the intellectual framework for the mapping aspect of the project. As such it is an entirely separate publication, making its own independent contribution to our understanding of the multinational corporations that form so major a part of the present-day globalization process.

Neither publication could have come into existence without the financial and moral support of the Ford Foundation and the Rockefeller Brothers Foundation. Lance Lindblom, who was program officer at Ford (he is now President of the Nathan Cummings Foundation), not only oversaw the grant and gained the support of the President, Susan Beresford, but participated in the entire planning of the project. Colin Campbell, President of the RBF at the time (he is now the head of the Williamsburg Foundation), has been a believer in the NGH initiative since its beginnings and a source of constant strength. Would that all foundations were headed by such far-seeing and capable individuals!

Although we are responsible for the contents of this book and for the editorial decisions, Jeannette Hopkins was of incalculable assistance in the actual editing of the volume, aided by India Tresselt. In its final stages, the book reflects the work of Kenneth Weisbrode; without his calm and steady editing of the final version, the book would not be in your hands.

Among those who contributed to the thinking behind *Leviathans*, we wish to give special thanks to John H. Dunning and John Stopford.

At Cambridge University Press, it was Frank Smith who saw the importance of the book and supported it through all the stages of its publication. He made several informed and carefully explained suggestions, which have made this a far better book than when it was first submitted to him. By rights he should be listed as one of the coeditors. Instead, he will have to settle for our profound thanks.

Alfred Chandler and Bruce Mazlish

Contributors

Alfred Chandler is Isidor Straus Professor Emeritus of Business History, Harvard Business School.

Bruce Mazlish is Professor Emeritus of History at MIT.

Neva Goodwin is Codirector, Institute for Global Development and Environment (GDAE), Tufts University.

Geoffrey Jones is Professor of Business Administration at the Harvard Business School.

Stephen J. Kobrin is William H. Wurster Professor of Multinational Management at The Wharton School, University of Pennsylvania.

Sara McKinney is Senior Consultant, Roberts Research Group, in Australia.

Robert A. G. Monks is the founder of the Institutional Shareholder Services and of the investment fund LENS.

Elliott R. Morss is the President of the Asia Pacific Group.

Brian Roach is a Senior Researcher at the Institute for Global Development and Environment (GDAE), Tufts University.

Sei Yonekura is Professor at the Institute of Innovation Research, Hitotsubashi University, Japan.

Mira Wilkins is Professor in the Department of Economics, Florida International University.

Zhu Jia-Ming is a principal in the Asia Pacific Group.

Introduction

ALFRED CHANDLER AND BRUCE MAZLISH

This book and the project of which it is part were inspired by a United Nations statement a few years ago that of the 100 entities with the largest gross national product (GNP), about half were multinational corporations (MNCs). This meant that by this measure these big MNCs were larger and wealthier than about 120 to 130 nation-states.[1] They still are. An atlas depicts continents and nation-states, their boundaries, their leading features, geographies, and geological characteristics such as mountains, rivers, and so forth. The MNCs do not exist on traditional maps. Convinced that these new Leviathans must be acknowledged, identified, and located, we produced *Global Inc.*, an historical atlas that shows their outreach.[2] This book, which is the atlas's conceptual counterpart, seeks to make MNCs more visible and more understandable to the mind's eye.

Thomas Hobbes' seventeenth-century book *Leviathan* tried to provide a metaphoric analysis of the notion of a commonwealth or state. The model he used to conceive his new body politic, its "Matter, Forme and Power," was the automaton – an artificial creation, representing a physical body and a human mind and soul. Thus, he spoke of sovereignty as "an artificial *soul*," and magistrates as "artificial *joints.*" In short, the state was the product of art – that is, artifice. Hobbes co-opted the term "leviathan" from a biblical allusion. Webster's *New Collegiate Dictionary* defines "leviathan" as, alternatively, a great sea monster (adversary of Yahweh); a large ocean-going ship; a vast bureaucracy; or something "large or formidable." In Psalm 74:14, Leviathan

---

1. The figures given are, in fact, based on revenue rather than value added, that is, how GDP is measured. Thus, the role of MNCs is actually exaggerated. Yet the general point about the growing power of MNCs relative to the nation-states is correctly symbolized in the U.N. statement.
2. Medard Gabel and Henry Bruner, *Global Inc.: An Atlas of the Multinational Corporation* (New York: The New Press, 2003).

1

is a name of a dragon subdued by Yahweh, who crushed its head and fed him to wild animals when the creation began.

Today, a new kind of Leviathan has risen from the depths of humanity's creative powers – the multinational corporation. In its embryonic state, it is found in multinational enterprises (MNEs), the first wave of the modern global economy, which began in the 1880s in the wake of the Industrial Revolution and modern empires. It took mature shape in a second wave in the multinational corporations (MNCs) of the 1970s. Both in number and power, these multinational phenomena have made a qualitative change in our economic world by the time of the new millennium.

Unlike the nation-state, the new Leviathan makes no pretension to godly origin, though sometimes it seems to appeal to divine protection and legitimacy. Its corporate body is grounded in law, as is its "Matter, Forme and Power." It is recognized as artifact and generally treated as an artificial person. It is as much historical invention – innovation – as the communication and transportation systems on which it depends. It increasingly challenges the power of the nation-states and of regional entities.

When this project of mapping began in the 1990s, about 37,000 MNCs existed. As of 2002, there were around 63,000. Their power and effects are almost incalculable – not only to the economy but also to politics, society, culture, and values. Multinational corporations have an impact on almost every sphere of modern life from policymaking on the environment to international security, from issues of personal identity to issues of community, and from the future of work to the future of the nation-state and even of regional and international bodies and alliances.

New Global History attempts to analyze globalization both as an historical phenomenon and as an ongoing process. In the new "global epoch," many enterprises, not economies alone, transcend existing national boundaries in an intensive and extensive fashion albeit with deep roots in the past. Among such factors are humanity's step into space; the satellites circling the globe that provide almost instantaneous communications; the struggle against viruses, mutant genes, and nuclear and other pollutants that drift across national boundaries; environmental dangers that cross all local lines; the new concern with *human* rather than merely parochial, national, or tribal rights; and the growth of global culture that transcends traditional cultures. The spread of MNCs and their influence and activities are such a factor. All are marked by a synergy and synchronicity hitherto unknown.[3]

---

3. Cf. *Conceptualizing Global History*, ed. Bruce Mazlish and Ralph Buultjens (Boulder: Westview Press, 1993) – especially the Introduction.

Some scholars have sought to trace MNCs back more than 2,000 years. In an original and significant book, *Birth of the Multinational*, Karl Moore and David Lewis see multinational enterprises stretching as far back as Ashur, the religious capital of ancient Assyria, to the age of Augustus.[4] Still, the term "multinational" is an anachronism, for "nation" today has a far different meaning from Assyria or the Roman Empire. And even "corporation," a relatively recent term, is also grounded in continuing legal philosophy and practice. Although Moore and Lewis speak of multinational enterprises rather than of corporations (as do many other commentators on the subject), we believe that to do so ignores one of the key characteristics of the new Leviathans.

The multinational corporation does have a history, and the MNCs do change over time, as Mira Wilkins so convincingly shows in Chapter 2. Thus, she identifies a line stretching from the British and Dutch East India Companies of the 17th century to the leviathans of our own time. Keeping a sharp eye out for what is persistent and what is changing, we may see a general shift from trading companies to resource extraction, then to manufacturing, and then to service and financial service companies as the dominating types of MNCs – a shift both gradual and incorporative. The earlier forms do not disappear but continue as part of the economic scene.

What is a multinational corporation aside from its arising in a setting of nation-states and corporate law? One of the simplest definitions is that MNCs are firms that control income-generating assets in more than one country at a time. A more complicated definition would add that an MNC has productive facilities in several countries on at least two continents with employees stationed worldwide and financial investments scattered across the globe. Whether an MNC is privately owned or can also be publicly owned by a government, and whether its forms and practices can be either unique to its own nation or transnational are questions to be considered. The answers modify the definition.

By the simplest common denominator, the growth of the MNCs has been phenomenal. There has been increasing concentration at the top, marked by mergers and acquisitions, resulting in huge global corporations whose size (measured by value added) rivals that of many nation-states. However, of the *Fortune* 500 list in 1980, 33 percent no longer existed autonomously a decade later.[5] By 1995, another 40 percent were gone – a situation reminiscent of the post-Westphalian (i.e., after 1648) absorptions and disappearances

4. Karl Moore and David Lewis, *Birth of the Multinational: 2000 Years of Ancient Business History – From Ashur to Augustus* (Copenhagen: Copenhagen Business School Press, 1999).
5. See Chapter 8 in this volume.

of various states. In the perspective of New Global History, it may be possible to see certain constants in the emergence of MNCs, but also visible is constant change and perhaps a dynamic that may have a distinct direction.

The New Global History perspective compels us to recognize that the MNCs are not mere economic entities but part of a complex interplay of factors. The economic is not the whole of globalization, though some commentators seem to imply that it is. Thus, MNCs have a profound impact, intentional and unintentional, on the environment. Some MNCs are destructive of resources and of the general ecology of the planet. Yet they also alert us to global environmental crisis through the satellites circling overhead and reporting on the pollution and the depletion that transcend national boundaries, and some of these satellites are operated by the very MNCs that are part of the problem. MNCs and their executives, in practice and in principle, not only can cause but also can and sometimes do take steps to reduce the severity of these environmental problems.

For better or worse, consumerism is spread via the same satellites that operate on behalf of global multinationals; taste and trade are both promoted by the ubiquitous advertisements transmitted in all countries. World music, for example, is circulated by multinational media corporations. Whatever the sins of Microsoft, it makes possible, via the computer network, the mobilization of opinion worldwide, which then brings pressure on governments everywhere. In pharmaceuticals, too, MNCs play a multifaceted role; the producers of wonder drugs that heal are the same companies that often conspire to rig the market and constrain their use worldwide. Human rights' scope and power are dependent on the same communications links.

MNCs, therefore, embody contradictory impulses and play multiple roles, often producing results unintended by the actors themselves. MNCs, as with other factors of globalization, must be studied in a sustained empirical fashion, in an historical perspective, and with a constant effort to move back and forth between theory and data. We need better knowledge before we pass judgment on our new Leviathans.

We must ask, for example, whether increased globalization is inevitable: Does it result inexorably from the competitive nature of the MNCs with their werewolf appetite for profits (to quote Karl Marx on the nature of capitalism)? Thomas Friedman of the *New York Times* proclaims that those who suggest that globalization can be stopped – for example, by organized protesters in Seattle, Davos, or elsewhere – are wrong. Globalization, he tells us, is, indeed, "inevitable."[6] A respondent to Friedman denies that

6. Thomas Friedman, *New York Times*, February 2, 1997.

globalization is irresistible, sweeping all before it. He sees MNCs as a result of choices:

Multinational corporate executives are making conscious marketing and production decisions [such as Nike producing shoes in Vietnam in sweatshop conditions] to globalize their operations. They could only make their choices in a legal and regulatory framework that permits unimpeded capital mobility, maintains low tariffs and provides stable trading rules like those set by the World Trade Organization and the North American Free Trade Agreement.[7]

In trying to understand the MNCs' role in globalization, it seems useful to take account of the nature of business competition and also the fact that competition does not take place in a vacuum. Political and social conditions requisite for MNCs to operate as they do may provide a stable context and, at the same time, be subject to change – changes that, in turn, respond to the shifting play of culture as well as of forces like migration and technological innovation. Leviathans, though artificial constructs, take on a life of their own, but they are also subject to human decisions. This is so at the level of company decisions such as that of the Ford Motor Company and its policy of making its management global and of building a "world car." When that effort was unsuccessful, Ford reversed its policy. On a more complex level, market bubbles and protectionist policies might still undo much of present economic globalization as in the earlier decline in indicators of globalization that occurred between the worldwide Depression of the 1930s and the end of the Second World War.

Closely connected to the question of inevitability (its other face?) is predictability. Might globalization falter and go into reverse, as occurred in the period between the two world wars? An economic meltdown might occur – a failure of MNCs worldwide. Or might continuing economic success result in terrible global effects – environmental, for example – that could, in turn, precipitate a major collapse of political and social structures and even the possibility of effective governance?

Globalization as a process is nonetheless likely to continue even if there were to be a collapse in its economic underpinnings, for economic forces, especially in the shape of MNCs, are but one factor in globalization. We can speculate that the transcending of national boundaries in culture, political interventions, human rights movements, and so forth will continue even in the face of a weakening of the "material" base.

Our aim in this book is to consider the MNCs as they actually are, not to praise or blame. We need to look at the myths or propositions about them.

7. Letter to the Editor, *New York Times*, February 6, 1997.

We might inquire into the assertion that the nation-state itself is in the process of being displaced by the MNCs, losing its authority to those "more sovereign than the state." Arguing against this view, William Keller and Louis Pauly assert that "huge, sprawling commercial hierarchies are not replacing states as the world's effective government." Their argument goes further to what some scholars call the "myth of the global corporation." "The global corporation, adrift from its national political moorings and roaming an increasingly borderless world market, is a myth." They see that corporations are nation-state, not globally, based and reflect national cultures, national traditions, and national social structures – some more distinctly than others. German and Japanese firms, for example, possess a clearer sense of distinct national identity than American firms. So too, Keller and Pauly write, the European continental companies lean more toward national protectionism and against global free markets. Thus, Keller and Pauly conclude, "the 'global corporation' is mainly an American myth."[8] MNCs are not replacing the nation-state in terms of political power.

Without judging this contention before further empirical research, we can nonetheless inquire whether this is at the heart of the matter: Is the current process of globalization creating a sort of vacuum in which all kinds of market and currency movements are uncontrolled – neither by nation-states nor MNCs?[9]

Another proposition is that MNCs are not truly global. Almost all MNCs do have boards composed of one set of nationals. In the United States, for example, the election a few years ago of a Japanese businessman to the board of General Motors was almost a first. In Japan, there is probably no comparable example. A similar "nationalism" exists country by country. In opposition to the thesis is the assertion of many CEOs that their interests are indeed "global" and so is their company. Are such statements merely fashionable or representative of the actual state of affairs? A global elite has emerged operating in a largely transnational manner, meeting in "global" settings such as Davos, and concocting policies and political aims such as those embodied in the World Trade agreements and the North American Free Trade Agreement (NAFTA). New elites based on specialized policy and technological expertise may be framed by more genuinely global rather than merely international perspectives.

8. Paul N. Doremus, Louis W. Pauly, Simon Reich, and William Keller, eds., *The Myth of the Global Corporation* (Princeton: Princeton University Press, 1999), 371, 375, 370, 373.
9. Cf. David Held, "Democracy, the Nation-State and the Global System," in *Political Theory Today*, ed. David Held (Stanford, CA.: Stanford University Press, 1991).

If such a global elite exists, as we believe it does, is it homogeneous? Is it made up of different segments, such as business, media, military? How do such segments relate to one another? The MNC elite is connected to the other elites. National elites will increasingly interact with a developing global elite having dual identities and with the same individuals moving from national to global elite status. We need to revisit Keller and Pauly's first thesis about the unchanging relation of existing nation-states and MNCs.

On the question of homogenization, it is frequently said that MNCs are imposing themselves everywhere in a more or less single and convergent form, which, in a new version of imperialism, disseminates their values and exports their ways of operating worldwide. The same product is promoted in all countries by the same advertisements and the same films. Instead of heterogeneity, we are given the equivalent of Velveeta cheese – one cheese for all purposes.

Homogenization, in turn, it is said, is identified with Americanization. In the eyes, for instance, of many of the French, there has been "Coca-Colazation" or Americanization of the world. More recently, McDonald's has come to symbolize an American homogenization of the planet. Of the more than 18,700 outlets serving 33 million people every day a few with 3,200 new restaurants opening each year, about two-thirds of the new branches were to have been outside America.[10] McDonald's has even become the basis for a new social science "law." Thomas Friedman, in the *New York Times*, has claimed that no country with a McDonald's outlet has ever gone to war with another country having the same restaurant chain. The reasoning behind this Golden Arches theory is that the restaurants involved are only to be found in countries that have reached a sufficient level of economic well-being and political stability to make war unattractive. This is an intriguing thesis: a new, globalizing version of the long-held view that trade brings peace.

Alarm about homogenization may, however, be a misplaced fear about the character of industrial society at large and its loss of particularity in the face of mass production. Simultaneously, increased heterogeneity has also occurred. All societies at all times alternate between homogenization and heterogeneity with a balance between them. If all McDonald's have golden arches, they serve different menus in different countries. For example, in addition to homogeneous Big Macs, there are also special fish Macs in Japan, and so forth. So, too, global production is often carried out in small

---

10. *The Economist*, June 29, 1996, 61.

innovative settings. In northeastern Italy, one of the fastest growing and richest regions in Europe, the economy is based on small and medium-sized entrepreneurs who are operating successful trading and manufacturing enterprises. Even more to the point, MNCs are turning increasingly to small-batch production, working to satisfy individual tastes, and moving away from Fordism. Ideological a priori myths and hypotheses all need confirming evidence based on detailed empirical inquiry.

As for the issue of Americanization, the hypothesis that it is equivalent to globalization must also be carefully tested and considered. There is no denying that the United States is the most important player in globalization in terms of its economic muscle – its MNCs – its political power, its cultural reach, and, especially, its military capacity. The United States today militarily is the only truly global power. But this by itself does not constitute Americanization of the globe. Indeed, a shift has been occurring in the national character of MNCs. About 25 years ago almost all of the 500 largest industrial MNCs were American or European; today about one-third have their headquarters in Asia and Latin America. Globalization itself, in the form of MNCs, has been becoming increasingly global. Of course, it is still true that in India, for example, with its more than one billion population, only one company, Indian Oil Co., is ranked among the world's 500 largest firms.

Americanization itself is not what it used to be. As a culture, the United States is increasingly experiencing other modes of being. Here, again, what is needed is detailed research concerning MNCs and their role. The outcome, of course, may confirm the view that globalization equals Americanization. On the other hand, it may not. (As our brief remarks suggest, we believe that it will not.) If McDonald's has spread overseas, overseas food has come to America. Within the increasingly porous borders is a bewildering array of Chinese, Thai, Japanese, Indian, Mexican, French, Italian, and other restaurants. One encounters the "other," too, in the form of world music drawn from African reggae, Mexican, Brazilian, and similar "exotic" traditions. The outside enters as well in the shape of films, fashion, and philosophy – French postmodernist thought, largely ignored in its "home" country (where it drew largely upon German inspirations), has been widespread in American academia. The United States is a country in which black and white may still separate the races, albeit unofficially, but it has not done so in its intellectual discourse. Americanization, both inside and out, is Janus-faced.

The notion of the "transparency" of MNCs derives from a term more familiar in politics – a concept linked to the French Revolution and its demand for openness in government. Before 1789, the reigning political concept (with a partial exception in Great Britain) was that the monarch's rule was separate from the people's will because royal power derived from God, ancestry and tradition, or all three. The guiding principle was *raison d'état*, which was not to be shared with the public and needed no defense other than the king's assertion of it. In short, it was secret and nondemocratic. With the fall of the Bastille, transparency – openness – was demanded in regard to both an individual's heart and the workings of institutions. In Rousseau-like fashion, individuals were expected to experience interior private revolutions that mirrored the revolution taking place in the state. Similarly, the state was to be open in its own dealings with all its workings and reasonings available to public inspection.[11]

The demand for transparency was, and is, clearly linked to democracy. Can it be translated to MNCs, whose officials are not elected by public vote but, at best, by directors and shareholders? John Browne, chief executive of British Petroleum, believes that corporations have public responsibilities as well as private ones, that MNCs that do not engage in the "business" of pollution control as well as profit taking will lose their legitimacy. As one account of his activities puts it, "The continuing process of globalization . . . has made business transparent." Or, in Browne's own words, "Business must keep projecting the fact that on balance, it is a good thing."[12] To be a good thing means that one must show what one is doing, that is, be transparent, for how else can a business be held to account for its public actions and efforts as well as for its private money-making? Increasingly, it is MNCs and not governments alone that are engaged in public actions of great import. Within the corporation a struggle often exists between the CEO or the managers' desire for secrecy – and thus for unaccountability – and the stockholders' and other stakeholders' demand and wish for information. In the public role of corporations and their desire to hide information there are public implications. Witness the tobacco companies' foot-dragging in the face of the polity's need for transparency.

If MNCs are, in fact, the new Leviathans of our time, much more thought and analysis must be given to transparency, but political scientists, for one, seem to have chosen to ignore the subject. Two scholars looking at the

11. Cf. Jean Starobinski, *Jean-Jacques Rousseau: Transparency and Obstruction*, trans. Arthur Goldhammer (Chicago: University of Chicago Press, 1988).
12. Quoted in Youssef M. Ibrahim, "International Briefs: Praise for the Global Warming Initiative," *New York Times*, December 12, 1997.

Web site that posts a thousand abstracts of the American Political Science Association's meeting in 2000 and using a good search engine discovered only two hits for the word "corporation."[13] This suggests that political science has not yet caught up with the political importance of the new Leviathan.

The other key concept derived from political power that relates to MNCs is sovereignty, which is a term accorded much attention by political scientists, although their attention is confined almost solely to the sovereignty of nation-states. The idea that MNCs as political actors might also need to be examined in terms of the notion of sovereignty appears quite foreign to most work in the field of political science as well as in economics.

Like transparency, sovereignty, too, is a relatively new concept. It can be traced back to the seventeenth century and the emergence of the modern state system, which is customarily dated from the Peace of Westphalia in 1648 at the end of the Thirty Years' War. In that treaty, several countries' sovereignty over territories was confirmed. A century earlier, the eminent theoretician of the idea, the French writer and jurist Jean Bodin, in his *Six Books* (1576) on sovereignty, had laid down the lines along which discussion subsequently proceeded. Bodin saw sovereignty as indivisible – a state's power vested in a single individual or group. Thus, sovereignty now generally means, as Webster's *New Collegiate* puts it, "supreme power esp. over a body politic: freedom from political control." But it is useful to distinguish the internal from the external exercise of power. Internally, sovereignty means exercising power (e.g., the control of violence) in a relatively uncontested way even though, in fact, there are always oppositional groups. The government, in other words, exercises "supreme power." As Hobbes put it, "there had to be a supreme authority that enforced the law and adjudicated conflict."[14] External sovereignty is even more complicated. It requires, in the Westphalian state system, that a state be recognized by other states and be accepted as a juridical equal with a corresponding right to enter into treaties, alliances, and international institutions. But, in such a system, no sovereignty is ever absolute; it is always balanced by other sovereign states. Yet, for international purposes, the smallest state deserves representation, for example, in the United Nations as much as a large state such as China. This model of sovereignty is, as one recent scholar of the subject puts it, based on two principles:

---

13. Public e-mail posting by Focus on the Corporation, a weekly column written by Russell Mokhiber and Robert Weissman, September 20, 2000. <http://www.sfpg.com Focus>.
14. Quoted in Josef Joffe, "Rethinking the Nation-State," *Foreign Affairs*, November/December 1999, Vol. 78, No. 6, 123.

"territoriality and the exclusion of external actors from domestic authority structures." Further reduced, this idea can be stated as the "principle of nonintervention."[15]

The activities of MNCs, although not threatening the authority of states, do challenge their control (the other part of sovereignty). On matters of global power, the flow of goods, pollutants, and currencies and even human rights and broad factors like global migratory movements appear to escape the control of "sovereign" states. Such flows do not respect national boundaries; they "transgress" across them or transcend them. These characteristics have enormous regulatory and governance aspects.

The sovereignty of MNCs themselves seems, as we have stated, to have been neglected by scholars. Yet the "principle of nonintervention," an aspect of state sovereignty, has been breached in recent years not only by transnational global forces, such as currency movements, but also by concerted and intentional military, political, and judicial action as in Kosovo. In an increasingly globalized world, no nation is an island unto itself.

What is and should be the "sovereign" power of an MNC and when and how is intervention warranted? A *New York Times* full-page advertisement headed in large letters, "Invisible Government," goes on to speak of MNCs at one remove, that is, of their proxy, the World Trade Organization. "The World Trade Organization (WTO) is emerging as the world's first global government. But it was elected by no one, it operates in secrecy, and its mandate is this: 'To undermine the constitutional rights of sovereign nations.'"[16] Here, in obviously polemical – some might say hyperbolic – terms are reflected all of the issues of transparency, sovereignty, and democracy mentioned earlier.

By reflecting on such questions, we hope to stimulate thought about the issues surrounding the rise and expansion of multinationals not just as business entities but as institutions that influence social, cultural, and political conditions around the world and that have, in consequence, provoked increasing and even violent public protests. By providing an interdisciplinary perspective on the history, nature, and purpose of multinational corporations, we seek to contribute to laying a rigorous foundation for constructing policies that affect these firms and to help stimulate an informed and diverse debate about the role multinationals can and will play in the future. Such overall, is the "global" reach of our project.

15. Joffe, 124.
16. Advertisement in the *New York Times*, November 29, 1999, A15.

II

Having outlined the perspective in which we believe that our new Leviathans should be viewed, we turn now to the individual efforts to realize parts of this vision. The first chapter is Brian Roach's primer, which demonstrates that the magnitude of economic activity attributed to MNCs is, indeed, significant and increasing. In Roach's judgment, traditional economic theories, such as economies of scale and scope, are insufficient to explain the recent growth of MNCs. Modern MNCs freely seek low-cost inputs to production and a favorable regulatory environment across national boundaries. Firms with greater transnational mobility thus are able to gain a competitive advantage by lowering costs and externalizing negative spillover effects. The global marketplace does not ensure that the actions of MNCs accord with the broader goals of society. Thus, Roach argues, greater corporate transparency and accountability are required for the voices of all stakeholders to be represented. Current attempts to influence MNC behavior are inadequate, relying on national regulations or voluntary practices. An international approach, implemented through trade agreements and treaties, is needed to guarantee that MNCs explicitly recognize the broad social and environmental context in which they now operate.

The next three chapters are largely historical accounts of the emergence of MNCs in the West and in Japan. Mira Wilkins's chapter, "Multinational Enterprise to 1930: Discontinuities and Continuities," reviews in detail and depth the central role played by the multinational enterprises in creating the first global economy and emphasizes continuities and discontinuities. Geoffrey Jones's "Multinationals from the 1930s to the 1980s" carries the story forward as he describes the disintegration of the first global economy during the Great Depression and World War II and the rising barriers to trade subsequently. In the years between 1945 and the 1970s, two-thirds to three-quarters of all the world's foreign direct investment (FDI) was accounted for primarily by the United States.

Yonekura and McKinney's "Innovative Multinational Forms: Japan as a Case Study," is divided into two parts. The chapter begins by describing how Japan's unique trading companies permitted this country, after 200 years of isolation from the West and therefore from modern technology and institutions, to enter the first global economy. Then in the 1970s Japan's new modern multinationals began to capture world markets from the long-established multinationals of the United States and Europe. The authors' basic message is that Japan's modern economy has been created almost entirely through the activities of multinational enterprises operating in two time periods and in two very different ways. The Japanese trading companies, the *sogo shosha*, made possible the country's participation in the first global economy. Their successors, the MNCs, were part of the process by which, in the 1980s, Japan became the world's second largest national economy in terms of GNP and the most dynamic player in the shaping of the second global economy.

In "The Social Impacts of Multinational Corporations," Neva Goodwin looks at the issue of globalization through two different lenses: that of economic theory, which predicts and welcomes competition, and that of the myriad real-world forces that seek shelter from competition. She explores how this tension is worked out in the arena of MNCs with particular attention to the experience of workers and the effects of MNC-led economic development. Her hypothesis is that the increasingly globalized nature of business competition that has evolved since the 1970s still contains shelter within which excess revenues can be generated but that an increasing share of these revenues has been captured by owners and top-level managers at the expense of the workers. These issues are explored within two overarching questions: Is social welfare generally increased or decreased by the expanding role of the MNCs? How does their role affect the total size of the global money economy and the way the fruits of that economy are divided among the different economic actors?

In the chapter, "A Global Elite?," Bruce Mazlish and Elliott Morss attempt to define the term "elite" in an historical sense. Recognizing that there have been elites of various kinds in the past – for example, local, regional, and more recently national – they ask whether now something that can be called a global elite is emerging. Such an elite would correspond to the globalization process taking place so vividly before our eyes. How does one research such a topic? Emphasizing that theirs is a preliminary and exploratory effort, the authors mention various sites such as the World Bank and the IMF and venues such as Davos and the Trilateral Commission and even offer a more extended analysis of the Davos attendees, using the membership list of the year 2000. Going further, Mazlish and Morss hypothesize that there is not one but four global elites needing examination: the first derives its status from social and family backgrounds, the second receives its power from developing and implementing profit-making ideas, the third from holding a senior position in a global organization such as the World Bank, and the fourth from the managers of global organizations trained in Western business and technical schools. The task of further work is to analyze these elites in great detail, searching for evidence of a common life style and a common view, and then to look at how they relate to one another, asking finally whether there is any justification for talking about them as a singular "global elite."

What of the governance of MNCs? What are the issues of responsibility in regard to them? Robert Monks speaks to these questions in his "Governing the Multinational Enterprise: Emergence of the Global Shareowner." In this chapter he takes up the history of the global shareowner and then turns his attention to such matters as the characteristics of the global shareowners, the responsibilities of the owners, shareholder activism and value, and the conflict of interest. Lastly, he addresses the problem of proof and the nature of corporate power and the state and then concludes by looking at the possibility of positive change within the scope of existing laws.

In the chapter "The Financial Revolutions of the Twentieth Century," Zhu Jia-Ming and Elliott Morss address the dramatic changes that have occurred in the financial services industry over the last several decades. Specifically, they document the global expansion of pension funds, insurance companies, and mutual funds and how they have increasingly taken over from commercial banks as the primary vehicles for personal savings. Zhu and Morss explain how these institutions have contributed to the emergence of two new financial services subindustries: investment services and risk adjustment. The chapter then concludes with speculations about the need for new global controls over the financial services industry.

Stephen Kobrin's chapter, "Multinational Corporations, the Protest Movement, and the Future of Global Governance," focuses on the broad response to the coming of the second global economy. He begins by comparing the protests of the 1970s to those of the 1990s. They differ in that the latter involved a much larger number of people and concentrated on social and cultural issues as well as on economic ones; however, the basic theme of the protest remained the power and dominance of the MNCs. Kobrin follows his analysis of what he terms the antiglobalization angst by inquiring in the context of several national polls whether it represents broad public opinion. He concludes by saying that "the dramatic increases in the scale of technology, the internationalization and integration of production and especially the digital revolution . . . will be impossible to reverse. . . . The genie cannot be put back into the bottle: over the long run globalization is a one-way street."

As can readily be seen, the book as a whole tries to indicate the scope of the multinational phenomena in various of its dimensions. The Introduction and Chapter 1 provide the large picture, and the focus then narrows to the historical, the social, and the governance questions. Throughout, the aim is to secure a better grasp of the phenomenon of present-day globalization with the emphasis on the new Leviathans of our time: the multinational corporations. Though they may someday disappear, for the foreseeable future they will only grow larger. Our knowledge of their nature and their effects on all parts of our society must increase as well. It is as a contribution to that goal that this volume has been conceived and the individual chapters commissioned. The resultant whole, we hope, will be more than the sum of its parts, shedding a special light on both the multinationals and on the environment of globalization in which they move and have their life.

PART ONE

The Scope of the Multinational Phenomenon

1

A Primer on Multinational Corporations

BRIAN ROACH

A FIRST LOOK AT A MODERN PHENOMENON

The modern multinational corporation (MNC) is an economic, political, environmental, and cultural force that is unavoidable in today's globalized world. MNCs have an impact on the lives of billions of people every day – often in complex and imperceptible ways. The importance of large MNCs is illustrated in this chapter using data measuring the economic magnitude of these firms. In this context, the leading explanations for why some firms have grown so large are summarized. However, it is important to recognize that the scope of MNCs extends beyond the economic realm. Within the nations in which they operate, large corporations exert political influence to obtain subsidies, reduce their tax burdens, and shape regulations. What especially differentiates the modern MNC from earlier large firms is its great mobility to seek low-cost inputs to production. This transnational mobility implies that firms may be able to set nations against one another in an effort to obtain a favorable regulatory environment. Even further, recent international trade agreements may enable corporations to circumvent national sovereignty entirely.

The second section of this chapter describes the general economic significance of MNCs in today's world, and the final section addresses their political influence as well as their environmental and social impacts and responsibilities. The chapter ends with some observations on the requirements for bringing the goals of MNCs more closely into line with long-range social goals based on the interests of all stakeholders. First, however, we describe the activities of a single MNC to anchor our later, more sweeping look at this extraordinary modern phenomenon.

Looking Inside a Major Multinational Corporation

Consider a consumer in the United States who purchases a pint of Ben & Jerry's ice cream. To many people, Ben & Jerry's represents the antithesis of a large multinational corporation, which is an entity assumed to be focused exclusively on profit maximization. In contrast, Ben & Jerry's is well known for its support of environmental and social causes, its involvement in local communities, and its fair labor practices. What the purchaser of this brand of ice cream may not know – and cannot determine by reading the packaging – is that it is now produced by a major MNC. In 2000, Ben & Jerry's was purchased in a semihostile takeover[1] by Unilever, one of the largest consumer goods manufacturers in the world. No longer an independent company, Ben & Jerry's has become just one of more than 400 brands produced by Unilever.

A brief look at the history and structure of Unilever provides some insight into the operations and impacts of a major MNC. The company's roots can be traced back to the British soapmaking firm Lever Brothers, which was founded in the 1880s.[2] Using mass-production techniques and recognizing the effectiveness of advertising, this firm was the largest soap manufacturer in England by the turn of the century. Cofounder William Lever did not hesitate to expand the firm into foreign markets – first throughout Europe and later to the United States. To ensure supplies of raw materials, Lever Brothers purchased coconut plantations in the Solomon Islands in 1905 and several African trading companies over the next several years. In an attempt to fix prices in the soap market, the company sought to form a loose trust with several of its major rivals. When a public outcry forced abandonment of the plan, Lever Brothers instead purchased most of its major rivals between 1910 and 1920. By 1921, Lever Brothers was producing more than 70 percent of the soap sold in England.

Lever Brothers began manufacturing margarine in 1914 at the request of the British government, which was concerned about food shortages at the outbreak of World War I. In yet another attempt to reduce competition,

---

1. During the takeover battle, an attempt was made by Ben & Jerry's cofounder Ben Cohen to arrange the purchase of Ben & Jerry's by a socially responsible group of investors. The board of Ben & Jerry's appeared willing to accept this offer even though the price was less than that being offered by Unilever. When Unilever increased its price, the board felt it had no choice but to accept the offer or face lawsuits by stockholders (Marjorie Kelly, "The Legacy Problem," *Business Ethics*, Summer 2003:11–16).
2. Historical information on Unilever obtained from Alfred D. Chandler, Jr., *Scale and Scope: The Dynamics of Industrial Capitalism* (Cambridge, MA: The Belknap Press of Harvard University, 1990); Philip Mattera, *World Class Business* (New York: Henry Holt and Company, 1992); and Unilever's Web site, <http://www.unilever.com>.

Lever Brothers merged with the Dutch margarine manufacturer Margarine Unie in 1929. This was the largest international merger until World War II. In a complex arrangement, the two firms retained a degree of independence. To this day, Unilever is organized into Unilever Ltd., a British company, and Unilever NV, a Dutch company. This dual-country structure has provided the company with certain tax and political advantages over the years.

After World War II, Unilever moved into new markets – especially food products, perfumes, detergents, and toothpastes. In the 1980s the firm focused attention on expanding its prominence in U.S. markets by purchasing Chesebrough-Pond in 1986 and several fragrance lines, including Faberge and Calvin Klein. By the end of the 1990s, Unilever was producing more than 1,600 brands worldwide. In 2000 the firm began a major restructuring effort, selling off many of its underperforming brands and smaller operations with the goal of retaining only 400 brands by 2005.

Despite the recent divestiture of many holdings, Unilever still produces a wide range of brands. According to Unilever, its products are used each year by an estimated 99 percent of the households in Canada, 95 percent of Indonesian households, 99 percent of households in the United Kingdom, and 95 percent of households in Vietnam. Again, many people may not associate these brands with Unilever despite nearly universal brand recognition. Unilever produces Lipton, the world's leading brand of tea and iced tea, and Hellmann's, the world's top brand of mayonnaise. Their Rexona deodorants, available in 90 countries, are also the world's top brand. Unilever's biggest brand is Knorr, which includes a range of sauces, snacks, frozen foods, and other food products. Other well-known Unilever brands include Vaseline, Dove soaps, Thermasilk shampoos, Bertolli oils, Close-Up and Mentadent toothpastes, Slim•Fast diet products, and Calvin Klein fragrances. Ben & Jerry's was not their first ice cream brand, for Unilever owns Breyer's ice cream as well as other brands. In addition to brands that are marketed throughout the world, Unilever produces some products for regional or even national markets. Their Ala laundry detergent is sold only in Brazil. The Findus brand of frozen foods is primarily Italian. The Continental brand of soups, sauces, and snacks is sold in Austria and New Zealand.

In 2002 Unilever was number 66 on the *Fortune* Global 500 list of the largest corporations in the world ranked by revenue. Their 2002 revenue of about $46 billion was well below the largest corporations (Wal-Mart was number 1 with revenues of nearly $247 billion) but greater than such well-known corporations as Time Warner, J. P. Morgan Chase & Co., Sears Roebuck, and BMW. Unilever's global employment of around one-quarter million makes it the 29th largest employer in the world. Ranked by total

Table 1-1. *Geographical Distribution of Unilever Employment, Revenue, Profits, and Assets, 2001*

Region	Employees (%)	Revenue (%)	Profit (%)	Assets (%)
Europe	27	39	41	35
North America	8	26	27	38
Africa, Middle East	18	7	5	3
Asia and Pacific	32	15	15	5
Latin America	14	13	12	19

Source: <http://www.unilever.com>.

assets, Unilever is the 181st largest capital owner in the world.[3] Although still a very large corporation, Unilever is not the industrial standout it once was. In 1970 it was the second largest industrial corporation outside of the United States on the *Fortune* list and the ninth largest in the world. In 1990 it was still ranked the 21st largest corporation in the world, but in the following decade it was surpassed by a several other firms in the *Fortune* Global 500 ranking.[4]

Unilever calls itself a "multilocal multinational." It is a conglomerate composed of numerous companies, each with some degree of independence and its own management structure. According to Unilever's 2002 Annual Report, the Unilever Group includes nearly 200 principal companies in almost 90 countries. Table 1-1 illustrates the penetration of Unilever into labor, goods, and asset markets throughout the world. Revenue and profits are highest in Europe. The most assets are to be found in North America, although employment there is quite low. Employment is disproportionately concentrated in Asia and the Pacific even though Unilever owns few assets there.

Any large MNC that produces consumer or wholesale goods must also be a complex financial institution. The Unilever Group includes a separate company, the Unilever Capital Corporation (UCC), to obtain credit in international debt markets.[5] The transnational mobility of UCC means it can seek out funds in nations with low interest rates and favorable currency exchange rates. In 2002, Unilever reported total debt obligations exceeding $20 billion. These debts were owed in various currencies, including U.S. dollars, euros, Japanese yen, Swiss francs, and the Thai baht. Through risk management and hedging, Unilever seeks to protect itself from volatility in

3. Revenue, asset, and employment rankings from "Global 500," *Fortune*, July 21, 2003, and July 22, 2002.
4. Corporate ranking data from various editions of *Fortune*.
5. For more on international financial markets, see Chapter 8 in this volume.

international currency markets. Protection from supply-chain price changes is provided through forward contracts for raw materials. Unilever manages its employees' retirement accounts, financing them through equities (57% of pension assets), bonds (27%), and other investments (16%). In 2002, Unilever reported about $13 billion in pension plan assets with pension liabilities of about $17 billion. Given the time lags involved in pension management, the company calculates its liabilities and assets based on assumptions about rates of return on investments, inflation rates, and salary growth. Unilever's ability to meet its long-term pension obligations depends heavily on whether these assumptions turn out to be accurate.

Unilever, like other major MNCs in recent years, has become more transparent by publishing reports on its environmental performance and social responsibilities in addition to the usual reports on financial performance. (The three together are increasingly being referred to as "the triple bottom line.") The company has undertaken three major sustainability initiatives concentrated on issues of agriculture, fisheries, and water quality. Unilever helped organize a marine catch sustainability certification program and has set a goal of purchasing all its fish from sustainable sources by 2005 (as of 2002 it was purchasing about one-third of its fish from sustainable sources). The company has set environmental targets for reductions in hazardous wastes, energy use, carbon dioxide emissions, and other environmental parameters – meeting some targets but failing to meet others. It has initiated programs to combat HIV and AIDS in Africa, plant wildflowers and shrubs in Canada, eradicate child hunger in the United States, and provide educational opportunities in Brazil. Overall, the corporation contributes about 1 percent of its pretax profits to community initiatives.

Like any large MNC, Unilever is a complex organization that cannot simply be described as an entity seeking only to maximize profits. Not only do MNCs pursue multiple objectives, but situations will frequently arise in which the objectives of different parts of the organization conflict. Consider that Unilever has long been an advocate of international trade liberalization. On October 16, 2001, the *Financial Times* revealed that more than $1 million donated by Ben & Jerry's, part of Unilever, to the Ben & Jerry's Foundation was given to organizations associated with the antiglobalization movement. Thus, Unilever was simultaneously lobbying for further globalization and funding antiglobalization protests. Executives at Unilever who were aware that donations to the foundation would likely be used to fund antiglobalization efforts decided against attaching caveats to their contributions and respected the independence of the Ben & Jerry's Foundation.

THE ECONOMIC SCALE AND IMPACT OF MNCs

Unilever is just one type of MNC. There is enough variation among these complex organizations that no single firm could be called typical of them all. To obtain a broader perspective on the role of MNCs in the world, we now turn to an overview of this kind of institution. The remainder of this chapter introduces several issues that must be considered if one is to understand the scale and power of multinational corporations. This section emphasizes issues that can be understood primarily in economic terms.

The Numbers and Geographical Distribution of MNCs

The terms "multinational corporation," "transnational corporation," and "global corporation" are often used interchangeably. The United Nations Conference on Trade and Development (UNCTAD) defines a transnational corporation as an entity composed of a parent enterprise that controls the assets of entities in countries other than its home country plus the foreign affiliates of that parent enterprise. This definition will be applied to the term multinational corporation as well. According to the UNCTAD, some 65,000 MNCs existed as of 2000, and the parent enterprises of about 50,000 were located in developed countries.[6] This represents a significant increase in the number of MNCs from 1990, when there were only 35,000.[7] Growth has been especially dramatic in the Third World. Although the number of MNCs in developed countries increased by 63 percent between 1990 and 2002, the number of MNCs in developing countries increased by 258 percent during the same period.

Despite this recent trend, the geographical distribution of MNCs is highly skewed toward Western Europe. Perhaps surprisingly, the country hosting the parent company of the most MNCs is Denmark (about 14% of all MNCs).[8] Denmark is followed by Germany (13%), Sweden (7%), and Switzerland (7%). The United States hosts only 5 percent of all the world's MNCs. Of the more than 13,000 MNCs in developing countries, more than half are located in South Korea. Other developing countries with significant numbers of MNCs include South Africa, Brazil, and the Czech Republic.

When we consider the geographic distribution of only the very largest MNCs, the corporations become much more concentrated in the United

6. UNCTAD (United Nations Conference on Trade and Development). *World Investment Report 2002* (New York: United Nations. 2002).
7. UNCTAD (United Nations Conference on Trade and Development). *World Investment Report 1992* (New York: United Nations. 1992).
8. UNCTAD, 2002, annex table A.I.3.

States and Japan, although this has also been changing in recent decades. About 64 percent of the largest 250 industrial companies were headquartered in the United States in 1960. Except for a handful in Japan, all the rest of this group were located in Europe.[9] Coming forward to 2002, we find only about 38 percent of the *Fortune* Global 500 firms headquartered in the United States; Japan was second with 18 percent, then France with 8 percent, and Britain and Germany with 7 percent each. Several of the top 500 corporations are now located in developing countries, including China, Brazil, India, Malaysia, and Mexico.

MNCs have become more "transnational" in recent years. A common metric used to measure the activity of MNCs in foreign markets is foreign direct investment (FDI). FDI is investment by an entity, such as a corporation, in productive activities occurring in any nation other than its declared home. FDI outflows grew slowly from the mid-1970s to the mid-1980s.[10] FDI then nearly tripled between 1984 and 1987 and continued to grow steadily at a rate of around 20 percent per year during the first half of the 1990s. There was a dramatic growth spurt in FDI during the late 1990s at a rate of more than 40 percent annually before it began to fall significantly in 2001 as a result of the global economic slowdown. The growth of FDI outflows in current prices during the period 1982–2001, an absolute increase of more than 2,100 percent, has far outpaced the growth in exports (257%) and world output (195%).

The Size of MNCs: Different Ways of Assessing Size

The data presented in the previous section have generally ranked MNCs based on annual revenues as in the case of the *Fortune* Global 500 list. Revenues are only one way to assess economic magnitude, and different modes of assessment are useful for different purposes.

The *Fortune* Global 500 list received combined annual revenues in 2002 of about $13.7 trillion. This amount is equivalent to annual expenditures of $2,200 by *every* individual on the planet on the products of these 500 corporations. The 50 largest corporations accounted for close to a third of these sales, and their combined revenues were nearly $4.4 trillion.

A common comparison made by some researchers is to relate the revenues of MNCs to the gross domestic product (GDP) of countries. For example, a recent report indicates that 51 of the world's 100 largest economies are

---

9. Calculations on large industrials in 1960 made from various editions of *Fortune*.
10. Historical FDI data obtained from various editions of UNCTAD's *World Investment Report*.

companies whereas 49 are countries.[11] This report also states, with much emphasis, that the revenues of the world's 200 largest corporations were equivalent to 27.5 percent of world GDP in 1999. However, there are serious conceptual problems with such comparisons because corporate revenue is not equivalent to GDP, which is measured in terms of value added. To make the comparison valid, one should also measure the economic impact of corporations as value added (defined as the sum of salaries, pretax profits, and depreciation and amortization). When this is done, 29 of the world's 100 largest economies are companies.[12] In 2000 the world's largest MNC by value added was ExxonMobil with a value added of $63 billion. This is larger than the GDP of such countries as Pakistan, New Zealand, Hungary, and Vietnam. Although the revenues of the 100 largest corporations constitute nearly 20 percent of world GDP,[13] the more relevant comparison, using the value added metric, indicates that the 100 largest corporations account for 4.3 percent of world GDP.

The UNCTAD ranks MNCs by the value of their foreign assets. On the basis of this metric, the world's largest MNC is the English telecommunications corporation Vodafone followed by General Electric and ExxonMobil. The final common metric one could use to rank corporations is employment. The world's largest corporate employer, according to the *Fortune Global 500*, is Wal-Mart, which employs 1.3 million workers.

Table 1-2 presents data on the world's 10 largest corporations using each of these 4 metrics. The world's largest corporations by revenues and value added are quite similar; 9 of the top 10 by revenues are among the top 10 by value added. There is less overlap in the foreign assets ranking; 6 of the top 10 by revenues also appear on this list. The world's 10 largest employers, except for Wal-Mart, are not among the 10 largest companies by revenues.

How MNCs Are Growing in Scale and Scope

The portion of the world's economy attributed to the largest corporations is increasing. The amount of revenue received by the world's 200 largest corporations was equivalent to 25.0 percent of world GDP in 1983 but had risen to 27.5 percent by 1999. The growth is proportionally larger when we consider value added; in 2000 the world's top 100 MNCs accounted for 4.3 percent of world GDP up from 3.5 percent in 1990. Again, on the basis

11. Sarah Andersen and John Cavanaugh. *Top 200: The Rise of Corporate Global Power* (Institute for Policy Studies, 2000).
12. This and the following statistics come from UNCTAD (2000).
13. Calculation made from table 3 of Anderson and Cavanaugh.

Table 1-2. *The World's 10 Largest Corporations Ranked by Revenues, Value Added, Foreign Assets, and Employment*

	Ranking by Revenue		Ranking by Value Added		Ranking by Foreign Assets		Ranking by Employment	
Rank	Company	Revenue ($ bil.)	Company	Value Added ($ bil.)	Company	Foreign Assets ($ bil.)	Company	Workers (1000)
1	Wal-Mart	$247	ExxonMobil	63	Vodafone	221	Wal-Mart	1300
2	General Motors	187	General Motors	56	General Electric	159	China National Petroleum	1146
3	ExxonMobil	182	Ford Motor	44	ExxonMobil	102	Sinopec	917
4	Royal Dutch/Shell	179	DaimlerChrysler	42	Vivendi Universal	93	U.S. Postal Service	854
5	BP	179	General Electric	39	General Motors	75	Agricultural Bank of China	491
6	Ford Motor	164	Toyota Motor	38	Royal Dutch/Shell	75	Siemens	426
7	DaimlerChrysler	141	Royal Dutch/Shell	36	BP	57	McDonald's	413
8	Toyota Motor	132	Siemens	32	Toyota Motor	56	Industrial and Commercial Bank of China	405
9	General Electric	132	BP	30	Telefonica	56	Carrefour	397
10	Mitsubishi	109	Wal-Mart	30	Fiat	53	Compass Group	392

Sources: Revenue and employment data are for 2002 from *Fortune* Global 500; value added and foreign asset data are for 2000 from UNCTAD 2002.

of the value added, in 1990 24 of the world's largest economies were countries; as noted earlier, by 2000 this had risen to 29.

Other analysis supports the claim that the economic strength of the world's largest corporations is expanding. It was estimated in the early 1990s that one-quarter of the world's productive assets were owned by just 300 corporations.[14] Between 1983 and 2001, world GDP increased by about 173 percent.[15] Revenues for the world's 50 largest firms grew at a pace similar to that of world GDP – a 179 percent increase between 1983 and 2001. More indicative of economic power, the value of capital assets owned by the world's 50 largest corporations increased by an astonishing 686 percent during this time.[16]

The phenomenal growth in revenues and assets was not matched by a comparable growth in employment. In 2002, the *Fortune* Global 500 corporations employed about 47 million people – an average of nearly 100,000 each. With a global labor force of more than three billion, these 500 firms employed 1.6 percent of the world's labor force.[17] Although the profits of the world's 50 largest corporations increased by 167 percent between 1983 and 2001, employment in the largest 50 firms increased by only 21 percent.[18]

Explaining the Growth of MNCs

Most of the world's largest corporations started as relatively small enterprises. Unilever began as a soapmaking enterprise run by two brothers in 1885. Ford Motor Company was started in a small factory in Detroit in 1903. Wal-Mart began with a single store in Arkansas in 1962. These companies have become large MNCs because of a combination of circumstances specific to these firms and an economic environment that created conditions for very large firms to develop in certain industries.

The two traditional economic explanations for the growth of business enterprises have been economies of scale and economies of scope. Economies of scale arise when a firm can lower its per-unit production cost of a single good or service by producing in greater quantity. Division of labor through specialization is one reason per-unit costs can decrease as scale increases. Adam Smith noted in the 18th century that a pin factory will increase its

---

14. Richard J. Barnet and John Cavanaugh. *Global Dreams* (New York: Simon & Schuster, 1994).
15. Calculation made using the World Bank's World Development Indicators Online, <http://devdata.worldbank.org/dataonline/>.
16. Calculations made using various editions of *Fortune*.
17. Global labor force data from the World Bank's World Development Indicators Online, <http://devdata.worldbank.org/dataonline/>.
18. Calculations made using various editions of *Fortune*.

production significantly, and thus decrease per-unit costs, if each worker repeatedly performs a specific task in the production process rather than having each worker independently complete the entire production process. In the late 19th century, Frederick Taylor introduced the concept of "scientific management" – analysis that identifies the specific division of labor in a process that would maximize production efficiency. Henry Ford consulted with Taylor in designing the world's first large-scale moving assembly line in 1913.

In modern MNCs, economies of scale occur not only through the division of labor but by combining, and often replacing, human labor with mechanized production. Investment in large-scale capital equipment and the latest production technologies often requires significant up-front costs. These investments may be affordable only for firms with substantial retained earnings or access to credit. Thus, firms that are already large can gain further competitive advantages over smaller firms that must rely on older and higher-cost production technologies. In industries in which the minimum efficient scale[19] is very large, one would expect that, over time, the industry would become dominated by a small number of producers. This has occurred in such industries as automobile production and petroleum exploration and distribution; note the presence of several such firms in Table 1-2.

Economies of scope arise when a firm can lower average costs by expanding the range of goods and services it produces. Normally, a firm will expand its production line along related products, taking advantage of existing marketing or distribution networks. For example, a telephone company may expand into providing Internet services or an ice cream producer may add yogurt to its product line (as was done by the ice cream manufacturer Breyer's, a company that is now part of Unilever). Firms may also achieve economies of scope through the production of seemingly unrelated products. An example is the conglomerate General Electric, which produces goods such as aircraft engines, home appliances, medical equipment, wind power turbines, and televisions; it also provides financial services to businesses and consumers and owns the television network NBC. Conglomerates may expect to achieve economies of scope savings through managerial efficiency, financing flexibility, political power, or the centralization of research and marketing.

In a related strategy, a firm may achieve cost savings through expansion by vertical integration. Rather than purchasing raw materials and other

---

19. The minimum efficient scale is the minimum production level necessary to obtain the minimum long-run average cost.

inputs externally, a firm expands vertically by taking on additional steps in a production process. In essence, vertical integration entails removing production steps from the free market and adding them to the internal economy of a corporation. This allows profits previously earned by suppliers to be captured internally and increases the reliability of supplies. These were the expected (and actual) benefits that led, for example, to the purchase of coconut plantations by Unilever in the early 20th century.

Although these conventional factors explain the historic growth of most large corporations, the most significant competitive advantage of MNCs in recent years is considered to be international mobility – the ability to transfer resources across national borders. In the decades immediately following World War II, the "internationalization" of corporations, primarily American, took place through the establishment of foreign affiliates intended to serve the markets in which they were located. However, with trade liberalization and falling transportation costs, firms increasingly looked abroad not only for new output markets but for low-cost production opportunities. Initially attracted by inexpensive manufacturing labor and capital markets, a growing proportion of foreign investment by MNCs is now being directed toward services and knowledge-based resources. MNCs that take advantage of low-cost foreign labor (as an especially common example) gain a competitive advantage over less mobile firms that remain dependent on higher-cost inputs. Low-cost foreign labor is a significant factor explaining the growth of MNCs in such sectors as electronics and apparel.

Savings from the use of low-cost foreign inputs are increasingly achieved through contracts with external suppliers rather than through vertical integration. For example, not a single employee of Nike, the world's largest apparel retailer, makes shoes.[20] All of Nike's shoes, clothing, and other gear are manufactured by foreign firms under contract with Nike – mostly in Indonesia, China, and Vietnam. Relying on subcontractors offers MNCs advantages over internal vertical integration. First, unburdened by capital investments, firms can quickly shift to contracts in other countries in response to fluctuating input prices. Second, MNCs can avoid demands for instituting fair labor practices and meeting environmental standards by claiming these are at least jointly the duty of the subcontractors. Although MNCs benefit economically from high levels of flexibility, this can also exacerbate negative social and environmental externalities – an issue to which we turn in the next section.

---

20. Charles Derber, *Corporation Nation: How Corporations Are Taking over Our Lives and What We Can Do about It* (New York: St. Martin's Press, 1998).

It is worthwhile to note that large MNCs have not arisen in all industries. Industries heavily focused on the provision of services in which human labor is the major cost and the consumer receives the services through direct, in situ contact with the supplier are most likely to remain local. In low-wage sectors such as repair services, food service operations, and child care and housekeeping, the minimum efficient scale tends to be relatively small, and a large MNC would have little, if any, advantage over a smaller local firm. Local identity is an advantage that can be lost in scaling up. Restaurants provide good examples of the circumstances under which local identity is, and is not, an advantage. The customer whose main concern is price or who is traveling quickly and prizes familiarity over specialness may prefer McDonald's, but those who go out for a "dining experience" are more likely to want something unique to one particular place.

The medical care industry contains few MNCs, though the pharmaceutical products it uses are most often produced by major MNCs. Although there is considerable international mobility among medical workers and the enhanced health that is the ultimate product will travel near or far with the discharged patient, at the time of purchase health care services are consumed on the spot by the patient. The relatively low profits achieved in this industry (which, indeed, includes many not-for-profit firms) may also explain why it has not tended to expand to multiple locations. Until recently these generalizations also fitted another major service industry – education. Although there is no immediate likelihood of K–12 or preschool education becoming attractive to large corporations (except those that supply pedagogical materials), developments in long-distance learning technologies and in technologies that can be used for long-distance management are prompting some universities to experiment with the establishment of "brand name" branches in foreign countries.

POLITICAL POWER, SOCIAL RESPONSIBILITY, AND WAYS OF AFFECTING MNC BEHAVIOR

Assessing the Political Power of MNCs

Many critics of MNCs remark on the huge political power of corporations and worry that this power is increasing.[21] Despite ample anecdotal evidence of corporate power, little empirical research is available to support the claim

---

21. See, for example, William Greider, *One World, Ready or Not: The Manic Logic of Global Capitalism* (New York: Simon & Schuster, 1997) and David C. Korten, *When Corporations Rule the World*, 2nd edition (Bloomfield, CT: Kumarian Press, 2001).

of increasing power. One of the problems is that no universally accepted metric exists to measure corporate power easily and reliably. We will consider several of the measures that have been proposed, noting, in relation to each measure, its theoretical limitations and whether the data it requires are available.[22]

Industry concentration ratios measure the proportion of total industry revenues accruing to the largest firms in the industry. Common ratios measure the sales of the largest 4, 8, or 20 firms divided by total sales in the industry. As a rule of thumb, if the four-firm concentration ratio in an industry is higher than 0.40, the industry is considered to be oligopolistic – that is, dominated by a small number of firms with significant market power.[23] Increasing concentration ratios over time could indicate a rise in power among the largest firms in an industry. Concentration ratio data from the United States suggest that many industries are oligopolistic, including petrochemicals, cellular telecommunications, credit cards, waste treatment, and natural gas distribution.[24] However, concentration ratios in the United States have changed little in recent decades; some industries have become more concentrated whereas others are more dispersed.

National concentration ratios have two major limitations as a measure of corporate power: (1) they fail to measure the impact of foreign competition, and (2) they do not account for the power of conglomerates that operate across a range of industries. However, an attempt to measure global concentration ratios reveals results similar to the U.S. data.[25] The unweighted average global concentration ratio across 15 industrial sectors was 0.42 in 1990 (ranging from 0.29 to 0.67).[26] Across 12 service sectors, the average concentration ratio was 0.36 in 1990 (ranging from 0.20 to 0.63).[27] Although many of these sectors could be described as global oligopolies,

22. Options for assessing corporate power described in Randy R. Grant, "Measuring Corporate Power: Assessing the Options," *Journal of Economic Issues* 31(1997): 453–60. This chapter does not discuss all seven options considered in the Grant article. The four described here (industry concentration ratios, aggregate concentration ratios, corporate tax revenue proportions, and union membership) are those with the most theoretical support or available data.
23. David Colander, *Economics*, 3rd edition (Boston: Irwin McGraw-Hill, 1998).
24. U.S. Census Bureau. "1997 Economic Census – Concentration Ratios," 10 December 2001 <http://www.census.gov/epcd/www/concentration.html> (16 September 2003).
25. John H. Dunning, *Multinational Enterprises and the Global Economy* (Wokingham, England: Addison-Wesley Publishing Company, 1993), 45.
26. Concentration ratio calculated as the sales of the largest 3 firms in the sector divided by the sales of the largest 20 firms in the sector. For 7 of the 15 sectors, data were available for fewer than 20 firms. For these sectors, the ratio was calculated as the sales of the largest three firms divided by the sales of the maximum number of firms with available data (7–19 firms). Ibid.
27. Concentration ratio calculated as the sales of the 3 largest firms in the sector divided by the sales of the largest 15 firms in the sector. Ibid.

time-series data again show that concentration ratios did not increase between 1962 and 1990.

Sector-specific concentration ratios do not reveal an increase in corporate concentration, but the aggregate corporate data presented earlier do suggest a recent increase in corporate power. Recall that the proportion of global revenues and value added attributed to the world's largest firms increased during the 1990s. In particular, global productive assets are becoming increasingly concentrated in the largest MNCs. Recall the increase in the value of capital assets owned by the world's 50 largest corporations of 686 percent between 1983 and 2001. Although no reliable data are available on total global capital assets, data from the U.S. Bureau of Economic Analysis indicate that total fixed, nonresidential assets in the United States only increased by 77 percent during this same period. These data suggest, but do not prove, a dramatic increase during the 1990s in the concentration of productive assets in the hands of the world's largest corporations.

Corporate power can also be assessed by considering the strength of countervailing forces that seek to limit the influence of corporations. Perhaps the most significant countervailing force to corporate power has historically been labor unions. In 1956, John Kenneth Galbraith optimistically cited such countervailing powers as effective limits to the excessive growth of corporate power. However, during the period 1980–94, union membership declined in 13 of 19 OECD (Organisation for Economic Co-operation and Development) countries. Averaged across all countries (unweighted), union membership in the workforce declined from 46 percent to 40 percent during this period. The decline in union membership has been particularly pronounced in the United States, where membership has declined from a peak of around one-third of the workforce in the mid-1950s to around 10 percent today.[28]

Another way to measure corporate power is to look at the proportion of total tax revenue obtained from corporate taxation. The theoretical assumption behind this measure is that corporations use gains in political power to reduce their tax burden – effectively shifting the burden of taxation away from themselves and onto other taxpayers. Data from 30 OECD countries again show mixed results.[29] Averaged across all 30 countries, the percentage of taxation derived from corporate taxes remained relatively constant between 1965 and 2000. The corporate tax share generally declined in

---

28. Henry S. Farber and Bruce Western, "Round Up the Usual Suspects: The Decline of Unions in the Private Sector, 1973–1998." Princeton University Industrial Relations Section Working Paper #437 (April 2000).
29. OECD, 2002.

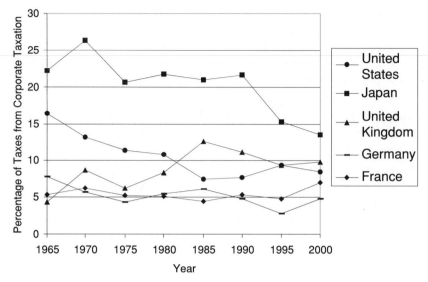

Figure 1-1. Corporate Tax Share as a Percentage of Total National Taxation, 1965–2000.

North America and the Pacific countries, whereas it increased in Europe. Figure 1-1 presents historical corporate tax shares for the five countries with the most *Fortune* Global 500 companies. The data for 1965–2000 indicate that the corporate tax share declined in the United States and Japan, remained relatively stable in France and Germany, and increased in the United Kingdom. Thus, corporations do not appear to be equally effective at reducing their tax share in all countries.

In addition to achieving tax reductions, corporations can exert power by obtaining other political favors and directly influencing elections through campaign contributions. For example, large corporations benefit from direct public subsidies called "corporate welfare." Estimates of corporate welfare in the United States range from $87 billion more than $170 billion per year.[30] Consider the public subsidies that benefit the pharmaceutical industry, one of the most profitable sectors in the economy as well as one of the most active in political lobbying. In the United States, the National Institutes of Health (NIH) funds a substantial amount of medical research designed to produce new drugs. However, pharmaceutical companies obtain the patents for these drugs and reap large profits. For example, the world's leading glaucoma drug,

---

30. Low estimate from Stephen Slivinski, "The Corporate Welfare Budget Bigger than Ever." Cato Policy Analysis No. 415 (10 October 2001), and high estimate from Citizens for Tax Justice. "Surge in Corporate Tax Welfare Drives Corporate Tax Payments Down to Near Record" (April 17, 2002).

Xalatan, was developed using $4 million in NIH funds. The exclusive rights to Xalatan were obtained by Pharmacia Corporation (recently acquired by Pfizer) for no more than $150,000.[31]

The power of MNCs today must be assessed in light of their tremendous mobility. Corporations lobby national governments to obtain political favors such as tax breaks and a sympathetic regulatory environment. This is not a new phenomenon, but the mobility of modern MNCs means that corporations can effectively bring nations into competition with each other for corporate investment and employment opportunities. A critic of MNCs has said that multinationals "are, in effect, conducting a peripatetic global jobs competition, awarding shares of production to those who make the highest bids – that is, the greatest concessions by the public domain."[32] Examples that support this claim include the country of Malaysia, which attracted manufacturing operations from several semiconductor MNCs in the 1980s by promising them no taxation on earnings in the country for 5 to 10 years and a guarantee that electronics workers would be prevented from forming independent unions. As another example, the U.S. state of Alabama attracted a Mercedes factory in the early 1990s by providing tax breaks and other subsidies amounting to about $200,000 for each job that would be created by the factory, including a promise to purchase 2,500 Mercedes sport utility vehicles for $30,000 each.[33]

The mobility of MNCs also allows them to shift production and profits across national borders in an attempt to reduce their tax burden. An analysis of the corporate financial reports from 200 U.S.-based corporations in the 1980s revealed evidence of tax-motivated income shifting.[34] Again, this creates an environment in which nations compete against each other by offering MNCs low tax rates and breaks on the taxation of capital and other investments. Ireland and several Asian countries have attracted MNC production facilities in recent years primarily through offering low tax rates. Other countries such as Bermuda and the Cayman Islands are recognized as tax havens, and MNCs are able to avoid taxation in other countries simply by legally incorporating in these havens without moving any production facilities there. Corporate profits in countries classified as tax havens rose

---

31. Jeff Gerth and Sheryl Gay Stolberg, "Medicine Merchants: Birth of a Blockbuster; Drug Makers Reap Profits on Tax-Backed Research," *The New York Times*, 23 April 2000, sec. 1, p. 1.
32. Greider, 82.
33. Examples of Malaysia and Alabama from Greider, 91–3.
34. David Harris, Randall Morck, Joel Slemrod, and Bernard Young, "Income Shifting in U.S. Multinational Corporations." In *Studies in International Taxation*, edited by Alberto Giovannini, R. Glenn Hubbard, and Joel Slemrod (Chicago: The University of Chicago Press, 1993), 277–302.

735 percent between 1983 and 1999, whereas profits in countries that are not tax havens grew only 130 percent.[35]

In addition to benefiting from competition by nations, MNCs may be able to override national sovereignty through provisions in recent international trade agreements. Perhaps the most controversial example is the Chapter 11 provisions of the North American Free Trade Agreement (NAFTA). This states that parties to the agreement (Canada, Mexico, and the United States) may not "take a measure tantamount to nationalization or expropriation" of a foreign investor without sufficient compensation. In practice, this provision has provided foreign corporations the opportunity to challenge the sovereign decisions of nations or localities – rights that are unavailable to domestic corporations. As of 2001, there were at least 17 cases in which corporations had filed complaints against NAFTA signatories under the Chapter 11 provisions, most of these claiming economic losses related to environmental regulations. Some of these Chapter 11–based challenges have been successful, including suits against Canada's proposed ban on the import of the gasoline additive methylcyclopentadienyl manganese tricarbonyl (MMT), a Mexican municipality's refusal to grant a construction permit for a hazardous waste site, and Canada's ban of polychlorinated biphenyl (PCB) exports. Although the overall economic and environmental impact of these few Chapter 11 cases is relatively minor, the greater impact may be that national and local regulators are reluctant to set new public safety regulations over concerns about corporate challenges – an effect known as "regulatory chill."

The Environmental and Social Responsibility of MNCs

By virtue of their sheer magnitude, the activities of MNCs can have significant spillover effects on society. The conception of corporations as merely economic entities is being replaced by a view that places corporations in a broader economic, social, and environmental context. Large corporations implicitly recognize this interconnection in their donations to nonprofit organizations. The Web sites of nearly all large corporations include a section detailing their efforts to support such causes as the environment, education, or disaster relief. For example, Wal-Mart donated a total of $200 million in 2002 to thousands of organizations.

The negative side of the interconnections between corporations and their social and physical environment is sometimes expressed in the economic

---

35. David Cay Johnston, "Key Company Assets Moving Offshore," *The New York Times*, 22 November 2002, sec. C, p. 3.

term "externalities." Negative externalities are costs resulting from the actions of an individual or an organization that are not borne by the entity generating the cost but by some part of that entity's external environment. Examples include the costs of pollution, worker injuries, and infrastructure. The only plausible estimate of the total of public costs incurred to support the operations of private corporations was made in 1994 by Ralph Estes, a careful statistician whose work carries considerable credibility even in this difficult area. The total he calculated for the United States was $2.6 trillion per year.[36]

When corporations manage to externalize some of the costs of doing business, they are then not part of the market feedback loop that tells the firm "do less of that – the costs are too high in proportion to the returns." When significant costs have been externalized in the form, for example, of environmental or cultural pollution, a wedge is placed between corporate behavior that maximizes shareholder returns and behavior that (in the simple textbook picture of the competitive firm) would maximize the overall welfare of society. "Given the close relation between minimizing costs and maximizing profits, it is natural to assume that an organization that seeks profits and has significant political power will feel some motivation to use that power to externalize costs, where possible. This motivation may be held in check by ethical considerations, by regulation, or by a fear of backlash from groups that might harm the organization; for example, consumer groups, or others who could mobilize effective public opinion."[37]

An emerging corporate responsibility paradigm that is still being articulated seeks to move toward "internalizing the externalities" by giving all affected parties – not only shareholders – a voice to influence the behavior of large corporations formally or informally. These "stakeholders" include all parties affected by corporate decisions. Stakeholder concerns begin with a requirement for corporate transparency to allow them to make informed decisions. The next requirements are for mechanisms to allow stakeholders to express their preferences and empowerment to enable them to actually affect corporate behavior.

Consumers are one of the significant stakeholder groups. Several effective efforts have been undertaken to empower consumers to influence corporate behavior directly through boycotts, protests, and other direct action. For example, public outcry over "sweatshop" labor being used to produce Nike and Reebok shoes in China, Vietnam, and other countries has led to

---

36. Ralph Estes, *Tyranny of the Bottom Line: Why Corporations Make Good People Do Bad Things* (San Francisco: Berrett-Koehler Publishers, 1996).
37. Neva Goodwin, personal communication, September 2003.

some reforms, including higher pay, increased transparency, and removal of antiunion practices. These movements can only continue if consumers are able to make informed decisions.

Transparency is also necessary to allow investors (including both potential and actual shareholders) to make decisions that reflect values in addition to the desire to maximize returns. When provided with relevant information, investors have proven (as, for example, in the South Africa divestment movement during the 1970s and 1980s or in preferences regarding income derived from tobacco products) that their concerns about corporate behavior are multidimensional. The amount of money dedicated to socially responsible investing in the United States nearly doubled between just 1997 and 1999 from $1.2 trillion to $2.2 trillion.[38]

A trend with potentially significant implications is the concentration of corporate stock held by institutional owners, including mutual funds and pension plans. In the early 1970s, individuals owned about 75 percent of corporate stock in the United States. By 2000, institutions owned about 60 percent of the stock in the 1,000 largest U.S. corporations.[39] In contrast to the earlier (between the late 19th and mid–20th centuries) trend for stocks to be owned by increasingly dispersed individuals, the rise in institutional ownership provides an opportunity for organized and effective influence in matters of corporate governance. Although, to date, institutional influence on corporations has primarily been used to promote the interests of shareholders, the influence of institutional owners continues to increase and could be used to promote the interests of other stakeholders as well.

Other stakeholders include workers, creditors, and "neighbors" – that is, the individuals, municipalities, and other social groups (including future generations) that are affected by MNCs' activities. One way in which that voice has been given to these stakeholders is through the formal integration of some of their representatives into corporate management. In several European countries, particularly Germany, work councils composed of elected workers are intended to "institutionalize worker rights to information and consultation on the organization of production and, in some cases, codetermination of decision making."[40] In Japan, corporate boards often include representatives from their creditor banks.

38. Social Investment Forum, "1999 Report on Socially Responsible Investing Trends in the United States," SIF Industry Research Program (4 November 1999).
39. James Hawley and Andrew Williams, "Some Implications of Institutional Equity Ownership," *Challenge* 43 (July/August 2000):43–61.
40. Kevin Gallagher "Emerging Patterns of Industrial Relations: Overview Essay." In *The Changing Nature of Work*, edited by Frank Ackerman, Neva R. Goodwin, Laurie Dougherty, and Kevin Gallagher (Washington, DC: Island Press, 1998), 220.

Regardless of whether a firm's objectives for improving its social and environmental reputation are ultimately self-interested or altruistic, a significant change in the transparency of MNCs is occurring. Annual reports published by large corporations no longer focus exclusively on financial performance. A notable effort to increase the transparency and consistency of corporations' environmental and social performance is the Global Reporting Initiative (GRI). The GRI, founded in 1997, seeks to "develop and disseminate globally applicable sustainability reporting guidelines . . . for voluntary use by organizations for reporting on the economic, environmental, and social dimensions of their activities, products, and services."[41] The GRI has published reporting guidelines for firms wishing to participate in the project.[42] So far, more than 300 corporations have adopted these guidelines in preparing reports, including AT&T, Ford Motor Company, Nike, Nissan, and Shell.

High standards of environmental and social performance do not necessitate a reduction in economic performance. Until the stock market downturn beginning in 2000, the majority of research suggested that firms with high social performance, as measured by various indices, also have better-than-average economic performance. However, about one-third of the studies comparing economic and social performance have found a negative relationship between the two variables. Further research is needed – particularly on the validity of techniques for measuring social and environmental performance.

Affecting the Behavior of MNCs

The objective of ensuring that corporate behavior is aligned with the broader goals of society rests on two central concepts already discussed: transparency and accountability. To achieve this objective, corporate actions must be transparent not only through accurate financial reports but in reports showing their impact on workers, the environment, social and cultural issues, political activities, and subcontractor policies. They must be accountable not only to shareholders but to all stakeholders.

At the least, it is necessary that corporations obey existing regulations. Recent scandals involving such companies as Enron, WorldCom, and Tyco International have shown the need for greater transparency and accountability even in standard financial accounting. Although financial reporting by

---

41. GRI (Global Reporting Initiative), "Sustainability Reporting Guidelines," Boston: Global Reporting Initiative, 2002, 1.
42. See the GRI Web site at <http://www.globalreporting.org>.

corporations is required by law, social and environmental reporting remains primarily voluntary. The GRI represents a positive step toward standard-ization in this area, but most consumers and noncorporate stakeholders are unaware of such reports. There is a need for information on corporate en-vironmental and social behavior that is more succinct and visible than the necessarily lengthy reports of firms that are complying with GRI require-ments. One system that can provide such information is "eco-labeling." Eco-labels either indicate the overall environmental impacts of a product or identify those products that pass certification criteria. Eco-labeling is now common in such industries as major home appliances, forestry products, and organic foods.

Making such labeling a requirement for a broad range of products and using consistent standards could greatly increase the transparency of corpo-rate environmental and social activities. Absent such a legal regime, after an eco-label has been established, the problems of how to get companies to adopt it – and how to get them to adopt reputable labels created and monitored by disinterested third parties rather than those emerging from industry-controlled groups – remain. Here nongovernment organizations (NGOs) have been playing an important role. For example, the NGO Forest Ethics recently encouraged the large copying and printing chain Kinkos to commit to buying paper from sustainable sources. The Rainforest Action Network has also extracted significant promises from the lumber company Boise Cascade to stop logging and purchasing trees from endangered forests. That is not, however, the whole story; important pieces of the puzzle de-pend on the relationships among corporations – especially the pressure that a firm can exert on a supplier. In the cases just cited, once Kinkos had made its commitment, it pressured Boise Cascade to follow suit.[43]

Consumers, NGOs, and other stakeholders, in addition to responding to eco-labels, can make their preferences known through boycotts and protests. Consumer boycotts and public information campaigns have been instru-mental in effecting corporate change in some instances such as the pack-aging used by McDonald's and the fishing techniques used to harvest tuna. The nascent protest movement, which is commonly referred to as "global democracy" and is epitomized by the Seattle protests at the World Trade Organization's ministerial conference in 1999, emphasizes the goal that all stakeholders be fairly represented in international trade negotiations.

It is unlikely that MNCs will fully align their behavior with the broader social and environmental goals of society solely through voluntary responses

---

43. Jim Carlton, "Boise Cascade Turns Green," *Wall Street Journal*, 3 September 2003, p. B6.

to stakeholder preferences. Rules and regulations on national or international levels will be necessary if the interests of stakeholders are to be formalized. We conclude with a brief discussion of some types of regulations that can influence corporate behavior – first at the national level and then at the international level.

Corporate taxation is a way to collect fees from corporations to finance public services and to compensate for external costs imposed on society. Existing loopholes in national tax policies allow some corporations to achieve very low – even negative – rates of taxation on profits. For example, in 1998, 24 large U.S.-based corporations actually received a tax rebate despite making large profits. These included Enron, Texaco, Pfizer, and WorldCom. One analysis estimates that corporate welfare payments actually exceeded corporate tax payments for 2002 in the United States.[44]

Closing tax loopholes such as accelerated depreciation, excessive tax credits, and deductions for stock options would help ensure that profitable corporations pay what society deems to be their fair share of taxes. It is in the fiscal interest of nations to enact legislation that reduces the ability of MNCs to shelter their profits in off-shore tax havens. The benefits of such tax avoidance accrue to a small portion of any society, whereas the loss of tax revenue means that the majority suffer from loss of services or from the need to pay other taxes to support these services. The absence thus far of significant debate on the prospect of outlawing the use of off-shore tax havens is persuasive evidence for the deep political power of the MNCs.

Enforcement of antitrust laws is another traditional way to limit the power of very large corporations. More rigorous enforcement of antitrust laws could be used to increase competition in industries with high concentration ratios. Greater scrutiny of proposed mergers is another measure for preventing the concentration of market power.

In the political arena, campaign finance and lobbying reform can limit the power of corporations. The data that are available on these issues relate primarily to the United States. Lobbying expenditures in the United States for 1999 are estimated to be about $1.5 billion, and the top contributing industries are pharmaceuticals, insurance, electric utilities, and oil and gas. A similar amount of money is raised annually, on average, for the funding of federal elections,[45] and the MNCs are among the major contributors to these campaigns. The largest corporate lobbying spenders include Philip

---

44. Citizens for Tax Justice, 2002.
45. Lobbying and campaign fundraising data from "Influence, Inc., 2000 Edition," Center for Responsive Politics, <http://www.opensecrets.org/pubs/lobby00/index.asp> (16 September 2003).

Morris, ExxonMobil, Ford, and General Electric. All of these corporations were among the top recipients of corporate tax breaks in the late 1990s.

As corporations increasingly operate in a global market that transcends national boundaries, the possibility of using their mobility to avoid national regulation is enhanced. Thus, the regulation of MNCs is often best approached at the international level through treaties, international institutions, and the coordination of national policies. "Government laws and agencies are needed to regulate markets, but there is no world government with enforceable laws for markets. Hence international agreements are needed to develop civil governance."[46] The key to an effective global corporate regulatory regime does not necessarily require international rules and oversight. Distinct national regimes can be effective if structured within a flexible and enforceable international framework. Consider the current regime of national tax policies. International competitiveness for corporate investment can lead to inefficient corporate behavior as firms spend resources to shift income across national boundaries in an attempt to lower their taxes. There is a need for nations "to harmonize the taxation of business income, and methods of settling transfer pricing and cost allocation disputes."[47] Tax policies should be similar enough across nations to discourage corporate mobility that has no productive or efficient purpose but incurs significant human, and some financial, cost simply to move to the lowest tax area.

Bilateral trade agreements (between two nations) are proliferating, and currently about 300 treaties are in place. Although more bilateral treaties are likely in the future, these are limited in two respects. First, bilateral agreements can conflict with broader regional or international trade agreements, complicating the negotiation process. Second, many bilateral agreements are between nations having disparate bargaining positions with one country maintaining an absolute advantage. The broader international trade agreements that are derided by many in the global democracy movement are nonetheless likely to provide the most effective means to regulate MNCs. "Developing a broad framework for international investment would help stabilize the global economic system while giving direction and coherence to the regulatory environment facing transnational business."[48]

The key to international trade agreements that improve corporate accountability and transparency is that all stakeholders be represented. Progress is slowly being made to include noncorporate interests in international trade

---

46. Severyn T. Bruyn, *A Civil Economy: Transforming the Market in the Twenty-First Century* (Ann Arbor: The University of Michigan Press, 2000), 200.

47. Dunning, 511.

48. John M. Kline, "International Regulation of Transnational Business." In *Companies without Borders: Transnational Corporations in the 1990s*, UNCTAD, Division on Transnational Corporations and Investment (London: International Thomson Business Press, 1996), 305.

negotiations and advisory committees. However, a look at the composition of trade advisory committees in the United States reveals a striking imbalance. Of the 111 members of the 3 major trade advisory committees in the early 1990s, 92 represented individual corporations and 16 represented trade industry associations. Only two represented labor unions, and one represented environmental advocacy groups. Although the Clinton administration did little to decrease the imbalance in existing committees, it did create a separate Trade and Environment Policy Advisory Committee. Still, half the membership of this committee includes industry representatives.[49]

The prospect for international trade agreements that direct corporations to adopt social and environmental objectives once again rests on the issues of accountability and transparency. Unfortunately, international trade policy is currently conducted under circumstances that are deficient on both counts. Trade representatives are appointed, not elected, and the meetings of the World Trade Organization (WTO), the primary international trade agency, are conducted behind closed doors.

Two forces are pushing for greater transparency and accountability in the regulation of international trade. One is the global democracy movement, which is still loosely organized, comprising primarily single-issue groups dedicated to the environment, workers' rights, women's issues, or health topics. This movement is also hampered by being perceived as a group of radical elitist protesters rather than one that offers logical discourse. The second force is the trade preferences of developing countries. Poor countries are desperately in need of economic development but are generally suspicious of the trade rules proposed by the industrial countries and MNCs. The developing countries oppose proposals by industrial nations to expand the WTO regulations beyond trade issues into investor rights along the lines of Chapter 11 of NAFTA. But the developing nations are also fractured, disagreeing about what constitutes fair trade rules. If these two forces were to provide an effective counterweight to the trade interests of the industrial countries, which are heavily influenced by the MNCs, they would need to settle their internal differences, join together, and present a coherent alternative to the current picture of globalization.

CONCLUSION

The importance of multinational corporations has been illustrated along several fronts. Their economic scale is increasing – particularly when measured

49. Public Citizen, "On Procedures for Obtaining Trade Policy Advice from Non-Governmental Organizations," public comments submitted in response to 65 Federal Register 19423, 10 July 2000.

according to their ownership of productive assets. Although economies of scale and scope have contributed to the growth of MNCs, the dominant characteristic of modern MNCs is their transnational mobility in seeking low-cost labor and capital inputs.

MNCs wield significant political power, but precise measurement of this power remains elusive. Corporate power appears particularly evident in the United States, where corporations have lobbied to lower their share of total taxes, to receive substantial subsidies, and to impose externality costs on society. The political power of MNCs is also expressed in international trade agreements under which corporations can challenge the regulations of democratic sovereign governments.

Pressure from several directions is pushing MNCs to become more transparent and accountable regarding their social and environmental impacts, but much more needs to be done. Convergence of MNC objectives with the broader goals of society is unlikely to be realized by internal reforms or national regulations. The transnational mobility of MNCs implies that international regulation is required. The difficulty is that MNCs exert significant influence over international agreements. Only if the interests of all stakeholders are represented in these agreements will meaningful change occur.

2

Multinational Enterprise to 1930

Discontinuities and Continuities

MIRA WILKINS

A multinational enterprise (MNE) is a firm that extends itself over borders to do business outside its headquarters country. It operates across political boundaries. It is a firm as economists define "the firm:" an allocator of resources, a producer of goods and services.[1] Most MNEs have only one home (the headquarters country); some come to have more than one – as with Royal Dutch Shell and Unilever. Some MNEs never extend beyond a single foreign host country; others remain within a region. Some expand slowly, whereas others do so rapidly to become truly global multiproduct, multiprocess enterprises operating around the world that are horizontally and vertically integrated. By 1930, several firms had foreign direct investments on six continents.[2]

To measure the extent of MNE activity, some scholars have looked at the percentage of business done abroad (certain early, quite small companies would qualify as substantial MNEs under this criterion). Others have considered the number of countries in which a firm does business and the absolute size of assets, sales, employment, or profits outside the headquarters

I wish to express my debt in developing this chapter to several individuals who stimulated my thinking, including Alfred Chandler, John Dunning, Jean-François Hennart, Geoffrey Jones, and the late Raymond Vernon. I greatly appreciated the comments of the other participants at the Mapping Multinationals Conference of 1999 – particularly those of Herman van der Wee, Steve Kobrin, and Bruce Mazlish.

1. I prefer the term "enterprise" to firm, company, corporation, or buinsess because the entity over borders is often a cluster of firms, companies, corporations, or all of these; "business" implies both the institution and the activity. For the across-border activity, I favor the term "multinational" over "transnational" because states are not transcended, and over "global" given that evolving enterprises never begin with global coverage. I like the word "multinational" better than "international." Nonetheless, I use the nouns (enterprise, firm, company, corporation, and business) and the adjectives (multinational, transnational, global, and international) interchangeably. Note that I define "enterprise" as a producer of goods and services; I do not confine myself to businesses that produce only goods.

country.[2] A firm fits my definition of an MNE if it extends itself over borders, internalizing business in two or more locales within the firm that are at the time under different sovereignties.[3] I survey the process of internationalization, that is, how firms have evolved while engaging in business outside their home country.

Most of the earliest MNEs began with a single operation abroad in a single host location; typically, however, MNEs invest in more than one host country. The MNE has a presence abroad, however small; it does not merely export to (or through) other unaffiliated firms or to consumers. It retains a headquarters at home. The significance of the MNE for the study of global history is that, through time, such an enterprise provides ongoing intrafirm connections – a tissue that unifies on a regular, not on a one-time, basis. The MNE is an institutional governance structure that serves as a framework for interchanges and relationships, including further mobilization of investments, exports and imports, technology, knowledge, general information transfers, and, most important, management itself. It is thus crucial for historians to focus not on a single function such as foreign direct investment flows but on how the entire firm operates over borders through time.[4]

PRECURSORS OF THE MODERN MULTINATIONAL ENTERPRISE

Karl Moore and David Lewis write that "the businesses operated by the ancient Assyrian colonists [in the second millennium B.C.] constituted the first genuine multinational enterprises in recorded history." They suggest that the Phoenician organizational structures resemble modern forms.[5]

2. A U.N. group (now under the aegis of UNCTAD – the United Nations Conference on Trade and Development) has prepared an index of transnationality for business firms "calculated as the average of the ratios: foreign assets to total assets, foreign sales to total sales and foreign employment to total employment." UNCTAD, *World Investment Report 2002*, 88. In 2000, on the basis of this index, no U.S.-headquartered firm ranked in the top 10 in "transnationality." By contrast, if ranked by size of "foreign assets," 3 U.S. firms are in the top 10. Ibid., 86–88.

3. Multilocation investments within the Austro-Hungarian empire, for example, were domestic before 1914, but at the end of the First World War a business (with no change in operations) might become international with the redrawing of borders. I include in the designation of "different sovereignties" overseas empires, and thus I classify an English company's investment in India before independence as a "foreign" investment as well as a French company's one in Algeria.

4. The foreign direct investment flows from the parent do not reflect the nature of the multinational enterprise activities. Finance is only one function of the multinational enterprise. What makes a multinational enterprise is the firm's extension over borders and its continuing presence abroad. The level of foreign direct investment, although a good measure to use, is only one gauge and can fail to capture the dynamic processes.

5. Karl Moore and David Lewis, *Birth of the Multinational: 2000 Years of Ancient Business History – From Ashur to Augustus* (Copenhagen: Copenhagen Business School Press, 1999), 27, 33, 60ff. Ibid., 79, gives the "golden age of Phoenician business between 1000 and 600 B.C." Moore and Lewis indicate

The records are fragmentary, yet, clearly, business requirements for out-posts abroad emerged as the result of trade. How long individual "multina-tional enterprises" persisted is unknown. From the businesses of the ancient world – those of the Assyrians, Phoenicians, Greeks, and Romans – to medieval Europe is a progression, albeit one with sharp discontinuities. It seems evident that in the interim trading firms headquartered in Asia and the Middle East (and perhaps elsewhere) extended over borders long before the Middle Ages and had structures somewhat akin to modern MNEs. Yet none of the ancient MNEs that Moore and Lewis describe nor, as far as I can determine, the subsequent merchant houses from Asia and the Middle East appear to have had any continuity with the businesses over borders that took shape in medieval Europe.[6]

Within medieval Europe itself, many businesses invested across political jurisdictions. As Rondo Cameron has written, Italian bankers had a pres-ence in England in the thirteenth and fourteenth centuries.[7] The Hanseatic League's loose representation abroad might have qualified it as an MNE. The Medici bank in the fifteenth century – with a headquarters in Florence – had branches throughout Italy and as far afield as Geneva, Lyons, Basel, Avignon, Bruges, and London.[8]

that such enterprises operated on three continents: Asia, Europe, and Africa. While preparing the initial draft of this chapter, I read in the press (*Miami Herald*, June 24, 1999) of the findings of Robert Ballard, who, using Navy nuclear submarines, located two Phoenician shipwrecks in the Mediterranean, dating from 750 B.C., each carrying 10 tons (!) of wine in ceramic jugs. If accurate, this would suggest sizable commerce and would probably justify the assumption of some regular contacts in distant parts to receive, to store, and to sell (to distribute) the jugs, their contents, or both. Herman van der Wee has noted that it is strange to talk of "multinational enterprise" in the era before there were nations. The point is well taken.

6. Historical analysis of recent years has become less Eurocentric. A recognition has arisen that forms of doing business may share certain common features. Jack A. Goldstone, "Review Essays: Whose Measure of Reality?" *American Historical Review* 105 (April 2000): 503–5, considers, for example, merchants around 1300, arguing that there was nothing exceptional about Western merchants. He bases this conclusion on studies of Chinese, Indian, and Arabian merchants of prior years. See also Karl Moore and David Lewis, *Foundations of Corporate Empire* (London: Prentice-Hall, 2000), 120–134. None of the work I have seen shows a direct link between early Chinese, Indian, and Arabian mercantile organizations and those that emerged in medieval Europe.

7. Rondo Cameron, "Introduction," in *International Banking, 1870–1914*, ed. Rondo Cameron and V. I. Bovykin (New York: Oxford University Press, 1991), 3; see also Charles Wilson, "The Multinational in Historical Perspective," in *Strategy and Structure of Big Business: Proceedings of the First Fuji Conference*, ed. Keiichiro Nakagawa (Tokyo: University of Tokyo Press, n.d.), 265–66.

8. Mira Wilkins, "Modern European Economic History and the Multinationals," *The Journal of European Economic History* 6 (Winter 1977): 5 (Hanseatic League). The Hanseatic League's lengthy existence, its changes through time, and its alliance structure fit awkwardly into an analysis of MNEs and their governance. The material on the Medici Bank is from Cameron, "Introduction," 3. For more on banks as multinationals in the 15th and 16th centuries, see Wilson, "The Multinationals," 266, and Charles P. Kindleberger, "International Banks and International Business in Historical Perspective" (1983), reprinted in Charles P. Kindleberger, *Multinational Excursions* (Cambridge: MIT Press, 1984), 155–56.

The age of exploration brought forth new MNEs, including the large trading companies. For the first time, a conception of the world emerged. William McNeill describes 1500 as the advent of the modern era – in world as well as European history – characterized by explorations linking "the Atlantic face of Europe with the shores of most of the earth."[9] The 16th- and 17th-century chartered trading companies, which used the corporate form, have been studied as MNEs.[10] Merchant trading houses (partnerships) also invested over borders, as did other types of businesses.[11]

With preindustrial-revolution MNEs, as with the modern MNE, no farmers integrated forward into distribution abroad. Unlike the modern MNE, no mining companies in a source-of-capital country integrated vertically or horizontally. More important, unlike the modern MNE, no preindustrial-revolution manufacturing company appears to have extended across borders to distribute its own goods, to manufacture its own products, or even to seek its own sources of supply. There were, however, preindustrial-revolution foreign direct investments in agriculture, mining, and manufacturing, but these were made by bankers, traders, and entrepreneurial individuals.[12]

In the Middle Ages, Tuscan merchant bankers financed the silver mining industry in the Balkans – and seem to have arranged for its development. In the 15th and 16th centuries, the Fuggers of Augsburg (Germany) invested in silver and copper mines in the Tyrol and Hungary.[13] The giant chartered companies and merchant trading houses invested over borders in mining and in manufacturing. Ann Carlos and Stephen Nicholas note that

---

9. W. H. McNeill, *The Rise of the West* (Chicago: University of Chicago Press, 1963), 619. I would argue that until there is a "conception of the world," there can be no world economy.

10. For example, Ann M. Carlos and Stephen Nicholas in "Giants of an Earlier Capitalism: The Chartered Trading Companies as Modern Multinationals," *Business History Review* 62 (Autumn 1988): 398–471, believe that the "sixteenth- and seventeenth century trading companies – the English and Dutch East India companies, the Muscovy Company, the Hudson's Bay Company, and the Royal African Company . . . had a geographical reach rivaling today's largest multinational firms. . . . " This was hyperbole, for none operated on all six continents. See also Mira Wilkins, "Modern European Economic History and the Multinationals," 5–6, for the suggestion that these firms fit some definitions of multinational enterprise and Mira Wilkins, *The History of Foreign Investment in the United States to 1914* (Cambridge: Harvard University Press, 1989), 3–13, on the Virginia Company, the Plymouth Company, and other chartered companies as foreign direct investors in America.

11. The trading houses often involved interlocking partnerships. In the mid-seventeenth and eighteenth centuries, English, French, and Dutch mercantile families dispatched relatives to America and to the West Indies as representatives of their firms. By the mid-18th century, American merchants were following the same pattern of sending family members abroad to represent the firm. Mira Wilkins, *The Emergence of Multinational Enterprise: American Business Abroad from the Colonial Era to 1914* (Cambridge: Harvard University Press, 1970), 3–5.

12. I use the word "traders" broadly to include both the large corporate trading companies and the merchant trading houses.

13. Cameron, "Introduction," 3–4 (on the Tuscan merchant bankers and the Fuggers).

the Muscovy Company in the mid-16th century set up a rope house in Russia that employed English craftsmen. The Dutch East India Company in 1641 opened a plant in Bengal to refine saltpeter and engaged in other manufacturing outside of the Netherlands; by 1717 the Dutch East India Company in Kaimbazar, Bengal, "employed" 4,000 silk spinners.[14] In 1632, two Dutch merchants were reported to have established a water-powered ironworks south of Moscow. In the 1760s, Peter Hasenclever (a partner in a merchant trading house) made sizable investments in iron manufacturing in the American colonies of New York and New Jersey.[15]

Individuals also set up companies to extend businesses abroad. The Principio Company, whose origins go back to 1715, was headquartered in London and had been formed by British iron masters; it was not an integration of an existing British business but was managed from England until the American Revolution as a British mining and processing investment in Maryland and Virginia.[16]

In the late 18th and in the first half of the 19th century, coincident with the British Industrial Revolution, mercantilist regulations began to break down. Charles Jones writes of the "elasticity of nationality," and of migration in that period:

Continental merchants and bankers settled in London and the textile regions of the North of England. Sons of British and European manufacturers and merchants traveled the world in search of export markets and often settled in some foreign trading port only to develop a business quite tangential to the original family concern. The mercantile diaspora embraced all the trading and manufacturing nations: Catalans, Basques, Germans, Danes, Chinese, Parsees, Jews, Armenians, Portuguese, Greeks, Dutch, North Americans, Scots and English. The outcome was a cosmopolitan trading community centered in London in which nationality was often very blurred.[17]

14. On the large trading companies' investments abroad in manufacturing, see Carlos and Nicholas, "Giants," 399.

15. John Dunning, *Multinational Enterprises and the Global Economy* (Workingham, UK: Addison-Wesley, 1993), 98 (citing John McKay on the Dutch merchants in Russia); Wilkins, *The History of Foreign Investment in the United States to 1914*, 23, on Hasenclever, a German who, in 1748–49 had established a commercial house in Cadiz, Spain. His family's Westphalian trading firm, founded in 1632, was active in Paris and Amsterdam in the mid-eighteenth century. In 1763, Hasenclever had been the founding partner of Hasenclever, Seton, & Crofts (Charles Crofts was associated with a firm in Amsterdam). This type of complicated partnership arrangement was apparently frequent among merchant firms of the 17th and 18th centuries. Partners changed as deaths occurred, as sons inherited, and as new families were brought into the groupings.

16. Wilkins, *The History of Foreign Investment in the United States to 1914*, 20–23 (on the Principio Company). By 1752, the Principio Company owned four furnaces, two forges, and 30,000 acres in Maryland and Virginia, serving both colonial and mother-country markets.

17. Charles A. Jones, *International Business in the Nineteenth Century* (Brighton, England: Wheatsheaf Books, 1987), 27–28.

Although this late 18th- and early 19th-century "mixing" of peoples of which Jones writes was a prerequisite for the rise of the modern MNE, it was not identical with it. Migration encouraged contacts, new ideas, trade, international investment, and technology transfers, but nationality was not blurred as MNE activities evolved. The MNE internalized the operations and management of the firm over borders; a parent firm persisted.[18] Although some partnership relations with no defined head office continued into the 19th and the 20th centuries (e.g., the family connections between the Rothschilds in London and Paris), the site of the headquarters far more frequently was specific as with the Italian bankers of the 13th, 14th, and 15th centuries and the chartered trading companies of the 16th and 17th centuries.[19]

There is no continuity to the present from any of the medieval banking firms. Of the large chartered companies that Carlos and Nicholas studied, only one (the Hudson's Bay Company) continued on into the 20th century. Even most of the merchant houses of the 17th and 18th centuries lacked continuity into the 19th and 20th centuries, although some that developed

18. More than three decades ago at a 1972 conference on the evolution of international management structures I commented on a paper by Charles Wilson titled "Multinationals, Management, and World Markets: A Historical View." Wilson emphasized "several different nationalities – Dutch, British, German, Swedish, and Swiss . . . " that were part of the "home" company experience of Imperial Chemical Industries; I focused on how different was the evolution of U.S. corporate management. See our discussion in *Evolution of International Management Structures*, ed. Harold F. Williamson (Newark: University of Delaware Press, 1975), especially 191, 217. America was a country of immigrants. It is all well and good, for example, to consider Du Pont as a French business in America at its origin in 1801, for the company used French management, capital, machinery, and workmen but did not remain French; there was no headquarters in France; the Du Ponts settled in America; the stock held abroad was returned to Americans; the firm became domesticated. Wilkins, *The History of Foreign Investment in the United States to 1914*, 44, 66. On the other hand, to suggest that Andrew Carnegie's late-nineteenth-century steel business was that of a Scottish MNE in America is bizarre. MNEs repeatedly provided a conduit for migration; an individual who worked for an MNE would decide to stay in the country of an MNE affiliate. Once an owner migrated, once there was no longer "a headquarters abroad," the MNE relationship no longer existed.

19. This is not to say that with the modern MNE ownership and headquarters cannot or do not change; they do – on occasion. Geoffrey Jones has written of the "migrating multinational." See Geoffrey Jones, "Origins, Management, and Performance," in *British Multinationals: Origins, Management and Performance*, ed. Geoffrey Jones (Aldershot, England: Gower Publishing, 1986), 7. Dual-headquartered multinationals (and there are some with three headquarters) are the exceptions rather than the rule. More important, in the history of MNEs, affiliates in a particular country become "domesticated" – sometimes through a natural process and sometimes through nationalization; when this happens the affiliate is no longer part of the MNE. The historical confusions over nationality and MNEs have their counterpart in the "Who Is Us?" debate at the beginning of the 1990s: see Robert Reich, "Who Is Us?" *Harvard Business Review* 68 (Jan.–Feb. 1990): 53–64, and Laura Tyson, "They Are Not Us: Why American Ownership Still Matters," *The American Prospect* (Winter 1991): 37–47. See also Mark Mason and Dennis Encarnation, eds., *Does Ownership Matter? Japanese Multinationals in Europe* (Oxford: Clarendon Press, 1994).

extensive multinational business did persist.[20] By contrast, there were continuities from the merchant bankers of the late 18th and early 19th centuries into the 20th century.[21]

I believe that to a significant extent there was a wide divide between the modern MNEs and their many precursors. The modern MNEs of the 19th (particularly late 19th) and 20th centuries have had a formidable impact on globalization. The MNE integrates the world economy in a manner that differs from trade, finance, migration, or technology transfer; it puts under one organizational structure a package of ongoing relationships – transfers of goods, capital, people, ideas, and technology. Moving internationally from the more advanced parts of the world through the MNE are business culture, practices, perspectives, and information along with products, processes, and managers.[22]

THE MODERN MULTINATIONAL ENTERPRISE AND THE "AMERICAN MODEL"

In the last third of the 19th century, the transportation and communications revolution (the spread of railroads, steamships, and cables) resulted in a vast expansion of MNEs as speed in delivering goods and information became feasible. Costs fell sharply, and organizational coordination and control within a firm became possible in ways earlier inconceivable.

MNEs did not merely touch the edges of countries but increasingly penetrated within boundaries, causing domestic change along with the international nexus and moving from a "shallow" to an ever deeper involvement in the process. The story line is not linear. "Exits" were many – some partial, some total. There were business retreats and failures, many new entries, and the growth of existing MNEs. Government policies, war, and revolution imperiled the MNE – especially after the Great Depression of the 1930s – but did not weaken their formidable influence on world economic development.

20. According to Richard Robinson, *Business History of the World: A Chronology* (Westport, CT: Greenwood Press, 1993), 72, 149, the Hanseatic League held its last assembly of six towns in 1669 but maintained "agents" in Bergen to 1775, in London to 1852, and in Augsburg to 1863. Geoffrey Jones, in *Merchants to Multinationals* (Oxford: Oxford University Press, 2000) documents the new set of merchant houses that emerged in the 19th and 20th centuries and their relationships with the earlier partnerships.
21. The Rothschilds, the Barings, and the Schroders, for example. By the twenty-first century, however, the Barings were no longer independent (now ING Barings); the Schroders were sold in 2000 to Salomon Smith Barney, which is part of Citigroup. The Rothschilds remain but are a shadow of their former glory.
22. I have put forward some of the ideas here in Mira Wilkins, "Multinational Enterprises and Economic Change," *Australian Economic History Review* 38 (July 1998): 103.

In what I call the "American model," the firm began at home in the domestic market, developed core competencies, and then, typically, if its product was unique, began to export, locate foreign agents, and soon establish foreign sales branches and subsidiaries. If barriers to trade, transportation costs, and such made markets abroad inaccessible or costly to reach, the firm would assemble, pack, bottle, or process near its customers and – at different paces in different markets and in different industries – would move into manufacturing abroad or integrate backward into buying or investing in raw materials at home, abroad, or both.[23] Many European and Japanese MNEs seemed to conform to this American model.[24]

Although my research into the history of foreign investment within the United States uncovered managed inward investments that fit perfectly into the American model, I found, in addition, managed cattle companies, mining firms, breweries, mortgage providers, and other investments with British parents that diverged from the American pattern – that is, they had not started with internalized core competencies and extended those competencies abroad, nor did a firm invest in the United States to fill its own supply needs. There were too many exceptions to the American model to be mere anomalies. I discovered similar British companies operating on a global scale and soon identified comparable French and Dutch businesses. Others have pointed out that many foreign direct investments in Latin America coincided with this pattern of British-managed investments

23. This was the pattern I found when studying American business abroad; see my history of Ford Motor Company's business abroad: Mira Wilkins and Frank Ernest Hill, *American Business Abroad: Ford on Six Continents* (Detroit: Wayne State University Press, 1964); Wilkins, *The Emergence of Multinational Enterprise*; and Wilkins, *The Maturing of Multinational Enterprise: American Business Abroad from 1914 to 1970* (Cambridge: Harvard University Press, 1974). See also John H. Dunning, *American Investment in British Manufacturing Industry* (London: George Allen & Unwin, 1958); Alfred Chandler, *Strategy and Structure* (Cambridge: MIT Press, 1962); Alfred Chandler, *The Visible Hand* (Cambridge: Harvard University Press, 1977); and Oliver E. Williamson, "The Modern Corporation: Origins, Evolution, Attributes," *Journal of Economic Literature* XIX (December 1981): 1537–68.
24. Raymond Vernon moved from his studies on American business abroad to studies of non-U.S. multinational enterprise. John Stopford in "The Origins of British-Based Multinational Manufacturing Enterprises," *Business History Review* 48 (Autumn 1974): 303–35, asked how ideas developed from research on American multinationals applied to the evolution of British firms. See also Larry Franko, "The Origins of Multinational Manufacturing by Continental European Firms," *Business History Review* 48 (Autumn 1974): 277–302, and his *The European Multinationals* (Stamford, CT: Greylock Publishers, 1976); Jones, ed., *British Multinationals*; Geoffrey Jones and Harm Schröter, eds., *The Rise of Multinationals in Continental Europe* (Aldershot, England: Edward Elgar, 1993); and Mira Wilkins, "Japanese Multinational Enterprise before 1914," *Business History Review* 60 (Spring 1986): 199–231. This was the approach in Alfred Chandler, *Scale and Scope* (Cambridge: Harvard University Press, 1990). I found the "American model" highly useful in understanding German chemical companies in the United States. See, for example, Mira Wilkins, "German Chemical Firms in the United States from the Late 19th Century to the Post-World War II Period," in *The German Chemical Industry in the Twentieth Century*, ed. John E. Lesch (Dordrecht, The Netherlands: Kluwer Academic Publishers, 2000), 285–321.

in the United States. Donald Paterson found differences between British and American direct investments in Canada. Jean-François Hennart noted evidence in British and French investments in tin in Malaya and other foreign investments in tin, and Geoffrey Jones concluded that the vast expansion of British international banks was not part of the overseas activities of the domestic commercial banks; instead multinational banks were set up for the specific purpose of overseas banking in a particular region.[25] Ideas developed on "the free-standing company – one that extends over borders but does not grow out of an existing home-based business operation."[26] These free-standing companies were in clusters, for without core competencies they had to draw on the talents of outsiders. Those free-standing companies that survived did come to internalize many of the needed skills.[27]

BASIC INFRASTRUCTURE AND MULTINATIONAL ENTERPRISE – TO 1930

Basic infrastructure set the foundations for a more closely knit world economy. Some MNEs invested in infrastructure whereas others did so in mining, plantations, or activities for which they had to supply the infrastructure. The MNEs that emerged were the "free-standing companies," the "American model" firms, and some that fit neatly into neither paradigm.

In the late 19th and early 20th centuries, MNEs contributed to two fundamental transportation needs: U.S. outward direct investments in transit routes across Nicaragua and Panama cut distances, whereas the opening of the Suez Canal Company in 1869 dramatically reduced the time between West and East by sea from London to Bombay (by about 40%) and from

25. On the relevance to Latin America, see Charles Jones, "The Origins of Modern Multi-National Corporations: British Firms in Latin America, 1850–1930," in *Foreign Investment in Latin America: Impact on Economic Development*, ed. Carlos Marichal (Milan, Italy: Università Bocconi, 1994), 27–37; for Canada, Donald G. Paterson, "The Failure of British Business in Canada, 1890–1914," in *Proceedings of the Business History Conference*, ed. Herman Krooss (Bloomington: School of Business, Indiana University, 1975), and idem, *British Direct Investments in Canada, 1890–1914* (Toronto: University of Toronto Press, 1975); for tin, Jean-François Hennart, "Transaction Costs and the Multinational Enterprise: The Case of Tin," *Business and Economic History* 16 (1987): 147–59; and on banking, Geoffrey Jones, *British Multinational Banking* (Oxford: Oxford University Press, 1993).
26. Mira Wilkins, "The Free-Standing Company, 1870–1914: An Important Type of British Foreign Direct Investment," *Economic History Review* 2d ser., 41 (May 1988): 259–82; Wilkins and Harm Schröter, eds., *The Free-Standing Company in the World Economy, 1830–1996* (Oxford: Oxford University Press, 1998). I acknowledge my huge debts to many scholars in developing these ideas.
27. In many ways the free-standing company paradigm seems more interesting in understanding the start of some MNEs and their early evolution than it does in explaining the firm's survival beyond its first decades.

London to Singapore (about 30%).[28] Because private enterprise had been unable to put together the resources for the Panama Canal, it was built by the U.S. government and opened in the summer of 1914. So, too, the British government invested in the Suez Canal Company, but, with its headquarters and administrative offices in Paris, it remained a private sector–managed, foreign, direct investment until the Egyptian nationalization of the canal in the 1950s.[29] The shortening of distances achieved by the building of both canals was crucial to the integration of the world economy.

The application of steam to ocean travel led to new steamship companies of many nationalities with the British in a dominant position. These companies typically stationed representatives in ports of their principal business and encouraged new investments in port facilities and docks or made such investments themselves. By the outbreak of the First World War, steamship companies were MNEs, and the large German steamship lines owned docks in U.S. ports.[30] Several British free-standing companies built docks (and undertook related construction projects) abroad.[31]

In the same period, insurance companies organized overseas operations to insure cargos. Marine insurance became associated with fire insurance (warehouses holding goods burned). Many British, French, German, Swiss, and other insurers established international businesses. Japanese insurance companies insured Japanese imports and exports.[32] In 1914, more than

28. The Nicaragua route, by carriage and boat, was run by an American-controlled company, the Accessory Transit Company, and was in operation from 1851 to 1855. The Panama Railroad had been chartered (in New York) on April 7, 1849, but was not in full operation until 1855, when it proved a superior way of getting to the American West (superior to the cross-Nicaragua route and the best connection between the American East and the American West until the transcontinental railroad was completed in 1869). Both were American businesses abroad. I have called the Panama Railroad the first truly large American direct investment abroad. See William Woodruff, *The Impact of Western Man* (New York: St. Martin's Press, 1967), 243, on the reduction of distances.

29. The Suez Canal Company is a fine example of a "free-standing company." There was no existing parent canal company that used its know-how to extend abroad. Rather, a new company was established that drew on the engineering talents, managerial skills, and financial resources of France and Britain to establish and to operate the canal for many decades. The administrative offices were in Paris.

30. Wilkins, *The History of Foreign Investment in the United States to 1914*, 517. When the steamship companies invested in docks in connection with their existing businesses, this conformed to the American model in that the investments arose based on their internalized core competencies. Other docks were built by the "great British contractors," who as MNEs extended abroad. See Wilson, "The Multinational," 271, and Marc Linder, *Projecting Capitalism: A History of the Internationalization of the Construction Industry* (Westport, CT: Greenwood Press, 1994), 66.

31. Often, what appeared to be "free-standing companies" were in fact closely integrated with MNEs.

32. On the large number of foreign insurance companies doing business in the United States before 1914, see Wilkins, *The History of Foreign Investment in the United States to 1914*, 528–535; Mira Wilkins, *The History of Foreign Investment in the United States, 1914–1945* (Cambridge: Harvard University Press, 2004) shows the importance of the international business of insurance companies in the years 1914–1945. Specifically, on Japanese insurers, see Wilkins, "Japanese Multinational

two-thirds of policies on American vessels were written by foreign insurers.[33] American life insurance companies had become MNEs before
the war.[34]

Railroads built in less developed countries were often constructed by
MNEs. Marc Linder writes that late-20th-century multinational construction firms had "their forerunners in the nineteenth-century English, French,
and German railroad construction and civil engineering firms that were integrated into a world market that they helped forge."[35] As Linder points
out, "the civil engineering knowledge and technology required to build
technically challenging mountain routes for many non-European railroads
generally exceeded the capacities" within many countries in which the railroads were being built.[36] In the United States, despite civil engineering
knowledge, Americans turned to British MNEs for difficult construction
endeavors such as railroad tunnels.[37]

British and Anglo-Belgian companies led in the spread of the railroad
system from Britain to Northern France and to Belgium (after the latter's
separation from Holland in 1831).[38] In developed countries, most railroads
could be financed through capital markets – through foreign and domestic[39]
portfolio investments – and there were qualified personnel to manage and to
run the railroads. Although some of the investments over borders in railroads
were in foreign-managed activities, much of the financing for U.S. railroads,
for example, came through London and Amsterdam; however, the railroads

Enterprise before 1914," *The History of Foreign Investment in the United States to 1914*, 227, and *The History of Foreign Investment in the United States, 1914–1945.*

33. Jeffrey J. Safford, *Wilsonian Maritime Diplomacy, 1913–1921* (New Brunswick, NJ: Rutgers University Press, 1978), 231. These foreign insurers would typically have operations in the United States.
On this, the annual issues of *Best's Insurance Reports (Fire and Marine)* are wonderful.

34. See Wilkins, *The Emergence of Multinational Enterprise*, 64–65, 103–7, and Morton Keller, *The Life
Insurance Enterprise, 1885–1910* (Cambridge: Harvard University Press, 1963).

35. Linder, *Projecting Capitalism*, 5.   36. Ibid., 15–16.

37. Wilkins, *The History of Foreign Investment in the United States to 1914*, 550.

38. Wilson, "The Multinational," 272. In this 1974 presentation to the first Fuji Conference in Japan,
Wilson puzzled as to whether it was appropriate to apply the term multinational to the British
activities in railroads on the European continent. He concluded that these railroad investments did
come within the possible definition of a multinational. And he added, "As far as I know, nobody
has investigated the nineteenth-century international railway system in Europe as a multinational
system." He pointed out that I had in my *Emergence of Multinational Enterprise* dealt with U.S. railway
investments abroad as associated with early American MNEs, Wilson, "The Multinational," 272,
288. There is still an absence of work that applies concepts of managed business investments and
MNEs to the emergence of railroads on a worldwide basis. Linder, *Projecting Capitalism*, 37–38,
shows the role of British contractors in the building of railroads on the European continent in the
1840s, 1850s, and 1860s.

39. In the early years of railroad building, English ironmasters, who sold iron rails to American railroad
companies, were often paid in securities; British merchant bankers created a market for such securities
in the United Kingdom. They did not result in foreign direct investment. Wilkins, *The History of
Foreign Investment in the United States to 1914*, 79.

were administered by Americans.[40] In other parts of the world, not only the construction but also the capital and the management came from abroad.[41] Sometimes, the ownership and control, initially in foreign hands, became national, as in Mexico, where principal railroads were nationalized between 1903 and 1910. Later, foreign investments were portfolio ones.[42]

Even though some Canadian railroads stretched over the border into the United States (and vice versa) and other existing railroads extended across national frontiers, elsewhere most railroads did not go over borders.[43] The great British contractors did become MNEs and built railroads outside of their home country.[44] A sizable number of free-standing companies participated in building and running railroads – some with long-lived investments and some rather short. Some railroads had no foreign "parent" but nonetheless were owned and administered by foreign investors.[45] So, too, several railroads in "Third World" countries, either at origin or later, came to be associated with primary products (United Fruit grew and transported bananas), and mining or oil concessions often included railroad building with the railroad concession acquired by foreign investors seeking to develop the primary product. Sometimes a trading company, such as W. R. Grace & Co., might play a role in obtaining financing abroad for a railroad. Other railroad building was connected with the search by iron and steel makers for export markets as in Krupp's obtaining a concession in the 1890s to build a railroad in Venezuela.[46] Sideline activities followed as railroad construction companies were required to develop manufacturing facilities.[47] Railroad

40. Wilkins, *The History of Foreign Investment in the United States to 1914*, Chap. 6.
41. Michael J. Twomey, "Patterns of Foreign Investment in Latin America in the Twentieth Century," in *Latin America in the World Economy since 1800*, ed. John H. Coatsworth and Alan M. Taylor (Cambridge: Harvard University Press, 1998), 171–72. It is important to look at both construction and railroad companies. The former often made direct investments while the construction was moving forward and then exited slowly, retaining securities as payment, or rapidly when the railroad had been built.
42. On Mexican railroads, see Reinhard Liehr and Mariano E. Torres Bautista, "British Free-Standing Companies in Mexico, 1884–1911," in *The Free-Standing Company in the World Economy, 1830–1996*, ed. Wilkins and Schröter, 261–62, and Wilkins, *The Emergence of Multinational Enterprise*, 119–20.
43. Wilkins, *The History of Foreign Investment in the United States to 1914*, 224–26.
44. Linder, *Projecting Capitalism*, is particularly good on this role. Contractors of other nationalities also built railroads abroad.
45. This seems to have been the case with some Argentine railroads.
46. Linder, *Projecting Capitalism*, 71–72. See also ibid., 72, on the French firm La Société de Construction des Batignolles founded in 1846, which produced locomotives and steel and integrated into railroad construction in numerous countries in order to sell its output.
47. With no available adequate French manufacturing facilities appropriate for the Le Havre–Rouen–Paris railroad, in 1841 the British builder Brassey cofinanced the construction in France of factories to produce rails and rolling stock. Linder, *Projecting Capitalism*, 37. In the early 1880s, The Alabama, New Orleans, Texas and Pacific Junction Railways Company Ltd. (a British free-standing company) built a creosote works in Louisiana to supply the New Orleans & North Eastern Railroad Company

building mobilized labor – usually within the country – but sometimes across borders.[48]

What does this add up to? By 1910, on a global scale, more than 640,000 miles of railroads were in place.[49] Do we know what percentage of global railroads involved participation of MNEs? No. A formidable amount of foreign investment appears to have been mobilized to build and run world railroads; however, only a limited amount of it was foreign direct investment, and much of this was concentrated in construction rather than subsequent management of the railroads.[50] Nonetheless, in certain host countries – especially less developed ones – the activities of MNE-type investors were undoubtedly crucial, including the impact of the great contractors and their international extension. Early MNE activities appear to have receded over time.

The first direct communication by cable between London and Paris came in November 1852 through the lines of the Submarine Telegraph Co. and the European and American Telegraph Co. with the British financing the enterprise. Between 1852 and 1855, the German company Siemens, important in the laying of cable, designed and put into operation a Russian telegraph system in European Russia – a system run by the Russian government. In 1866, an American company financed by British capital was successful in transatlantic cable communication. (Telegraph connections across the United States, completed in 1861, had not involved MNEs.) By 1870, the British Indian Telegraph Company had laid a direct cable from Bombay to England, and soon afterward the Great Northern Telegraph Company of Denmark extended the trans-Siberian line (finished in the late 1860s) from Vladivostok to Shanghai and Yokohama, tying in with the cables of the Eastern Extension Company and linking up India with China, Singapore, and Australia. The British-owned Pender group developed a global business. By 1914 London and New York were only minutes apart.[51] America's role

during the period when the British firm was involved in constructing the American railroad. See Alabama, New Orleans, Texas and Pacific Junction Railways Company Ltd., "Directors' Report, Nov. 20, 1883," 4–5, copy in the possession of Mira Wilkins.

48. British companies building railroads in East Africa, for example, brought in Indian contract labor.

49. A. G. Kenwood and A. L. Lougheed, *The Growth of the International Economy, 1820–1990* (London: Routledge, 1992), 13.

50. Herbert Feis, *Europe: The World's Banker, 1870–1914* (New York: W. W. Norton, 1930), 27, adapting George Paish's numbers, found 40.7 percent of the British capital "publicly invested" overseas in 1914 was in railroads with the largest portion (40.3%) in U.S. railroads, another 20 percent in the Dominions and colonies (excluding India), less than 10 percent in British Indian railroads (9.2%), and the remaining 30.5 percent in railroads in other foreign countries.

51. On the extension of the cables, see James Foreman-Peck, *A History of the World Economy: International Economic Relations since 1850* (Totowa, NJ: Barnes & Noble, 1983), 69–70; Wilkins, *The History of Foreign Investment in the United States to 1914*, 94; and Wilkins, *The Emergence*, 21, 47–48. On the

in cables grew – especially in Latin America – and, in 1920, the Central
and South American Telegraph Company became All American Cables, in
which International Telephone and Telegraph Corporation (ITT) acquired
a controlling interest 7 years later.[52]

In telephone communication it was American MNEs that transferred
U.S. technology abroad. The American-owned Edison Telephone Company, in 1879, began in London to install the first European telephone
exchange.[53] In Canada, in 1880 the American Bell Telephone Company
started and initially controlled the Bell Telephone Company of Canada;[54]
American Bell was convinced that "the whole field is far too large for us to
undertake to cover"[55] and planned to stimulate the involvement of Cana-
dians and Canadian capital. On a global basis, Germans, too, became active
(Siemens) and so did Swedes (Ericsson).[56] Telephone utilities were gradually
established worldwide and were sometimes linked with waterworks, electric
power and light, and electrical tramways.[57] After ITT was formed in 1920,
it began to expand markedly. It acquired Western Electric's international
manufacturing operations in 1925 – except for those operations in Canada.
By 1930, ITT operated telephone systems in Spain and in seven Latin American countries (Cuba, Mexico, Peru, Brazil, Uruguay, Chile, and Argentina)
and won telephone services concessions in Romania, Turkey, and China.[58]

role of Siemens, see Wilfried Feldenkirchen, *Werner von Siemens* (Columbus: Ohio State University
Press, 1994), 59 and passim. On Pender, see Hugh Barty-King, *Girdle around the Earth* (London:
Heinemann, 1979).

52. Wilkins, *The Emergence of Multinational Enterprise*, 48 n. Wilkins, *The Making of Multinational
Enterprise*, 27–28, 130.
53. Wilkins, *The Emergence of Multinational Enterprise*, 49–50.
54. Ibid., 50.
55. The quotation is from W. H. Forbes, President of American Bell, to C. F. Sise, the American
managing director of the Canadian enterprise, July 13, 1880, cited in ibid., 50.
56. In the early twentieth century, the Swedish telephone utility, linked in with L. M. Ericsson, got
telephone utility concessions in Moscow and Warsaw. By 1905, Ericsson (and the American Bell
Company) were installing telephones in Mexico. Wilkins, "Multinational Enterprises and Economic
Change," 108. See also James Foreman-Peck, "International Technology Transfer, 1876–1914," in
International Technology Transfer: Europe, Japan and USA, 1700–1914, ed. David Jeremy (Aldershot,
England: Edward Elgar, 1991), 122–52.
57. Thus, in the early twentieth century, the Delagoa Bay Development Corporation (a British free-
standing company) obtained a concession in Mozambique to operate a waterworks, telephone, and
an electrical tramway in Lorenzo Marques; this corporation had an interest in a separately established
power and light company. See Feis, *Europe*, 253. Similarly, in 1910 the Canadian-controlled Rio
de Janeiro Tramway, Light & Power Co. took over the Interurban Telephone Company, which
had the exclusive right to string lines throughout the state of Rio; this meant it had long-distance
lines to complement its domestic service in this important Brazilian city (and state). Christopher
Armstrong and H. V. Nelles, *Southern Exposure: Canadian Promoters in Latin America and the Caribbean,
1896–1930* (Toronto: University of Toronto Press, 1988), 174.
58. Wilkins, "Multinational Enterprises and Economic Change," 109 and 128, 37 n., and *The Maturing
of Multinational Enterprise*, 147 (on the sale of International Western Electric to ITT).

MNEs also introduced radio communication. Before the First World War, an affiliate of the British-owned multinational enterprise Marconi's Wireless Telegraph Company dominated this sector in the United States,[59] and Telefunken, a joint venture between Allgemeine Elektrizitäts Gesellschaft (AEG) and Siemens & Halske, was building a high-powered wireless station there in 1914.[60] After the First World War, determined not to leave this sector in foreign hands, the U.S. Navy arranged with General Electric for the Radio Corporation of America (RCA) to take over the Marconi broadcasting facilities,[61] and German-built radio stations in the United States were not returned to German control after the war. In the 1920s, RCA inaugurated long-distance wireless communication between the United States, Europe, and Asia, investing in high-power radio stations from Sweden to Poland, in China, and in Argentina. In other parts of South America and in Canada, RCA entered into joint ventures with British companies.[62] So, too, large MNEs operating in isolated locations in less developed countries supplied their own facilities; United Fruit, for example, had a radio company as a subsidiary.[63] The news services – the French predecessor to Agence France Presse, British Reuters, and the United Press (organized in 1907) – used the telegraph first and then the radio services to disseminate news globally.[64]

More information moved more rapidly than ever in history through the intermediation of MNEs. Motion pictures, until the advent of television, did more to unify the world economy than any other medium. In the age of silent film, the key MNE was the French Pathé, which by 1914 had outlets in more than 40 major cities worldwide. In the 1920s, when the "talkie" replaced the silent film, American movies were marketed internationally by U.S. MNEs.[65] The effect was dramatic. Thomas O'Brien writes that

the wondrous images bore testimony to the technological wonders and achievements of U.S. society. Film images of enormous factories, the skyscrapers of New York, spacious homes, and a plethora of consumer goods sent a graphic message of success through the American way to people across the Western Hemisphere. The films of the period suggested through their plot lines that human ills and unhappiness could be resolved through the ameliorating effects of consumerism.

59. Wilkins, *The History of Foreign Investment in the United States to 1914*, 520–23.
60. See ibid., 522, for the German involvement.
61. Mira Wilkins, *The History of Foreign Investment in the United States, 1914–1945*, 95–99.
62. Wilkins, *The Maturing of Multinational Enterprise*, 129.
63. Wilkins, *The Emergence of Multinational Enterprise*, 160 (United Fruit set up Tropical Radio Telegraph Company in 1913). See also Wilkins, *The Maturing of Multinational Enterprise*, 129–30.
64. Geoffrey Jones, *The Evolution of International Business* (London: Routledge, 1996), 160.
65. Wilkins, "Multinational Enterprises and Economic Change," 109. On Pathé, see Mira Wilkins, "Charles Pathé's American Business," *Entreprises et Histoire* 6 (Sept. 1994): 133–44.

Meanwhile, U.S. corporations enjoyed an important ally in their effort to make that vision a reality.[66]

In addition, and very basic, was the spread of light and power utilities. An early participant was the Imperial Continental Gas Company of the United Kingdom; by 1914, it operated gas (and in certain places also electrical) utilities in Austria-Hungary, Belgium, France, and Germany.[67] In the late 19th century and at the start of the 20th century, MNEs took part in installing and operating electric light and power facilities in urban areas around the world. (This, of course, made it possible to show the movies in the 1920s.) American, Canadian, British, Belgian, German, and Swiss MNEs were responsible for electrification's global reach.[68] In Russia, by 1914, most cities had electricity, and non-Russian-owned companies possessed and controlled about 90 percent of the public utilities.[69] Many of the new power plants provided for urban transportation (traction) as well as heat and light. Financial groups in Belgium, for example, moved rapidly from railroads to tramways and then to more general electrical activities.[70]

By the 1920s, the largest new U.S. direct investments abroad were in public utilities.[71] One U.S. company alone – the American & Foreign Power Company – at the end of that decade furnished 90 percent of Cuba's electric power, 75 percent of Chile's, 30 percent of Mexico's, 15 percent of Brazil's, and 13 percent of Argentina's. It also supplied electric power in China and India.[72] By 1930, the Japanese-owned South Manchuria Electric Company (formed in 1926) had taken over many of the power plants from the Japanese-owned South Manchuria Railway Company.[73]

Coal was a key input for transportation and industry. By the early 20th century, almost all the capital for India's large coal industry came from

66. Thomas O'Brien, *The Century of U.S. Capitalism in Latin America* (Albuquerque: University of New Mexico Press, 1999), 53.
67. Jones, *The Evolution*, 148, 155.
68. William Hausman, Peter Hertner, and Mira Wilkins ran a session at the 2002 International Economic History Congress in Buenos Aires on the role of MNEs in the introduction of electric power and light on a global scale.
69. Wilkins, "Multinational Enterprises and Economic Change," 106–7.
70. The Belgians specialized in tramway construction. Jones, *The Evolution*, 157, and Hermann Van der Wee and Martine Goossens, "Belgium," in *International Banking*, ed. Cameron and Bovykin, 125–27.
71. Measured by percentage increase in U.S. direct investment abroad during the decade 1919–29. This was pointed out to me by Robert Lipsey. For the figures, see Wilkins, *The Maturing of Multinational Enterprise*, 55. On the expansion abroad of American MNEs in power and light, see ibid., 131–34. See also William J. Hausman and John L. Neufeld, "U.S. Foreign Direct Investment in Electric Utilities in the 1920s," in *The Free-Standing Company*, ed. Wilkins and Schröter, 361–90.
72. Wilkins, "Multinational Enterprises and Economic Change," 108.
73. C. F. Remer, *Foreign Investments in China* (New York: Macmillan, 1933), 490.

investors in India itself. Nonetheless, the big coal companies there do appear to have been of British origin, and most of the well-known British trading houses in India had colliery interests.[74] British steamship companies – for example, the British India Steam Navigation Company – had coal mining interests in Bengal before the First World War.[75] Also, coal companies incorporated in South Africa had London offices with the majority of ownership in the United Kingdom,[76] and Harm Schröter found that before the First World War some German and Belgian free-standing companies in Bohemia (Austria-Hungary) participated in coal production.[77] The Japanese-owned South Manchuria Railway Company had major investments in coal mines at Fushun and Yeṇtai. In 1930, the Fushun mine was reputed to have been the greatest open cut coal mine in the world, serving the railroad but also providing exports to Japan. There were also other Japanese coal and iron direct investments in China.[78]

Far more global were MNE interests in oil, which, although important for the world economy from the late nineteenth and early twentieth centuries, did not replace coal until the 1960s as the world's principal source of energy. After oil was found in commercial quantities in 1859 in Titusville, Pennsylvania, America became the largest producer of crude oil and refiner of oil, and with the exception of a few years around the turn of the century when Russian crude oil output, developed by European capital, exceeded that of the United States, the United States led the world in crude oil production. From the start, Standard Oil companies were multinational, investing initially in selling and then refining abroad.[79] At first, the international oil companies served kerosene markets but with electrification turned to provide for new transportation needs (cars, trucks, buses, fuel oil for shipping and oil for tanks, ambulances, and airplanes) as well as oil for lubricants. By the late 1920s, the largest oil MNEs were investing in petrochemicals. By 1930, the leading companies in this fully internationalized industry were the predecessor of Exxon (Standard Oil of New Jersey), Royal Dutch/Shell,

---

74. Stanley Chapman, "British Free-Standing Companies and Investment Groups in India and the Far East," in *The Free-Standing Company*, ed. Wilkins and Schröter, 207, 210.
75. Jones, *The Evolution*, 152.
76. See Mira Wilkins, "The Impact of Multinational Corporations," *South African Journal of Economic History* 4 (March 1989): 11, 15, on whether these coal companies could qualify under the rubric of MNE.
77. Harm Schröter, "Continental European Free-Standing Companies: the Case of Belgium, Germany, and Switzerland," in *The Free-Standing Company*, ed. Wilkins and Schröter, 337.
78. Remer, *Foreign Investments in China*, 490–95.
79. The best history of the international oil industry is Daniel Yergin, *The Prize* (New York: Simon & Schuster, 1991); on U.S. oil multinationals, see Wilkins, *The Emergence of Multinational Enterprise* and *The Maturing of Multinational Enterprise*.

and the predecessor of British Petroleum. MNEs invested on six continents in selling, refining, transporting, producing, and exploring.

By 1914, new groups of trading companies had emerged to handle the vastly expanded trade.[80] Japanese trading companies came to have an important role. Because large general trading companies knew suppliers and markets, they could proctor quality control and identify and avoid fraud. Their activities cut costs in transactions and aided trade by reducing uncertainties.[81] The value of world commerce in primary products and in manufactured articles (measured in current dollars) grew steadily from the mid-1870s to 1929. Throughout these years the value of international trade in primary products exceeded that in manufactured articles.[82] With the development of the transportation, communications, and energy sectors came layered complementary trading arrangements – some within trading companies, some within major industrial companies, and some separate.[83] Standardized accounting procedures followed. The principal British accounting firms initially set up partnerships in the United States to audit investments, and then these firms came to serve the U.S. market.[84]

New international economic relationships and new globalization required international banking structures[85] as conduits for capital movement. Financial institutions moved monies and banks arranged new issues and priced

80. There were general trading companies and product-specific trading companies. It is important to view these as MNEs and as conduits in the integration of the world economy. See Jones, *Merchants to Multinationals*, and Geoffrey Jones, ed., *The Multinational Traders* (London: Routledge, 1998), on the nineteenth and twentieth centuries' traders.

81. See Wilkins, "Multinational Enterprises and Economic Change," 110. D. K. Fieldhouse, *Merchant Capital and Economic Decolonization* (Oxford: Clarendon Press, 1994), 4–5, is particularly good on the specialized skills of trading companies.

82. The figures are provided in League of Nations, *Industrialization and Foreign Trade* (Geneva: League of Nations, 1945), 17, 157. From 1926 to 1929, world trade (exports plus imports; annual average) in manufactured articles was $25.3 billion, whereas in primary products it was $40.5 billion. From 1876 to 1880, the figures were $4.8 billion (manufactured articles) compared with $8.3 billion (primary products).

83. This story is very product and very country specific. One large Japanese trading company, Mitsui & Co., in 1914 was responsible for almost 34 percent of all Japanese raw silk exports to the United States and 30 percent of U.S. raw cotton exports to Japan. These were the two major commodities in America's trade with Japan. Wilkins, "Multinational Enterprises and Economic Change," 110. Erich Pauer writes that "as in the period prior to World War I and also in the inter-war period, most of the German companies relied on German trading companies for the distribution of their goods in Japan. Most common were German trading companies acting as agents who were granted exclusive rights but had the obligation to be the exclusive agents for the products concerned." Erich Pauer, "German Companies in Japan in the Interwar Period," in *Foreign Business in Japan before World War II*, ed. Takeshi Yuzawa and Masaru Udagawa (Tokyo: University of Tokyo Press, 1990), 248.

84. Wilkins, *The History*, 536–46.

85. My mentors on international banking networks are Geoffrey Jones and Rondo Cameron. I have found particularly useful Richard Tilly, "International Aspects of the Development of German Banking," in *International Banking*, ed. Cameron and Bovykin, 90–112.

and marketed them; the securities were traded on stock exchanges. By 1914, the London stock exchange was an international market, as were the Amsterdam, Paris, Frankfurt, and Berlin exchanges. The New York Stock Exchange was fundamentally a domestic market before 1914, but in the 1920s it became an international market.[86] International business was often conducted through partnerships between and among houses in New York, London, Paris, Frankfurt and Berlin.[87] Large German, French, Belgian, and Swiss banks dealt internationally as issuers of securities and as sizable foreign investors; by 1914 most had representation in London. The Deutsche Bank set up certain banks abroad.[88] The war was disruptive. After the war, in the 1920s, stockbrokers provided for global investments; some stockbrokers' firms became MNEs.

International trade required financing. International trade is impossible without payments.[89] To carry on such activities, sometimes a little more representation abroad by bankers was required than was the case with the issue of securities.[90] Before 1914, the pound sterling was an international currency, and the British dominated the financing of international trade. Just as securities issues brought foreign countries into a global community so, too, trade finance linked nations.

International banks also arranged remittances home for immigrants: Italian banks, for example, were represented in Latin America and in the United States, where immigrants needed such services.[91] International banks, in addition, in certain countries, provided domestic commercial banking services with deep penetration within the domestic economy. British overseas banks introduced extensive domestic banking services for international and everyday domestic needs in many countries. By the start of the First World War, some 30 British banks owned and ran more than 1,000 branches and offices on 6 continents. British overseas banks, as multinational retail banks in

---

86. R. C. Michie, *The London and New York Stock Exchanges, 1850–1914* (London: Allen & Unwin, 1987). Mira Wilkins, "Cosmopolitan Finance in the 1920s: New York's Emergence as an International Financial Centre," in *The State, the Financial System, and Economic Modernization*, ed. Richard Sylla, Richard Tilly, and Gabriel Tortella (Cambridge: Cambridge University Press, 1999), 271–91.
87. See Paul H. Emden, *Money Powers of Europe in the Nineteenth and Twentieth Centuries* (London: S. Low, Marston, 1937).
88. Tilly, "International Aspects," 93, 94. Despite large French and other foreign interests in Russia, apparently the only foreign bank to maintain "branches" in Russia before the First World War was the Crédit Lyonnais, which opened an agency in St. Petersburg in 1879 and 2 years later added offices in Moscow and Odessa. These branches apparently were for "information"-seeking purposes. See B. V. Anan'ich and V. I. Bovykin, "Foreign Banks and Foreign Investment in Russia," in *International Banking*, ed. Cameron and Bovykin, 267.
89. Acceptances were the bread and butter of the British merchant banks.
90. Jones, *British Multinational Banking*, 5.
91. See Wilkins, *The History of Foreign Investment in the United States, 1914–1945*, 172.

Asia, Africa, the Middle East and Latin America, were often the first modern banks within those countries.[92] By 1913, three British banks attracted fully a third of the deposits in the entire Brazilian banking system.[93] Also in Brazil in 1913, five French, three German, two Belgian, two Portuguese, and one Argentine bank provided banking services.[94] Typically, the share of a foreign market held by banks from abroad declined as new domestic institutions substituted for the foreign banks. The copying was part of the impact. Thus, the foreign bank share of Argentine deposits, which was 39 percent in 1900, was 23 percent in 1914,[95] and by 1929 it declined even further.

Everywhere they operated, British overseas banks carried with them a reputation for honesty, integrity, and safety.[96] Their modern services were part of the integration of the world economy; the banks were the exemplar.[97] Likewise, European banks abroad provided services not otherwise available. American banks themselves were latecomers in the process of expanding abroad. Once U.S. law permitted it, however, National City Bank took the lead.[98] By 1929 it was truly multinational and had 93 branches in the principal cities in Central and South America, Europe, and Asia. It offered services for major U.S. MNEs, whose principals were on its board of directors (Sosthenes Behn – ITT; Gerald Swope – General Electric; E. A. Deed – National Cash Register; J. P. Grace – W. R. Grace & Co.; and C. H. McCormick – International Harvester).[99] For travelers, there was American Express, which supplied banking and travel services; Thomas Cook did the same for the British traveler. By 1926, American Express had 47 foreign branches.[100]

Other financial intermediaries furnished added connections in the world economy. British and Dutch mortgage companies provided credit on the advancing American frontier and did so through direct investments.[101] Large financial holding companies – some associated with the big German and

---

92. Jones, *British Multinational Banking*, 1, 56.   93. Ibid., 56–57.
94. Wilkins, "Multinational Enterprises and Economic Change," 109; Cameron and Bovykin, eds., *International Banking, 1870–1914*; and particularly Tilly, "International Aspects," 107.
95. Jones, *British Multinational Banking*, 97–99, 102. This was the period of great Argentine prosperity.
96. Jones, *British Multinational Banking*, 59–60.
97. This was true even as they lost relative position to domestic banks.
98. The Federal Reserve Act, passed in December 1913, for the first time allowed national banks to branch abroad.
99. Wilkins, *The Maturing of Multinational Enterprise*, 136. See also Harold van B. Cleveland and Thomas F. Huertas, *Citibank, 1812–1970* (Cambridge: Harvard University Press, 1985).
100. Wilkins, *The Maturing of Multinational Enterprise*, 136.
101. Wilkins, *The History of Foreign Investment in the United States to 1914*, 501–15.

Swiss banks (and with electrical manufacturing companies) – facilitated financing for the spread of public utilities on a global scale.[102]

On the infrastructure of education – the creation of human capital, of the social norms appropriate to newly industrializing societies, and the introduction of business cultures – Geoffrey Jones has made a major contribution in showing how foreign banks, in particular, developed a corporate culture that moved abroad with them.[103] His argument can be applied to all MNE activities. Companies that extended over borders brought with them on-the-job training, but of even greater significance than the specific skills was the "way things were done." Multinational corporations disseminated intangible institutional norms – a framework of new practices that might be called education in innovation, education in management, and education in processes and procedures. In some countries, transfer consisted of education in matters such as the meaning of a contract and an understanding of respect for private property and what it means to go to work for a regular working day and on time. The "brand" names of the MNE identified "known" quality.[104] A learning process circulated through the business abroad.

NEW RESOURCES, NEW PRODUCTS, AND NEW DEMANDS

Infrastructure was intimately associated with the opening up of new resources. Steamship, cable, and railroad connections meant newly identified primary agricultural and mineral products that could enter into trade. As world population and per capita income rose, as technological change multiplied, as new industries emerged and new products reached markets, consumer and producer demand grew with a rising call for basic commodities. Trading, banking, and insurance facilities, in turn, animated commerce.

The business structures connected with the expanding output of primary products and the bringing of these products into trade varied substantially by sector (and region). How MNEs fit – and which ones – is complex. Here we need to emphasize that unless there is a market and a means to get a primary product to that market there will be no development of production. Unless business institutions are available to find, develop, process, transport, and distribute the commodity, it has no economic value. In the late nineteenth and

---

102. Belgian financial and managerial intermediaries were particularly active in the spread of public utilities.
103. In Jones, *British Multinational Banking*.
104. See Mira Wilkins, "The Neglected Intangible Asset: The Influence of the Trade Mark on the Rise of the Modern Corporation," *Business History* 36 (January 1992): 66–95.

early twentieth centuries extensive development in output and trade took place in response to new demand. MNEs participated in providing the infrastructure that not only made this possible but that also made it feasible to do more.

International markets for meat (beef and lamb), for example, needed refrigerated shipping, and MNEs were involved in the beef industry in America and then in Argentina.[105] Bananas, too, depended on refrigerated shipping and on rapid distribution; MNEs participated in growing them as well as in shipping and selling. When the expanding electrical industry created a huge demand for copper, MNEs invested in mining that copper outside of the country in which it would be incorporated in the final product. And so it went.[106]

By 1929–30, the involvement of MNEs in production and trade in primary products was formidable. Although no figures are available on intracompany trade (there were none until 1977!), existing information suggests that intracompany trade was a far greater share of total trade in 1929–30 than at the start of the 21st century. By the end of the first three decades of the 20th century, foreign-based MNEs were responsible, for example, for more than 50 percent of the exports of Cuba, Chile, Peru, Venezuela, Northern Rhodesia, Iran, Malaya, and the Dutch East Indies. U.S. companies owned and controlled 32 percent of all mining and smelting in Canada. In 1930, three large trading companies handled between two-thirds and three-quarters of West African trade: the United Africa Company (a subsidiary of Unilever), the Compagnie Française de l'Afrique Occidentale, and the Société Commerciale de l'Ouest Africain.[107] The British Lipton bought its own tea, coffee, and cocoa plantations in Ceylon and set up agencies in more than 30 countries. Charles Wilson appropriately argues that Lipton "taught Americans to drink tea."[108]

When MNEs established plantations, mined, or drilled for oil, they brought new technologies and systematically managed organizations. They mobilized capital and assembled labor resources. They founded company towns, introducing modern urban life. They supplied the infrastructure there such as roads, power and light, and housing (usually for both foreign staff and local employees) and provided stores, schools, churches, hospitals, and recreational facilities in these towns. There has long been the assumption

---

105. Wilkins, *The Emergence of Multinational Enterprise*, 189–90.
106. Numerous different agricultural, pastoral, and mineral products were brought by MNEs into international commerce.
107. Wilkins, "Multinational Enterprises and Economic Change," 111.
108. Charles Wilson, *The History of Unilever*, vol. 2 (New York: Praeger, 1968), 259.

that these "enclaves" were fine for the MNE but worse than bad for the country in which such ventures were established.[109] In the early and mid-1960s, I visited some 31 company towns either owned by or once owned by American MNEs in Latin America, Africa, and the Middle East. What became clear to me was the failure of contemporary critics to recognize the linkage effects – domestic and international – that occurred as a consequence of such ventures around the world. This was before the major wave of nationalizations and expropriations, which was predicated on the belief that the presence of MNEs in primary product output was unnecessary and undesirable. Practically all the agricultural, mining, and oil-producing ventures had been established before 1930. It was investments by MNEs in producing for export that had served in a significant fashion to integrate the world economy.

Foreign direct investments in plantations and mining had long existed. What was new in the late nineteenth century, and particularly in the first third of the twentieth century, was (1) the extent of the investments, (2) the new commodities that went into trade, and (3) the integrated, managed MNE (from primary production to processing to sales to the final consumer abroad).

First, we will address the extent of investments. In the late nineteenth century and first third of the twentieth century, the size of MNE investments in plantation agriculture, mining, and oil production was unprecedented. The First World War created an awareness of the great need for rubber, copper, and oil in particular, hence, such international investments were encouraged by the war and in its aftermath. So, too, when the Russian Revolution cut off a major source of oil, companies had to find secure sources elsewhere.

The second factor is that the varieties of new commodities that went into trade expanded greatly as did the processes for producing and using them. Although vulcanization of rubber went back to 1839, the huge demand for rubber came only after the automobile and its call for rubber tires. Under the aegis of MNEs, rubber began to change from a native to a plantation crop.[110] Copper had been traded from ancient times, but demands from the new electrical industry altered the character of copper mining (from relatively small-scale to high-tech production that was capital intensive and

---

109. H. W. Singer, "The Distribution of Gains between Investing and Borrowing Countries," *American Economic Review* 40 (May 1950): 473–85, set the stage for discussions on enclaves. For a criticism of enclave theory as it applies to the modern plantation, see Edgar Graham, *The Modern Plantation in the Third World* (New York: St. Martin's Press, 1984), 33–36, 59.

110. Native production of rubber still constituted about 45 percent of the total world output in 1929. See Charles R. Whittlesey, "Rubber," *Encyclopedia of Social Sciences*, vol. xiii (1934), 454.

required new technologies). Oil was not found in commercial quantities until 1859; in the late 19th century oil was a new product.

Finally, the integrated, managed MNE with investments along the entire commodity chain – from producing the raw material to selling the manufactured product to consumers with experienced companies introducing new methods of primary product production – was unique to the late 19th and 20th centuries.[111]

When MNEs invested in plantation agriculture, linkage effects in the host economy were less than when such companies invested in mining or oil.[112] In each case, however, the MNEs created a commercial resource. Initially, the contribution seemed to be only one of furnishing jobs locally, although the existence of a cash wage meant the possibility that individuals in less developed countries could enter a market economy – often for the first time. Plantation companies typically bought from local producers, furnishing a market for their output. Mining and oil companies provisioned their company stores from abroad and then became markets for local sellers. American MNEs, very early, provided hospitals and clinics for their local employees: staff from abroad did not want to catch diseases from their employees and the MNEs preferred healthy employees. At the start, the enclaves imported most necessities, but, in time (with variations by country and community), goods were purchased locally not only to supply the company store but also to provide building materials for construction and for certain machines. Because most of these communities were in remote areas, the MNE was the means of connecting the distant locale with the outside world.

Although the early concessions resulted in little host government revenue, over time these economic activities furnished government income. Once established, the commodity produced had to be processed, transported, and directed to customers. The MNE provided those managed activities. In the beginning, management came exclusively from abroad, but, over the years

---

111. Much of what is included herein is grossly oversimplified. That each commodity's business structure was different becomes quite apparent in Steven C. Topik and Allen Wells, eds., *The Second Conquest of Latin America: Coffee, Henequen, and Oil during the Export Boom, 1850–1930* (Austin: University of Texas Press, 1998). In his fascinating discussion in *The Modern Plantation*, 38–47, Graham made the distinction between the "modern type of plantation which evolved towards the end of the 19th century and the New World plantations which have been most studied and have therefore tended to be regarded as the pattern." The distinction he claims lies in the crops and more specifically in the pattern that the sowing and harvesting of each crop imposes. It is clear that different crops imposed different requirements. For a truly interesting discussion of Lever and Unilever in the Belgian Congo, see Wilson, *The History of Unilever*, vol. 1, 167–79; Graham, *The Modern Plantation*, 41–42; and D. K. Fieldhouse, *Unilever Overseas* (London: Croom Helm, 1978), 498–522.

112. This is my own conclusion based on my research.

and at different paces, middle management began to be trained. Skills were upgraded; at company schools a generation of students in the host country became literate. The initial learning-by-doing involved simple activities from brick laying (to build homes in a company town) to driving trucks (to transport materials within the town). Later, as more of an industrial complex was introduced, the discipline of the workplace was also introduced.

In the 1970s, I taught a course in eastern Venezuela to a group of young master's degree candidates quite hostile to MNEs. They were first-generation college students who had grown up in oil company towns and attended company schools. Many of their parents had been illiterate. The company had taught their parents to drive trucks and similar skills; now their children were training to be the college professors of the 1980s. The students were surprised to discover that the MNE had made all that possible. What happened, gradually, was that MNE investments in primary products had immense impact – not only in bringing less developed countries into the world economy, but also in providing a ripple effect within certain economies that raised their standard of living.

Not all MNE investments in primary product production were of the integrated MNE variety. There were MNEs in raw materials that dealt only with production, or some were in processing (preparing raw material for export). Some MNEs were linked in a loose cluster with trading companies – specifically with the trading company responsible for bringing the commodity into trade. But, in all these instances, a new globalization occurred. A single MNE would develop diversified sources of supply for the primary product and then transfer its experiences in production in one part of the world to other regions.[113]

Also, although the oil investments of the first company in Iran (in the line of companies that eventually became British Petroleum) were originally in oil exploration, after oil was found the company began drilling and then went into refining and marketing; over the years it developed fully integrated international operations. This was only one of several typical routes to multinational behavior. Royal Dutch, too, began as an overseas oil producer. Shell (with which Royal Dutch merged in 1907), on the other hand,

---

113. The MNE might simply be a purchaser of the raw material in one locale, whereas in other countries it would be fully integrated into growing the raw material. International Harvester, for example, was closely associated with the development of henequen (sisal and hemp) production in the Yucatan (Mexico), but its relationships with local interests meant it had no need to invest in plantations; on the other hand, it did have plantations in the 1920s in Cuba and in the Philippines. (It needed the sisal for binder twine that was sold with harvesting equipment.) See Mira Wilkins, "An Alternative Approach," in *The Second Conquest of Latin America*, ed. Steven C. Topik and Allen Wells, 198–201.

started as a trading company. The Standard Oil group's first investments abroad were in marketing American refined oil; when, in 1911, standard oil was broken up into 34 separate companies (as the result of the U.S. Supreme Court antitrust decision), its multinational business was affected.[114] American oil companies' investments in producing abroad followed the initial investments in marketing. Thus, the first oil refining by American companies in Mexico entailed processing imported American crude oil. When American oil MNEs began to invest in crude oil production abroad – in Mexico, and then in Venezuela, and soon elsewhere – refining was near the oil-producing locale. In 1912, after Royal Dutch/Shell began its business in the United States in marketing imported oil, it quickly began to invest in U.S. crude oil production, in refining, and transporting and then made further marketing investments. By 1930, it had an integrated operation in the United States along with its global business. In such ways, the activities of MNEs in bringing primary products into world trade were vital to integration of the world economy.[115]

THE MANUFACTURING MULTINATIONAL

I have often heard it said that although there were, indeed, investments in raw materials and in primary products, the modern industrial MNE – in which the firm starts with manufacturing at home and extends abroad to manufacture in a variety of countries – is a post–Second World War phenomenon. This statement is wrong. The first foreign investments of Standard Oil were in marketing and refining (manufacturing) abroad. But, the skeptic will say that, although oil companies were multinational, other "industrials" were not. Once again, the skeptic is mistaken.

Industrialization spread in the late 19th and first third of the 20th century, but in 1930 agriculture was still more important than industry in much of the world. The spread of industrialization was such that in less than two handfuls of countries did the percentage of gainfully occupied population in manufacturing exceed that in agriculture – only the United Kingdom, the United States, Germany, Belgium, Switzerland, the Netherlands, Czechoslovakia, Austria, and Australia qualified. In France, on the other hand, 36 percent of the working population was employed in agriculture and 32 percent in manufacturing; in Sweden, 36 percent worked in agriculture and 31 percent

114. Wilkins, *The Emergence of Multinational Enterprise*, 84–85.
115. Did these investments always raise standards in the host country? Obviously not. At times, however, the linkage effects were impressive but at other times were far less so.

in manufacturing; in Japan, 50 percent in agriculture and merely 19 percent in manufacturing; in the Soviet Union, 67 percent of those employed labored in agriculture.[116] .

To a large extent, in the 19th and the early 20th centuries manufacturing multinationals went first to countries that were the most advanced in the transition from agriculture to industry. The MNEs then contributed to the pace of that transition. They went to these countries with distinctive products and processes. As far as I can determine, the first investment in manufacturing abroad by a company with manufacturing at home seems to have been by the Colt Patent Fire Arms Manufacturing Company of Hartford, Connecticut, which 4 years after its founding in 1848 built a London factory and introduced U.S. machinery and production processes. Samuel Colt, the firm's founder, exported his machinery to England from the United States because, so he wrote, no equipment made in that country "was exact enough for the work necessary to turn out the revolvers." Britain, it should be noted, was then the world's leading industrial nation! Colt set up his British factory to meet competition from "the destructive effects which would follow the introduction of . . . spurious arms into use in England, where he had no patent." Yet, he found that this branch plant, which opened in 1852, was in a year, "a constant drain on [his] resources and energies," whereupon in 1857, he sold it to a group of Englishmen.[117] Coordination and control over distance is not an easy matter.

Because there was no continuity in Colt's manufacturing abroad (subsequently, he licensed producers on the Continent), I do not want to label this company the pioneer manufacturing multinational. That title should probably be awarded to J. & P. Coats, the Scottish thread maker, which, by the 1830s, was selling in the United States, through exports to independent parties, about 60 percent of its Scottish output. In 1839, Andrew Coats (the youngest brother of James and Peter) traveled to the United States and remained for 21 years, building up a sales network and arranging for marketing.[118] Although Coats was not the first company to set up direct

---

116. League of Nations, *Industrialization and Foreign Trade*, 26–27. All the figures are for 1930 except the French figures (for 1931), German ones (for 1933), and Austrian ones (for 1934). The percentage distributions of the gainfully occupied population in agriculture and manufacturing for the listed countries were, respectively, as follows: United Kingdom, 7 and 32, United States, 22 and 30; Germany, 29 and 36; Belgium, 17 and 42; Switzerland, 21 and 45; Netherlands, 21 and 36; Czechoslovakia, 28 and 40; Austria, 32 and 33; and Australia, 20 and 30 percent. Other sectors indicated in the League of Nations figures are mining, commerce and transport, and "administration, domestic service, etc."

117. Wilkins *Emergence of Multinational Enterprise*, 29–30.

118. Wilkins, *The History of Foreign Investment in the United States to 1914*, 72. Dong-Woon Kim is the expert on J. & P. Coats. His work includes "The British Multinational Enterprise in the United

representation in the United States, there seems to have been discontinuity in the others' multinational growth. The sales network Coats put into place could be, and was, used by J. & P. Coats when, after the American Civil War, it made its first investments in manufacturing in the United States. In 1869, J. & P. Coats invested in an existing American thread company, the Conant Thread Company of Pawtucket, Rhode Island, which that year began to manufacture thread in America.[119] Even earlier, in 1865, Coats's Paisley, Scotland, competitor, J. & J. Clark, had built a mill for spinning and spool-thread manufacturing in Newark, New Jersey (in 1896 J. & P. Coats acquired the successor company to J. & J. Clark and, in the process, its U.S. manufacturing plant).[120] In 1886, Coats opened a selling branch in Russia and 3 years later entered into a joint venture to manufacture thread in that country. By 1913, Coats had roughly 36 individual investments in Europe, manufacturing thread in Russia, Italy, Belgium, Austria-Hungary, Spain, Germany, Portugal, and Switzerland; in Russia, it had six large manufacturing facilities. It also owned several U.S. manufacturing plants, and, before the First World War, this Scottish MNE manufactured in Brazil, Mexico, and Japan.[121]

Coats's Russian operation, under the aegis of its affiliate, the Nevsky Thread Manufacturing Company of St. Petersburg, in 1914 accounted for some 90 percent of Russian thread production. When it was taken over during the Revolution, of its six prewar plants, only two escaped confiscation – a mill in Riga (Latvia after the war) and one in Lodz, which became part of the newly independent Poland. In 1918, this "formerly Russian" Coats mill was the only large-scale thread producer in the new Poland, although the southern and western territories of Poland – formerly

States before 1913: The Case of J. & P. Coats," *Business History Review* 72 (Winter 1998): 523–51 (henceforth cited as Kim, "Coats in the U.S."); "J. & P. Coats in Tsarist Russia, 1889–1917," *Business History Review* 69 (Winter 1995): 465–93 (henceforth cited as Kim, "Coats in Russia"); "The British Multinational Enterprise on the European Continent: J. & P. Coats before 1914," unpublished paper presented at Glasgow, July 1999 (henceforth cited as Kim, "Coats in Europe"); and "J. & P. Coats as a Multinational before 1914," *Business and Economic History* 26 (1997): 526–39 (henceforth cited as "Coats before 1914." See Kim, "Coats in the U.S.," 527–33, on Coats' pre–Civil War business in the United States.

119. Wilkins, *The History of Foreign Investment in the United States to 1914*, 87, 130; Kim, "Coats in the U.S.," 532–33.

120. Compare Wilkins, *The History of Foreign Investment in the United States to 1914*, 129–30, with Kim, "Coats in the U.S.," 533–54. Because Andrew Coats arrived before George A. Clark, I have given the Coats firm pioneer status. If we gave it to the Clark firm, it would then transfer to Coats after the latter took over the Clark business in 1896.

121. Kim, "Coats in Europe," 2; Emma Harris, "J. & P. Coats Ltd. in Poland," in *Historical Studies in International Corporate Business*, ed. Alice Teichova, Maurice Lévy-Leboyer, and Helga Nussbaum (Cambridge: Cambridge University Press, 1986), 135–42; Kim, "Coats before 1914," 536 (manufacturing in Brazil, Japan, Mexico).

part of the Austro-Hungarian and German empires – "enjoyed established supply connections with other Coats mills and brands."[122] In the 1920s Coats was manufacturing not only in Latvia and Poland but also in Austria, Czechoslovakia, and Yugoslavia. During that decade, Coats maintained most of its vast international business outside Russia.[123] My students have never heard of the firm, and yet in 1919 it was the largest British company, measured by assets, and by 1929–1930 it was truly a global enterprise.[124]

Coats was by no means alone (or even rare) as an MNE, and there are thus other contenders for pioneer status. An early American MNE, R. Hoe & Co., maker of a newly designed printing press that revolutionized printing press production, opened an English factory in 1867.[125] I did not grant it first place because I can find no evidence that R. Hoe & Co. established a broader international business – apart from the U.S.–British interconnection – and no evidence of lengthy preliminary sales activity such as that characterizing the Coats expansion. A far better choice for U.S. pioneer status is a firm that established a plant in the United Kingdom in the same year, 1867, as did R. Hoe & Co. Like J. & P. Coats, Singer Sewing Machine was in an industry related to clothing a growing worldwide population, and in my view, it can be designated the "pioneer" American-headquartered MNE. In the 1850s, in its first attempt at business abroad, Singer sold its French patent to a French merchant; the patent sale was accompanied by a technology transfer agreement, and, by 1855, the merchant had a manufacturing plant in operation but was reluctant to pay the agreed-upon royalties. Singer learned from this experience. By 1858, the firm was appointing independent businessmen as foreign agents and exporting to these independents. By 1861, it sent a salaried representative to Glasgow and had a man in London. It developed a marketing operation abroad gradually and after the Civil War in 1867, in the face of rigorous competition, decided to manufacture in the United Kingdom.[126] Singer built up an impressive worldwide business, marketing on a global scale and with manufacturing in several countries. Before the First World War, its Scottish factory achieved larger production than its principal

122. Harris, "J. & P. Coats Ltd. in Poland," 135–36.
123. Kim, "Coats in Europe," 4; see Wilkins, *The History of Foreign Investment in the United States, 1914–1945*, for its U.S. business.
124. For the evidence on the size and importance of Coats, see Kim, "Coats in Russia," 551.
125. This factory was still operating in 1930, when it had a capacity equal to that of all its British competitors combined. Frank Southard, *American Industry in Europe* (Boston: Houghton Mifflin, 1931) xiii; Dunning, *American Investment in British Manufacturing Industry*, 18; and Wilkins, *The Emergence of Multinational Enterprise*, 46.
126. Wilkins, *The Emergence of Multinational Enterprise*, 39–41.

U.S. production plant.[127] By 1929, its operations were ubiquitous on a worldwide scale.

The Germans, too, pioneered with MNEs. The brother of Werner von Siemens, Wilhelm, moved to England in 1844; Siemens' first manufacturing investment abroad was in the United Kingdom in 1858. (A Russian subsidiary, which had been formed in 1855, built a Russian cable factory in 1882.) Siemens had some short-lived experiences with manufacturing in the United States before 1914,[128] but it was unable to resume important international business after the war. Another early German MNE was the Bayer Company. A Bayer Company history maintains that, because of high U.S. tariffs on dyes, that firm, which had been exporting to the United States, acquired a U.S. dyestuff plant in 1865. I think this is an error. It seems likely instead that Bayer was an exporter to the United States with U.S. representation and that not until 1871 did the Bayer Company make its first investment in American dyestuff manufacture.[129] Soon it was making other international investments; it started manufacturing in Russia in 1876.[130]

Following the success of J. & P. Coats, many other British MNEs emerged – including Lever Brothers (in 1929 absorbed into Unilever), Dunlop, and Courtaulds. Dunlop established its first factories in France and Germany in 1892, in the United States in 1893, in Japan in 1909, in Canada in 1927, and in Australia in 1928. The British Courtaulds was the first successful maker of rayon in the United States.[131] Following on

127. On Singer's international business, see Wilkins, *The Emergence of Multinational Enterprise*, 39–45; Fred V. Carstensen, *American Enterprise in Foreign Markets: Studies of Singer and International Harvester in Imperial Russia* (Chapel Hill: University of North Carolina Press, 1984); Robert B. Davies, "'Peacefully Working to Conquer the World': The Singer Manufacturing Company in Foreign Markets," *Business History Review* (1969): 292–325; Robert B. Davies, *Peacefully Working to Conquer the World* (New York: Arno Press, 1976); and Andrew C. Godley, "Pioneering Foreign Direct Investment in British Manufacturing," *Business History Review* 73 (Autumn 1999): 394–429. Godley is excellent in showing the importance of Singer's Scottish plant in its vast worldwide business.

128. On Siemens' international business, see Feldenkirchen, *Werner von Siemens*, especially xv, xviii, xxiii, and passim for its general international business. For Siemens in Britain, see Godley, "Pioneering Foreign Direct Investment Investment in British Manufacturing," 402–5 (the 1858 factory was very small). For Siemens in the United States, see Wilkins, *The History*, 433–38, and also Wilfried Feldenkirchen, "Die Anfänge des Siemensgeschäfts in Amerika," in *Wirtschaft Gesellschaft Unternehemen: Festschrift für Hans Pohl zum 60. Geburtstag*, ed. Wilfried Feldenkirchen et al. (Stuttgart: Franz Steiner, 1995), II, 876–900.

129. Compare Wilkins, *The History of Foreign Investment in the United States to 1914*, 131–32, 389–90, and Wilkins, "The German Chemical Industry," 290–91, with Erik Verg, Gottfried Plumpe, and Heinz Schultheis, *Milestones* (Leverkusen, 1988), 29. I made the same mistake in an earlier publication.

130. Verg, Plumpe, and Schultheis, *Milestones*, 48.

131. On the origins and growth of British manufacturing multinationals in general, see Jones, ed., *British Multinationals*. On Dunlop, in particular, see Geoffrey Jones, "The Multinational Expansion of Dunlop, 1890–1939," in ibid., 25. On Courtaulds' innovative role in the United States, see

the Singer Sewing Machine experience, many American industrials that sold nationally became international, marketing and manufacturing abroad. Among them were the Aluminum Company of America, American Radiator, American Tobacco, Eastman Kodak, Ford, General Electric, Gillette, H. J. Heinz, International Harvester, National Cash Register, Otis Elevator, United Shoe Machinery, and Western Electric.[132]

Besides Siemens and Bayer, other leading German electrical and chemical manufacturers as well as other companies became MNEs before the First World War. Orenstein & Koppel, a German machinery builder, had factories in the United States, Russia, Austria-Hungary, France, Switzerland, Holland, Spain, and South Africa. At war's end, only this company's sites in Vienna, Zurich, Amsterdam, and Madrid remained under its control, but it built anew or reacquired other plants in Hungary, Czechoslovakia, Romania, Yugoslavia, Poland, and Johannesburg, South Africa. It did not reenter the United States.[133] Although the war disrupted the international business of German companies, the British and American leaders persisted, and many German firms did resume substantial business abroad by the end of the 1920s. By 1929, German investments in the U.S. chemical industry were far more significant than they had been in 1914.[134]

Nor were such industrial MNEs confined to British, U.S., and German firms. There were, in addition, numerous French, Swedish, Swiss, Dutch, and Belgian manufacturing multinationals.[135] In fact, industrial MNEs

Wilkins, *The History of Foreign Investment in the United States to 1914*, 369–71, which is heavily dependent on D. C. Coleman, *Courtaulds*, vol. 2 (Oxford: Clarendon Press, 1969). Although Courtaulds met competition in the United States (from other non-U.S. MNEs and from du Pont), in 1930 it was still the front runner in the United States in rayon – the world's first synthetic fabric.

132. For these and many others that set up factories abroad before 1914, see Wilkins, *The Emergence of Multinational Enterprise*, 212–13. American Tobacco transferred its foreign factories to Imperial Tobacco and British–American Tobacco in 1902.

133. On German business abroad, see Harm G. Schröter, "Continuity and Change: German Multinationals since 1850," in *The Rise of Multinationals in Continental Europe*, ed. Jones and Schröter, 28–48; the case of Orenstein & Koppel is on p. 31; see also Peter Hertner, "German Multinational Enterprise before 1914: Some Case Studies," in *Multinationals: Theory and History*, ed. Peter Hertner and Geoffrey Jones (Aldershot, England: Gower, 1986), 113–34 (his case studies are of E. Merck [pharmaceuticals], Kathreiner's [malt coffee], Bosch [magneto ignitions], and Mannesmann [pipes]); and Franko, *The European Multinationals* (for a general overview of the historical course of German factories abroad).

134. Wilkins, "The German Chemical Industry," 306–310. See also Wilkins, *The History of Foreign Investment in the United States, 1914–1945*, chapter 5. For the expansion of German business in Central Europe in the interwar years, see *International Business and Central Europe, 1918–1939*, ed. Alice Teichova and P. L. Cotterell (New York: St. Martin's Press, 1983). Chandler, *Scale and Scope*, shows how MNE-type activities were part and parcel of the rise of major corporations in the United States, Britain, and Germany.

135. See contributions in Jones and Schröter, eds., *The Rise of Multinationals in Continental Europe* and in Hertner and Jones, eds., *Multinationals: Theory and History*. See also Franko, *The European Multinationals*. I think there has been an underestimation of late 19th- and early 20th-century

disseminated a wide range of new producer and consumer products around the globe. In a 1907 letter to an agent in Bangkok, Thailand, H. B. Thayer, vice president of Western Electric (A.T.&T.'s manufacturing subsidiary), wrote the following:

You speak of an anti-American attitude on the part of the [Government] Commission. We have offices and factories making our standard apparatus in Great Britain, Belgium, Germany, France, Russia, Austria, Italy, and Japan so that so far as this matter goes we are international rather than American. If there were time we could arrange to have the order go to any one of those countries that might be preferred.[136]

And a 1901 British publication observed that

the most serious aspect of the American industrial invasion lies in the fact that these newcomers have acquired control of almost every new industry created during the past fifteen years. . . . What are the chief new features of London life? They are, I take it, the telephone, the portable camera, the electric street car, the automobile, the typewriter, passenger lifts in houses, and the multiplication of machine tools. In everyone of these, save the petroleum automobile, the American maker is supreme; in several he is the monopolist.[137]

As I have written elsewhere, had the same Britisher penned this passage in 1914, he would have needed to add that, with the Model T, the American maker was also supreme as far as the "petroleum automobile" was concerned.

Ford Motor Company, founded in 1903, exported its sixth car and by its second year had established a manufacturing plant in Canada; by 1914 it was the leading manufacturer in the United Kingdom. In addition to manufacturing in Canada and England, Ford by 1930 had assembly plants

French MNEs; there were quite a few. Michelin, for example became a tire producer in England in 1904, in Italy (to serve Fiat) in 1906, and in the United States in 1907. Wilkins, *The History of Foreign Investment in the United States to 1914*, 423. For other French direct investments in manufacturing in the United States before the First World War, see Mira Wilkins, "French Multinationals in the United States: An Historical Perspective," *Entreprises et Histoire* 3 (May 1993): 17–19. There is a sizable literature on Swedish MNEs; among the best known were Ericsson and SKF. See Ragnhild Lundström, "Swedish Multinational Growth before 1930," in *Multinationals: Theory and History*, ed. Hertner and Jones, 135–56. Swiss MNEs included Nestlé, Hoffmann-LaRoche, Ciba, Sandoz, Geigy, and Brown-Boveri. The Swiss enterprises of the Robert Schwarzenbach group had silk manufacturing plants in Switzerland, France, Germany, and Italy at the turn of the century. See Mira Wilkins, "Swiss Investments in the United States, 1914–1945," in *La Suisse et les grandes puissances, 1914–1945*, ed. Sébastien Guez (Geneva: Droz, 1999), 91–139; Jean Heer, *World Events, 1866–1966: The First Hundred Years of Nestlé* (Lausanne, Switzerland: Imprimeries Réunies, 1966) on the vast expansion of Nestlé.

136. Wilkins, *The Emergence of Multinational Enterprise*, 200.
137. Ibid., 215–17. It was not only American MNEs that were attracted to investments in Britain. See Geoffrey Jones, "Foreign Multinationals and British Industry before 1945," *Economic History Review* XLI (1988): 429–53, for a roster of U.S., German, Swedish, Danish, Swiss, Dutch, French, and Italian manufacturing firms that invested in the United Kingdom before 1930.

in 18 other countries – in Europe, Latin America, Asia, Oceania, and Africa (Belgium, Denmark, France, Germany, Ireland, Italy, Spain, and Turkey; Argentina, Brazil, Chile, Mexico, and Uruguay; India, Japan, and Malaya; Australia; and South Africa).[138] In 1931, Frank Southard published a prize-winning volume, *American Industry in Europe*, which was intended as "a study of some aspects of the vast and complex fabric of American enterprise in foreign countries." He wrote only about Europe (including the British Isles) "largely because the author found that area quite large enough when he began going from factory to factory across its many countries."[139] It was evident that industrialization (and consumerism) spread through manufacturing MNEs, and this was not only true in automobiles but in a wide range of manufactured goods – products of the postindustrial revolution days unknown before the late nineteenth century.

THE DECADE AFTER THE FIRST WORLD WAR AND THE STATUS OF
MULTINATIONAL ENTERPRISE IN 1930

When, with the Russian Revolution, Russia became divorced from the world economy and the large MNE investments in that country were expropriated, it was the first of what would be major retreats of MNEs in the wake of expropriations.[140] Russia had been linked with the world economy; in 1914 MNE investment there had been dramatic. Although Russian associations with the rest of the world continued throughout its years as the Soviet Union, those ties tightened and eased but never compared with its integration into the world economic system before 1914. This true rent in the global economy was symbolized by the cutting off of MNE activities.

During the First World War the United States and Britain had taken over the properties of German MNEs present within their own borders. Their postwar disposition of these properties was connected in the 1920s with the steps taken to restore the world economy. Unlike in Russia, many of the companies based in a defeated Germany did reintegrate into the world economy by the end of the 1920s only to fracture once more in the 1930s, as the German government pursued autarchic policies, and then

138. Wilkins and Hill, *American Business Abroad: Ford on Six Continents*, 434–35 (table on when Ford began assembly and manufacture abroad, by country and date) and passim. In some countries Ford had more than one assembly plant. By 1930 General Motors was also an MNE.
139. Southard, *American Industry in Europe*, xiii.
140. The next major one would be the Mexican expropriation of its oil industry in 1938 – and it was sector specific.

with the Second World War. Nonetheless, in the 1920s the highly integrated world economy of 1914 that had been disrupted by the war and the Russian Revolution to a considerable degree was reinstated with new and impressive waves of international direct investments.

In the late 1920s, as international trade resumed, trading companies, insurance firms, shipping lines, and banks extended internationally to aid commerce. Japanese MNEs in these sectors took on added importance.[141] Although, with the end of the First World War the railroad era was over (with little new multinational enterprise activities in railroads), the 1920s experienced a global multiplication of MNEs in electric power, telephones, radios, automobiles, and rubber tires along with the many new products of the chemical industry, numerous branded processed foods, and cigarettes and matches.[142] MNEs expanded both in consumer and producer goods. Some companies were doing research abroad (Royal Dutch/Shell in the United States, for example); other companies were designing distinctive products for other countries' markets that would be manufactured in those markets (Ford, for example, by 1930). The oil MNEs made vast new international investments.[143] Many firms became both horizontally and vertically extended over borders. In the 1920s, America surged toward world supremacy; 42.4 percent of the world's manufacturing by 1929 occurred in the United States.[144]

---

141. Recently, at a conference in Japan (December 2003), there was a prevailing assumption that Japanese MNEs were all post–World War II. Overlooked were the important Japanese service sector MNEs that went back to the late nineteenth century, the development of which was enhanced rather than interrupted during the First World War.

142. In cigarettes the leading MNE was the British-American Tobacco Company (BAT). It had been formed in 1902 by American Tobacco and Imperial Tobacco to handle their international business. At the start, its head office was in England, but American Tobacco held the controlling interest. When in 1911 American Tobacco was broken up – in the antitrust case – it was forced to divest its interest in BAT. James B. Duke, however, became the chairman of BAT. Gradually, BAT drifted into British ownership and control. By the early 1920s it was clearly a British MNE with a vast international business. Wilkins, *The Emergence of Multinational Enterprise*, 92–93; Sherman Cochran, *Big Business in China: Sino-Foreign Rivalry in the Cigarette Industry, 1890–1930* (Cambridge: Harvard University Press, 1980); and Howard Cox, *The Global Cigarette: Origins and Evolution of British American Tobacco, 1880–1945* (Oxford: Oxford University Press, 2000). The giant MNE in matches was Swedish Match Company. In 1930, Swedish Match Group companies controlled over 40 percent of worldwide match production; another 20 percent of worldwide match production was by companies in which Swedish Match Company either had a minority interest (less than 50 percent) or by other collaborating companies. Hakan Lindgren, *Corporate Growth: The Swedish Match Industry in its Global Setting* (Stockholm: LiberFörlag, 1979), 110 (for the figures). Both BAT and Swedish Match had investments on six continents.

143. Royal Dutch/Shell: Wilkins, *The History of Foreign Investment in the United States, 1914–1945*; Ford: Wilkins and Hill, *American Business Abroad: Ford on Six Continents*, 358; Wilkins, *The Maturing of Multinational Enterprise*, 138–163, an overview on American business abroad in 1929. The book value of U.S. direct investments abroad equaled slightly more than 7 percent of the U.S. gross national product that year. Ibid., 163.

144. League of Nations, *Industrialization and Foreign Trade*, 13.

In raw materials, as international cartels were formed to push up the prices of rubber, copper, and oil, additional foreign direct investments protected sources of supply. By 1929–1930, American and European MNEs were ubiquitous.[145] Many operated on six continents. Their role in integrating the world economy had survived war, revolution, and expropriation.

145. In consulting David Fieldhouse's contribution to the history of the contemporary world – *The West and the Third World* (London: Blackwell, 1999) – I was struck by how the story I am telling does not fit comfortably into a tale of "imperialism." The MNE pattern was global. Empires did matter in the direction of certain investments; thus, British MNEs had a greater presence in the British empire than did the Dutch or the French. Empire, however, was not defined by location. American MNEs invested in the Dutch East Indies; Lever invested in the Belgian Congo. Moreover, in the late 19th century and first third of the 20th century, manufacturing multinationals invested in manufacturing in industrial countries far more than in less developed ones because that is where the largest markets were. My perspective on MNEs is global. New evidence on the broad scope of MNEs is in Hubert Bonin et al., eds., *Transnational Companies: 19th–20th Centuries* (Paris: Éditions P.L.A.G.E., n.d. [2002]).

3

Multinationals from the 1930s to the 1980s[1]

GEOFFREY JONES

MULTINATIONAL ENTERPRISES AND THE DISINTEGRATION OF A GLOBAL ECONOMY

At the end of the 1920s international business was extensive and widely spread around the world. It had grown rapidly for the previous half century in response to capital mobility and trade protectionism, demand for raw materials and foodstuffs generated by the second industrial revolution, the spread of colonialism, widespread acceptance of international property laws that reduced the risks of financial direct investment (FDI), and improvements in transport and communications. Many multinational enterprises (MNEs) were widely spread. Among them were Ford and General Motors, Nestlé and Unilever, and Shell and Standard Oil of New Jersey, but thousands of small and medium-sized firms had also invested abroad – sometimes in clusters or networks with other firms.

---

1. This chapter examines the changing composition and organization of international business from the 1930s to the 1980s. It does not seek to duplicate the standard works on the historical evolution of MNEs, including the still unsurpassed database generated by the Multinational Enterprise project conducted at Harvard Business School in the 1960s and 1970s; see Mira Wilkins, *The Maturing of Multinational Enterprise* (Cambridge: Harvard University Press, 1974); J. H. Dunning, "Changes in the Level and Structure of International Production: The Last One Hundred Years," in *The Growth of International Business*, ed. Mark Casson (London: Allen & Unwin, 1983); Geoffrey Jones, *The Evolution of International Business* (London: International Thomson Business Press, 1996). The results of the Multinational Enterprise project are published in James W. Vaupel and Joan P. Curhan, *The Making of Multinational Enterprise* (Cambridge: Harvard University Press, 1969); idem, *The World's Multinational Enterprise* (Cambridge: Harvard University Press, 1974); Joan P. Curhan, William H. Davidson, and Rajan Suri, *Tracing the Multinationals* (Cambridge: Harvard University Press, 1977). Based on a benchmark definition of MNEs as firms that control income-generating assets in more than one country, this chapter widens the focus from the large industrial enterprises that have preoccupied many past researchers to a more complex and varied world of firms that have engaged in international business and whose growth has been far from linear.

John Dunning has suggested that world FDI had reached around one-third of total world foreign investment, or $14,582 million, by 1914,[2] equivalent to around 9 percent of world output.[3] Despite the disruption of the war, FDI grew further in the 1920s; it had reached $26,350 million by 1938.[4] At the end of the 1920s, most of the stock of world FDI originated from a handful of Western European economies, especially the United Kingdom, accounting for around 40 percent of it. The United States accounted for no more than 25 percent of world FDI, though it had probably replaced the United Kingdom in flows during the 1920s. Latin America and Asia probably accounted for more than 50 percent of FDI stock. Wilkins identifies Canada and the United States among individual host economies as the two top hosts in 1929 followed by a cluster of developing countries.[5] Few countries, even the Soviet Union, were untouched by foreign enterprise.

The United States is the only country with plausible FDI estimates. Corporate forms used extensively in international business made no clear distinction between portfolio and direct investment. Much FDI was in colonies and a great deal of it in geographically proximate regions – like U.S. investment in Canada and Mexico and European investment in neighboring countries – and was perhaps more multiregional than multinational.

Nonetheless, although the quantification of world FDI remains problematic, its overall impact was striking.[6] By the 1920s many of the world's natural resources were produced, traded, and distributed by MNEs. In petroleum, most of the world's oil outside the United States was produced and marketed by a small number of large MNEs; in 1928 over 40 percent of the oil of Latin America was produced by two MNEs.[7] There was similar MNE concentration in other minerals, including aluminum, copper, and tin, which were industries characterized by high levels of intrafirm trade in the hands of vertically integrated MNEs. In renewable resources the picture was more mixed. Production of some commodities such as cotton and tobacco was outside foreign control, but in sugar cane, tea, bananas, and rubber, production and distribution were largely controlled by various multinational firms.[8]

2. Dunning, "Changes."
3. United Nations, *World Investment Report* (New York: United Nations, 1994), 130.
4. Dunning, "Changes."
5. Mira Wilkins, "Comparative Hosts," *Business History* 36 (1994): 21.
6. This chapter does not address portfolio capital flows, trade, emigration, and other features of a "global economy." See Michael D. Bordo, Alan M. Taylor, and Jeffrey G. Williamson (eds.), *Globalization in Historical Perspective* (Chicago: University of Chicago Press, 2003).
7. Wilkins, "Comparative Hosts," 37.   8. Jones, *Evolution*, 60–77.

Service sector MNEs during the nineteenth century had put in place the banking, trading, and informational infrastructure of the first global economy with significant social effects through the transfer of organizational and technical competencies to developing countries. Most multinational banking by the 1920s had taken the form of specialist "overseas banks," mostly headquartered in European countries, with branches in developing regions. In 1928 British multinational banks alone controlled more than 2,250 branches spread over Latin America, Africa, Asia, and Australasia, which financed international trade, undertook foreign exchange dealings, and provided retail banking services.[9] French, Dutch, and other European banks had less extensive branch networks; Japan's Yokohama Specie Bank had over 40 branches elsewhere in Asia, Europe, the Americas, and Australia.[10] Although the U.S. banking market was effectively isolated after the First World War and the 1920s, by 1930 the Citibank foreign network reached almost 100 branches – two-thirds of them in Latin America.[11]

On a par with multinational banking, European and Japanese multinational trading companies controlled large shares of international trade – especially, but not only, in commodities. The desire to overcome transactions and information costs led some firms to diversify into processing, resources, and other services. Many of the larger British trading companies with workforces of 100,000 to 150,000 by the late 1920s had become among the world's largest multinational employers.[12]

The global transportation and communications network put in place by MNEs, cable, and, later, wireless telegraph companies (e.g., MacKay, Eastern Companies, Marconi, I.T.T., and the Great Northern Telegraph Company) had become a global telecommunications infrastructure that lessened the risks of FDI by making the control of assets over long distances more feasible.

9. Geoffrey Jones, *British Multinational Banking, 1830–1990* (Oxford: Clarendon Press, 1993), 398–9.
10. Marc Meuleau, *Des Pionniers en Extreme-Orient* (Paris: Fayard, 1990); Yasuo Gonjo, *Banque Colonniale ou Banque d'affaires* (Paris: Comité pour l'histoire économique et financière de la France, 1993); Hubert Bonin, "Le Comptoir national d'escompte de Paris, une banque impériale (1848–1940)," *Revue Française d'histoire d'outre mer*, 78 (1991); Ben P. A. Gales and Keetie E. Sluyterman, "Outward Bound: The Rise of Dutch Multinationals," in *The Rise of Multinationals in Continental Europe*, ed. Geoffrey Jones and Harm G. Schröter (Aldershot, England: Edward Elgar, 1993), 68–9; Norio Tamaki, "The Yokohama Specie Bank: A Multinational in the Japanese Interest, 1879–1931," in *Banks as Multinationals*, ed. Geoffrey Jones (London: Routledge, 1990).
11. Thomas F. Huertas, "U.S. Multinational Banking: History and Projects," in *Banking Multinationals*, ed. Jones.
12. Geoffrey Jones, ed., *The Multinational Traders* (London: Routledge, 1998); idem, *Merchants to Multinationals* (Oxford: Oxford University Press, 2000); Shin'ichi Yonekawa and H. Yoshihara, eds., *Business History of General Trading Companies* (Tokyo: University of Tokyo Press, 1987); Shin'ichi Yonekawa, ed., *General Trading Companies* (Tokyo: University of Tokyo Press, 1987).

Large shipping companies had cut the costs and speed of oceanic transport by their global networks of steamship lines.

By the late 1920s, multinational manufacturing was also well established. Many companies were now manufacturing abroad – especially in industries characterized by proprietary technologies, brand names, and other intangible assets that gave rise to high transaction costs in market-based arrangements. Tariffs provided a stimulus to multinational manufacturing and, during the 1920s, growing protectionism was accompanied by new waves of multinational investment in industries such as automobiles.[13] Among these firms were the large industrial enterprises of the late 19th century that separated ownership from control and invested in production, marketing, and professional management.[14] Many of these companies integrated their international operations and, by the interwar years, several U.S. marketing affiliates in Britain were not simply supplying the domestic market but were engaged in exportation as well. U.S. and Swedish MNEs internationalized their technological activity to a high degree by this period.[15] Thousands of small and medium-sized enterprises (SMEs) that were often family owned and had one or more production facilities in a foreign country coexisted with larger ones.

But, between the 1930s and the 1970s, many of the key components of this first global economy were destroyed, dismantled, or diminished by a series of worldwide economic, military, and political shocks from the depression of the 1930s to the World War of the 1940s and the resulting political shifts that accompanied the end of the old empires and the spread of communism. The first such shock was the Great Depression, though the severe 1920–21 recession had had a larger impact on multinational trading companies.[16] The Great Depression's consequences created a new, more unfavorable environment for international business. Exchange controls, the collapse in capital mobility, protectionism, the decline in primary commodity prices, falling incomes in many developed countries, and the spread of nationalistic governments in Europe and Asia presented formidable challenges to international business. In a range of manufacturing and

13. Jones, *Evolution*, chapter 4; Wilkins, *Maturing*; Geoffrey Jones, ed., *British Multinationals: Origins, Management and Performance* (Aldershot, England: Gower, 1986).
14. Alfred D. Chandler, *Scale and Scope* (Cambridge, MA: Harvard University Press, 1990).
15. Geoffrey Jones and Frances Bostock, "U.S. Multinationals in British Manufacturing before 1962," *Business History Review* 70 (1996); J. A. Cantwell, "The Globalisation of Technology: What Remains of the Product Cycle Model?" *Cambridge Journal of Economics* 19 (1995).
16. Kazutoshi Maeda, "General Trading Companies in Pre-War Japan: A Sketch," in *General Trading Companies*, ed. Shin'ichi Yonekawa, 101–2; Keetie E. Sluyterman, "Dutch Multinational Trading Companies in the Twentieth Century," in *The Multinational Traders*, ed. Geoffrey Jones, 89–90.

resource industries, MNEs responded by forming international cartels as an alternative to FDI. A considerable proportion of world manufacturing became controlled by such agreements – often supported by European governments.[17] Cartels that regulated price and output flourished especially in industries with a relatively small number of producers as well as under depressed market conditions. Classic examples include the international cartels in chemicals, electric lamps, and steel, which, unlike many collaborative arrangements between firms, were sustained over long periods.[18] International cartels were few in fast-growing industries such as automobiles and branded consumer goods as well as in industries such as textiles that had numerous producers.

In resources, the problem of excess capacity and falling prices led to a virtual halt in new FDI and also to wide-ranging cartel agreements. The "Achnacarry Agreement," signed in Achnacarry, the Scottish home of the Camerons, in 1928 between the world's three largest oil companies (Shell, Esso, and British Petroleum) was a symbol of such interwar cartels. These three companies never succeeded in regulating the U.S. domestic market or in preventing "outside" supplies from undermining agreements elsewhere.[19] (By 1932 Mobil, Gulf Oil, and Texaco had joined, with resulting stable and higher prices.) The attempts by MNEs to cartelize the world copper industry were even less successful;[20] however, in tin, aluminum, and diamonds, small numbers and government support did lead to strong and sustained cartels.[21] In tea and rubber, but not in teak, European trading companies put in place successful cartels to support prices and restrict output.[22]

In the 1930s the MNEs of earlier decades did not disappear, however, nor did new investments cease as in automobiles and consumer goods industries and even in chemicals. There were almost as many new U.S. entrants into

17. Clement Wurm, *Business, Politics and International Relations* (Cambridge: Cambridge University Press, 1993).
18. Harm G. Schröter, "Cartels as a Form of Concentration in Industry: The Example of the International Dyestuffs Cartel from 1927 to 1939," *German Yearbook on Business History* (1988); Leonard S. Reich, "General Electric and the World Cartelization of Electric Lamps," in *International Cartels in Business History*, ed. Akira Kudo and Terachi Hara (Tokyo: University of Tokyo Press, 1992); Daniel Barbezat, "A Price for Every Product, Every Place: The International Steel Export Cartel, 1933–39," *Business History* 33 (1991).
19. J. H. Bamberg, *The History of the British Petroleum Company*, vol. 2 (Cambridge: Cambridge University Press, 1994), 107–17.
20. Thomas R. Navin, *Copper Mining and Management* (Tucson: University of Arizona Press, 1978), 132–37.
21. Jean-François Hennart, "The Tin Industry," in *Multinationals and World Trade*, ed. Mark Casson (London: Allen & Unwin, 1986), 232–34; George W. Stocking and Myron W. Watkins, *Cartels in Action* (New York: The Twentieth Century Fund, 1946); Debora L. Spar, *The Co-operative Edge* (Ithaca: Cornell University Press, 1994).
22. Jones, *Merchants*, chapter 9.

British manufacturing in the 1930s as in the 1920s, but there were also many more divestments than in the earlier decade.[23] Although certain large U.S. MNEs divested from European manufacturing, some of them opened new factories in Latin America, Asia, and Australia to take advantage of import substitution opportunities.[24] British-owned MNEs made major new investments behind tariff barriers in the 1930s – principally either in the politically safe Empire countries or in Latin America.[25] Companies with operations in countries that had tight exchange controls, such as in Nazi Germany, found themselves making "enforced investments" out of profits. Unilever, the Anglo-Dutch margarine and detergents MNE, which had inherited a large German business from its predecessor companies upon its formation in 1929, diversified into cheese, printing, ice cream, hair dyes, and even into shipbuilding to spend its trapped funds.[26]

Where there were few international cartels apart from shipping, foreign MNEs found themselves progressively blocked from activities reserved by governments for nationals or state-owned firms such as telecommunications, electricity, and transport utilities. Latin American and other governments had begun to exclude foreign firms from these services starting in the 1930s as well as airlines, which governments blocked from foreign ownership.[27] Canadian-owned utilities, on the other hand, retained substantial market shares in Mexico and especially in Brazil. For example, Brazilian Traction produced 60 percent of Brazil's power and 75 percent of its telephones in 1946.[28] The Soviet Union closed its borders to all forms of foreign enterprise, but Denmark's Great Northern Telegraph Company continued to own and operate the Trans-Siberian line throughout the 1930s.[29] On a much wider scale, despite the 1930s slump in international trade, some multinational trading companies flourished. Japan's unique trading companies, the *sogo shosha*, grew alongside Japanese exports, opening up new markets in Latin America, the Middle East, and the Soviet Union and thus creating "global sales networks."[30] Several Swiss trading companies, like André, grew rapidly in this period.[31]

---

23. Jones and Bostock, "U.S. Multinationals."   24. Wilkins, *Maturing*, 184–91.
25. Jones, ed., *British Multinationals*.
26. Charles Wilson, *The History of Unilever*, vol. 2 (London: Cassell & Co., 1954), 365–71.
27. Jones, *Evolution*, 169–72; Tetsuo Ato, "ITT's International Business Activities, 1920–40," *Annals of the Institute of Social Science* (1982).
28. Duncan McDowall, *The Light: Brazilian Traction, Light and Power Company Limited, 1899–1945* (Toronto: University of Toronto Press, 1988).
29. Kurt Jacobsen, "The Great Northern Telegraph Company: A Danish Company in the Service of Globalisation since 1869" (mimeographed).
30. Kawabe, "Overseas Activities and Their Organization," in *General Trading Companies*, ed. Yonekawa, 183.
31. Sébastien Guex, "The Development of Swiss Trading Companies in the Twentieth Century," in *Multinational Traders*, ed. Jones.

Perhaps the most significant consequence of the 1930s depression was not the decreased growth in multinational investment but the "nationalization" of MNEs. Trade barriers and exchange controls led to the increased autonomy of national affiliates, which were increasingly responsible for most of the value-added chain of their products.[32] Nationalism encouraged firms to strengthen their "local" identities. In Europe, U.S. producers like IBM, Ford, and General Motors responded to European competition by developing new products for major markets distinct from those they produced for their domestic markets.[33] Some U.S. MNEs sold part of the equity of their European affiliates mostly because of their liquidity problems at home, further enhancing the autonomous and quasi-independent standing of their subsidiaries.

The "older" forms of multinational business, which had been so important in the creation of the first global economy, moved in the same direction. European overseas banks responded to the decline in international trade by extending lending to businesses not related directly to trade and exchange. In Asia, the Middle East, and Africa, the British banks often modified their traditionally conservative regulations on collateral, sometimes making loans solely on the basis of reputation.[34] European trading companies, seriously affected by falling commodities prices and trade barriers, also deepened their involvement in local economies. In Latin America, as in the case of British trading companies in Chile, European trading companies responded to the growth of local industries by distributing the latter's products instead of foreign imports. These trading companies also redirected their business toward the goods in which international trade had still continued to grow such as branded consumer products and automobiles.[35] Dutch trading companies, like their British counterparts, sought to distribute Japanese goods and began to manufacture textiles and other products in their principal host region, the Dutch East Indies.[36]

The second shock to international business was the Second World War. The First World War had already changed the "policy environment" for MNEs by identifying the ultimate national ownership of firms as a political issue. The sequestration of German-owned affiliates by U.S., British, and other Allied governments at that time virtually reduced the stock of German FDI to zero and signaled the end of the era in which foreign companies could operate in most countries on terms more or less the same as

32. Wilkins, *Maturing*, 417–18.
33. Carl H. A. C. Dassbach, *Global Enterprises and the World Economy* (New York: Garland Press, 1989).
34. Jones, *British Multinational Banking*, 209–17.   35. Jones, *Merchants*, chapter 4.
36. Sluyterman, "Dutch Multinational Trading Companies," 89–90.

in their own. The government sequestration of foreign properties without compensation after the Russian Revolution in 1917 and the Mexican expropriations of foreign oil companies in 1938 further raised political risks of MNE investment. During the interwar years, German chemical and other firms sought to rebuild their international distribution networks and even their foreign production subsidiaries.[37]

The Second World War reinforced and intensified the political risks of FDI. The total loss of all German overseas assets once again led to an extremely subdued level of German FDI until the 1970s as German firms opted to export rather than engage in risking FDI. Although, during the interwar years Japanese FDI was small in absolute terms but considerable in comparison to the size of the Japanese economy, after the war a complex international business system involved worldwide Japanese trading and expansion of service sector companies as well as investments by Japanese cotton textile and mining companies in the markets and resources of Asia. After the loss of all Japanese FDI at the end of the war, Japanese firms, too, focused on exporting until the late 1970s.[38]

World FDI was far from being a "global" phenomenon after the Second World War. Between 1945 and the mid-1960s, the United States may have accounted for 85 percent of all new FDI outflows. Among the Europeans, only British and Dutch firms opted to make substantial FDI in the era of the postwar "economic miracles." As a result, between 1945 and 1980 from two-thirds to three-quarters of all world FDI stock was accounted for by firms from the United States, the United Kingdom, and the Netherlands.

The third exogenous shock to international business was the decline in receptivity to MNEs especially, but not only, in the developing world. The end of European colonial empires, the spread of communism, and growing state intervention in economies contributed to this trend. The 1949 Communist Revolution in China, one of the world's largest host economies before the war, led to the total exclusion of foreign MNEs until the late 1970s. Decolonization elsewhere was often followed by imposition of regulatory controls on foreign firms. Thus, in India, once a large host economy, first, high taxes and, from the 1960s, increasing control and regulations reduced foreign FDI by 1980 to minuscule levels as established foreign firms divested and new ones avoided the country. In the Middle East and Indonesia after the 1950s there was outright nationalization of foreign-owned oil fields, mines, and

---

37. Harm G. Schröter, "Die Auslandinvestitionen der deutschen chemischen Industrie 1870 bis 1930," *Zeitschrift für Unternehmensgeschichte* (1990).
38. T. Kuwahara, "Trends in Research on Overseas Expansion by Japanese Enterprises prior to World War II," *Japanese Yearbook on Business History* (1990).

plantations. Although, until the 1970s the political and military hegemony of the United States deterred mass expropriations of MNEs, the deluge began in that decade as the influence of the United States declined and some developing countries acquired the technical and managerial abilities to run their own industries. During the 1970s many expropriations occurred in the developing world, and virtually all MNE ownership of mining, petroleum, and plantation assets was wiped out.[39]

The nationalizations of the 1970s shattered the integrated MNEs that had once controlled so much of the world's resources. Vertical integration down to the production level was weakened or eliminated in most commodities with a corresponding decline in intrafirm trade flows. The resource MNEs had to switch from equity in contracts in order to access the resources of developing countries. In the oil industry, between 1970 and 1976 at least 18 countries, which accounted for three-quarters of international oil production, nationalized oil-producing operations, demolishing this industry's traditional structure. MNEs were able to preserve some elements of this structure by switching their exploration to the North Sea, Alaska, and other politically "safe" locations.[40]

During the three decades or so after the Second World War, therefore, MNEs lost the great importance they had once held in the developing world. The process often proceeded rather slowly as with the disappearance of Africa from the orbit of international business. State intervention in commodity marketing even before Nigerian independence and growing competition had obliged the United Africa Company (UAC), a diversified trading company 100-percent owned by Unilever, to withdraw from producing, marketing, and general trading during the 1950s. The UAC venture was reborn as an importer of specialist products such as automobiles and tractors; through joint ventures it became a major brewer and textile manufacturer. Although compelled by West African governments to sell part of its equity to local interests in the 1970s, UAC employed more than 70 thousand people in the 1970s and, at times, contributed one-third of Unilever's total profits.[41] Between the 1940s and 1980s UAC therefore remained Nigeria's – and West Africa's – largest modern business enterprise. Elsewhere in Africa,

---

39. M. L. Williams, "The Extent and Significance of the Nationalisation of Foreign-Owned Assets in Developing Countries, 1956–1972," *Oxford Economic Papers* (1975); Stephen J. Kobrin, "Expropriation as an Attempt to Control Foreign Firms in LDLs: Trends from 1969 to 1979," *International Studies Quarterly* (1984); Charles R. Kennedy, "Relations between Transnational Corporations and Governments in Host Countries: A Look to the Future," *Transnational Corporations* (1992).

40. James Bamberg, *British Petroleum and the Political Economy of International Oil* (Cambridge: Cambridge University Press, 2000).

41. D. K. Fieldhouse, *Merchant Capital and Economic Decolonization* (Oxford: Clarendon Press, 1994).

information asymmetries provided a continuing role for other European multinational trading companies such as CFAO (Compagnie Français de l'Afrique Occidentale) and Lonrho.

Still, during the postwar decades, multinational investment became progressively marginalized in much of the world. In many countries the natural resource and service sectors were closed to foreign firms. North America and Western Europe and indeed manufacturing as a sector remained open, but even the Japanese economy was largely closed to foreign firms because Japanese governments, until the 1970s, blocked most wholly owned FDI in favor of licensing or joint ventures.[42] For the first two decades after the end of the war, new FDI was largely a matter of U.S. firms' investment in Canada and Western Europe, and even in this case the flow was quite uneven geographically. In 1962, the United Kingdom alone accounted for more than 50 percent of the stock of U.S. manufacturing FDI in Europe. International business had shrunk in relative importance in the world economy from the late 1920s, and had declined in its "global" nature. In the 1930s, many firms preferred cartels to FDI, cartels becoming the principal form of international business in a range of industries. During the 1950s and 1960s, the growth of world FDI resumed but was geographically and sectorally constrained. The firms of many developed countries preferred exporting over foreign production, and large areas of the world restricted the operations of foreign firms within their borders. By 1980 the stock of world FDI amounted to a mere 4.8 percent of world output, which was significantly less than in 1914.[43]

THE MAKING OF A NEW GLOBAL ECONOMY

During the decades after the Second World War MNEs did begin to build a new global economy, but it was a somewhat protracted process, and only came to fruition during the 1980s and 1990s. In this process service sector MNEs were important, which is a significant fact that could be overlooked if one were to focus on FDI data alone. During the postwar decades there was a massive increase in the relative importance of manufacturing FDI until, by 1978, it accounted for just over 50 percent of total FDI stock (with services just under 25 percent), but these figures largely reflect the demise of capital-intensive FDI in transport and utilities in the developing world. Much of the new service sector multinational investment in business and

42. Mark Mason, *American Multinationals and Japan* (Cambridge, MA: Harvard University Press, 1992).
43. United Nations, *World Investment Report* (1994), 130.

professional services in developed economies either employed nonequity modes such as partnerships, franchising, and contracts or else was not capital intensive.

In the immediate postwar decades, multinational firms assumed an important role as conduits to the rest of the developed world of U.S. management practices and, more generally, of values and lifestyles. Multinational management consultancy can be traced back to the internationalization of accountancy in the nineteenth century, but during the interwar years consultancy firms like Bedaux, founded in the United States by the French immigrant Charles E. Bedaux, expanded internationally. Bedaux's establishment in interwar Britain and Germany was heavily dependent on the business of their U.S. client, Goodrich; U.S. firms often followed their domestic clients abroad. U.S. consultancies led by McKinsey, Booz Allen & Hamilton, and Arthur D. Little often followed their U.S. clients to Europe and developed a European client base, yet this evolutionary pattern was not universal. McKinsey, for example, invested in Europe in the late 1950s at the invitation of Shell, for which it had carried out an assignment in Venezuela. For a time British consultancies such as Urwick, Orr were also important internationally but largely serviced the countries of the British Commonwealth.[44]

The importance of management consultancies lay in their diffusion of American (and, from the 1980s, Japanese) management practices and structures. During the 1960s, McKinsey, in particular, played a major role in the spread of the M-form structure in Britain, France, and Germany even if, for institutional and cultural reasons, there was rarely a complete transfer of U.S. management practices to Europe or elsewhere.[45] Large European firms made repeated and extensive use of McKinsey and other consultancies, often calling them in when internal disagreements among senior managers blocked change.

Advertising agencies had also begun their internationalization in the interwar years, and some had done so even earlier. During the 1920s, J. Walter Thompson had an agreement with General Motors to open an office in

---

44. Matthias Kipping and Catherine Sauviat, "Global Management Consultancies: Their Evolution and Structure," *University of Reading Discussion Papers in International Investment and Business Studies*, ser. B, 9 (1996/7); Christopher D. McKenna, "The Origins of Modern Management Consultancy," *Business and Economic History* 24 (1995).

45. Derek F. Channon, *The Strategy and Structure of British Enterprises* (London: Macmillan, 1973); Heinz T. Thanheiser, *The Emerging European Enterprise: Strategy and Structure in French and German Industry* (London: Macmillan, 1976); Bruce Kogut and David Parkinson, "The Diffusion of American Organizing Principles to Europe," in *Country Competitiveness*, ed. Bruce Kogut (New York: Oxford University Press, 1993).

every country in which the U.S. car firm had an assembly operation or distribution; this practice drove the expansion of General Motors in Europe and elsewhere. After 1945, the U.S. agencies built on a series of innovations in market research and advertising techniques to dominate the world advertising industry, and, by the 1980s, they were operating in virtually every non-Communist country in the world.[46] Like the management consultancies, the advertising agencies "globalized" aspects of U.S. management practice, and, it is important to note, spread U.S. lifestyle. In the United Kingdom, U.S. breakfast cereal companies – Kellogg for one – spent large sums on market research and advertising services provided by J. Walter Thompson to decimate traditional British, and later other, breakfast habits of oatmeal, kippers, eggs and sausage, and such in favor of U.S.-style cereal consumption.[47]

Hotels and fast food retailers were among other service industries in which MNEs played a substantial role in diffusing "global" lifestyles. The hotel industry, which had been primarily national before the Second World War, internationalized after it as hotel groups such as Holiday Inn, Hilton, and Inter-Continental expanded abroad, usually employing management contracts and franchising. The fast food industry, with multinational growth from the 1960s, used the same modes. The British-owned J. Lyons acquired the international franchise of the "Wimpy Bar" of the United States, and, through the 1960s, licensed hamburger chains in Europe, Asia, and Africa. McDonald's led the globalization of food tastes. Although it only opened its first foreign restaurant in Canada in 1967, over the following two decades it conquered widely different culinary traditions worldwide; by 1990 there were more than 2,500 McDonald's restaurants in 50 other countries.[48]

The hotel and food industries were part of a wider process of the creation of global brands. Branding strategies were the product of the nineteenth century – in fact, much earlier.[49] By the interwar years some brands, such as Coca-Cola, were well established both in their home markets and abroad,[50] though most brands in industries as diverse as detergents and alcoholic

46. Douglas C. West, "From T-Square to T-Plan: The London Office of the J. Walter Thompson Advertising Agency, 1919–70," *Business History* 29 (1987); Vern Terpstra and Chwo-Ming Yu, "Determinants of Foreign Investment by U.S. Advertising Agencies," *Journal of International Business Studies* 19 (1988).
47. E. J. T. Collins, "Brands and Breakfast Cereals in Britain," in *Adding Value: Brands and Marketing in Food and Drink*, ed. Geoffrey Jones and Nicholas J. Morgan (London: Routledge, 1994).
48. Frank M. Go and Ray Pine, *Globalization Strategy in the Hotel Industry* (London: Routledge, 1995); Stanley C. Hollander, *Multinational Retailing* (East Lansing: Michigan State University Press, 1970); John F. Love, *McDonald's: Behind the Arches* (New York: Boston, 1987).
49. Mira Wilkins, "When and Why Brand Names in Food and Drink?" in *Adding Value*, ed. Jones and Morgan.
50. August W. Giebelhaus, "The Pause that Refreshed the World: The Evolution of Coca-Cola's Global Marketing Strategy," in *Adding Value*, ed. Jones and Morgan.

beverages remained primarily "national" until the 1950s and 1960s, when firms began to identify global brands. In alcoholic beverages, many leading brands had originated in the eighteenth and nineteenth centuries, but starting in the 1960s some brands began to be identified or promoted as global. The Cuban-based firm of Bacardi, which had sold its rum almost entirely in the United States before the owning family was expelled from Cuba by Castro in 1960, was now spread worldwide much assisted by the discovery that Coca Cola makes an excellent mixer.[51] However, the globalization of brands in many countries has been a slow process. In the food industry, many brands, customers, and competitors remained primarily local even up to the last decade of the century.

As in the creation of the first global economy, multinational banking and trading MNEs played a vital role in building, or rebuilding, a global infrastructure from the 1950s. The earlier phase of European overseas banking had left a legacy of thousands of multinational bank branches, mostly in the developing world, but only seven U.S. banks had any overseas branches; foreign banks had virtually no business in the United States. So, too, the heavily regulated nature of the industry worldwide left no room for new waves of multinational banking or indeed much innovation at all until the development of the Eurodollar markets in London from the late 1950s. Initially developed by British overseas and merchant banks eager to secure dollars and by Communist governments unwilling to repatriate dollars to the United States, the Eurodollar market grew thanks to the restrictions on interest paid on deposits (Regulation Q, 1970) in the United States. It captured a rising share of financial intermediation from the regulated domestic banking markets. The momentum of the market left its growth unaffected by the abolition of Regulation Q and by the disappearance of other initial reasons for its growth.

The new financial markets, increasingly important for the financing of MNE activities, had several curious features – especially their location and concentration in a small number of financial centers such as London or Singapore and Hong Kong in Asia, where the primary attraction was not the size of domestic markets but a combination of regulations, fiscal conditions, and political stability.[52] Multinational banking grew exponentially in size and, for the first time, attracted U.S. institutions on a large scale. During the 1960s, U.S. banks set up numerous branches in London to participate

51. Teresa da Silva Lopes, "The Impact of Multinational Investment on Alcohol Consumption since the 1960s," *Business and Economic History* (1999).
52. Howard Curtis Reed, *The Pre-Eminence of International Financial Centers* (New York: Praeger, 1981).

in the market; by 1985 U.S. banks had more than 860 branches abroad, although thereafter their international presence ebbed. Foreign operations of marginal concern to U.S. banks in 1960 by the mid-1980s had assets in their foreign branches equal to 20 percent of the total assets of all U.S. banks. In turn, European and, later, Japanese banks invested in the United States, ending the U.S.'s isolation from world banking. Foreign banks, which in the 1960s held an insignificant share of the American market, by the mid-1980s accounted for about one-fifth of the commercial and industrial loan market.[53] Conversely, by the 1980s the once enormous European overseas banking networks in Latin America, Africa, Asia, and Australia had largely disappeared.

The extent to which banking was globalized in the 1980s (and later) is debatable. Although the wholesale and Euromarkets became truly global, retail banking markets remained local. Few banks made a serious and sustained attempt to provide global banking services even at the retail level. The most important to do so, however, were Citibank of the United States and the Hongkong Bank (now HSBC), the British overseas bank in Hong Kong until 1993 that built on its core Asian and Pacific business by acquiring banks in the Middle East, the United States, Britain, and (in the 1990s) Latin America.

Trading companies also resumed a new importance in the postwar decades. The extensive business of the European trading companies in the developing world encountered considerable difficulties because government intervention in commodity trading, import and exchange controls, and pressure for local ownership of resources decimated many aspects of their traditional business. However, in regions and countries where political conditions permitted, these trading firms continued to evolve, sometimes investing in manufacture in their host economies or in related services. From the base of the British colony of Hong Kong, the British trading companies, such as John Swire and Jardine Matheson, survived the loss of all their extensive assets in China in 1949 and built new diversified trading and distribution businesses in the Asian and Pacific regions and elsewhere. The Swire Group established a new airline in the late 1940s (Cathay Pacific), invested in Coca-Cola bottling in Hong Kong and the United States in the 1960s and 1970s to become one of the world's largest bottlers, and developed disused land from its former dockyards and sugar refinery in Hong Kong into a vast real estate business in Asia and the United States.[54]

53. Michael R. Darby, "The Internationalization of American Banking and Finance," *Journal of International Money and Finance* 5 (1986).
54. Jones, *Merchants*.

Although such European trading companies developed as regional multi-national groups, other types of multinational trading firms built and developed global trading networks, benefiting from persistent information asymmetries – at least until the spread of the Internet during the 1990s changed the rules of the game – and in some cases from the opportunities to trade with Communist countries. Prominent among these firms were Japan's general trading companies (*sogo shosha*), which survived their dismantling by the Allied occupation after the Second World War to become the central players in both Japan's foreign trade and (until the 1970s) FDI as well as central components of Japan's horizontal business groups with a special role in financing and handling the foreign trade of Japanese SMEs. The *sogo shosha* accounted for more than 80 percent of Japan's total imports and exports during the 1960s and were counted as among the world's largest MNEs in terms of turnover.[55] In a regional context, the *sogo shosha* were important in the postwar decades through their alliances with overseas Chinese firms, enabling their local production and trading networks to be refocused toward Japan and the United States.

The postwar decades also saw the rapid international growth of commodity trading firms like Cargill, the U.S. grain trader and largest private company in the United States, which took advantage of increased government intervention in the marketing of commodities and the nationalization of mines and plantations.[56] By the 1970s a handful of commodity traders, including Cargill, Continental, Louis Dreyfus, Bunge & Born, and André, accounted for more than 90 percent of the European and U.S. wheat exports. Swiss-based trading firms, such as André and Glencore, built enormous global commodity and other trading links. By the 1990s Glencore had an annual turnover of more than $40 billion, trading in everything from base metals to soft commodities.[57]

During the 1950s, the international cartels of the interwar years were dismantled,[58] although U.S. manufacturing MNEs invested on a large scale in Western Europe – initially in response to the "dollar shortage" – encouraging U.S. firms to establish factories to supply customers in countries that lacked the dollars to buy American products.[59] In most industries,

55. M. Y. Yoshino and T. B. Lifson, *The Invisible Link: Japan's Sogo Shosha and Organization of Trade* (Cambridge, MA: MIT Press, 1986).
56. W. G. Broehl, *Cargill: Trading the World's Grain* (Hanover, NH: University Press of New England, 1992); idem, *Cargill, Going Global* (Hanover, NH: University Press of New England, 1998).
57. Guex, "The Development of Swiss Trading Companies," in *Multinational Trading*, ed. Jones.
58. H. G. Schröter, "Kartellierung und Dekartellierung 1890–1990," *Vierteljahrschrift für Sozial-und Wirtschaftsgeschichte* 81 (1994).
59. Wilkins, *Maturing*, 129.

U.S. firms held large "ownership advantages" in management and technology over their European counterparts, and their affiliates often achieved much higher productivity than their indigenous counterparts.

Between 1950 and 1962, at least 350 new U.S.-owned manufacturing affiliates were set up in Britain, the largest European host for U.S. manufacturing FDI. By the mid-1960s, U.S.-owned firms employed nearly 10 percent of the British manufacturing workforce and held large market shares in many products involving either high technological content or advanced marketing skills. U.S. firms accounted for between 30 and 50 percent of the British market for computers, rubber tires, soaps and detergents, instant coffee, refrigerators, and washing machines among many other products. Throughout the 1950s and 1960s the labor productivity of U.S. affiliates in Britain was estimated to be almost 33 percent higher than that of all British manufacturing.[60]

Although the fast growth of U.S. manufacturing affiliates was striking, there was little that could be considered global about multinational manufacturing in this era. On the one hand, this growth was little more than the story of U.S. firms shifting some of their production abroad – mainly to a few Western European countries. On the other hand, overseas affiliates remained very "national." There was little rationalized production, and intrafirm trade was very low. However, from the 1960s new strategies for the organization of multinational manufacturing began to involve both geographical and functional integration. By the postwar decades, the considerable autonomy given to national subsidiaries had given rise to extensive duplication of products and functions such as FDI. The worldwide lowering of trade barriers under the General Agreement on Tariffs and Trade (GATT), cost reductions in transportation, a convergence of consumer demand in some developed countries and sectors, and the formation of trading blocs beginning with the European Economic Community (later the European Union [EU]) in 1957 provided new opportunities for the integration of formerly isolated subsidiaries.

In practice, the process of building integrated productions systems was slow. U.S. MNEs took the lead in the integration of production, and among these IBM and Ford were the pioneers. Although IBM's foreign subsidiaries during the 1950s were hardly coordinated, this changed radically in 1964 with the launch of System 360, a broad line of compatible mainframe

---

60. J. H. Dunning, *American Investment in British Manufacturing Industry* (London: Allen & Unwin, 1958); Wilkins, *Maturing*; Vaupel and Curhan, *The Making of Multinational Enterprise*; idem, *The World's Multinational Enterprise*; Jones and Bostock, "U.S. Multinationals in British Manufacturing before 1962."

computers designed to be manufactured and sold worldwide. IBM in the United States took overall responsibility for development engineering and manufacturing, but responsibility for development of specific processes and peripherals was assigned to different laboratories in Europe and the United States. By the end of the 1960s, IBM had two regional production networks in North America and Europe. From the mid-1960s, Ford, too, began to integrate its manufacturing on a regional basis starting with the integration of production in the United States and Canada. Ford merged its European interests into Ford of Europe in 1967 and began to build a regionally integrated manufacturing system.[61] Not until the 1980s did Ford attempt to integrate design and production worldwide.

European-owned companies lagged far behind their U.S. counterparts in response to regional integration. The contrasting examples of Unilever and Procter & Gamble have acquired almost a textbook status.[62] Unilever had an extremely decentralized organization in the postwar decades reflecting, in part, the autonomy of national subsidiaries in Europe as a result of political developments in the 1930s and the Second World War and also Unilever's growing not as an organic company but through acquisitions and mergers. An organizational culture based on consensus also meant that senior management in the firm's twin headquarters in London and Rotterdam sought to avoid forcing their wills on local managers. The result was that this leading European-based MNE was remarkably decentralized. Within Europe, Unilever's national managers had the greatest possible freedom – that is, national products and brand names varied enormously and there was no integration of production between countries. Both its trading company subsidiary, United Africa Company, and its U.S. business functioned as almost autonomous operations. This development might have reflected a more general trend, for the many European manufacturing firms with operations in the United States in the postwar decades were often left largely alone for antitrust reasons and because of a belief in the uniqueness of the American market and the superiority of its American management.[63]

Unilever's position was severely challenged during the 1950s with the formation of the EU and the entry of U.S. MNEs led by Procter & Gamble and Colgate into Europe. Procter & Gamble, with relatively few international

61. Dassbach, *Global Enterprises*.
62. Christopher A. Bartlett and Sumantra Ghoshal, *Managing Across Borders: The Transnational Solution* (Boston: Harvard Business School Press, 1989).
63. Geoffrey Jones, "Control, Performance and Knowledge Transfers in Large Multinationals," *Business History Review*, 76, 3 (2002).
    The previous paragraphs draw on research for the author's forthcoming history of Unilever between 1965 and 1990.

operations before 1945, began its internationalization process at a time of falling trade barriers. Its management had a strong belief in Procter & Gamble's "way of doing things" and sought to structure its overseas operations as replicas of the U.S. business. It moved quickly to integrate its European plants, and, in 1963, established a European technical center to service the common research and development (R & D) requirements of its European subsidiaries.

Although Unilever lost market share in detergents rapidly following the assault by U.S. MNEs, its attempts to integrate production and achieve more cohesive organization were prolonged. In 1952 it appointed two "coordinators" (a term used to emphasize that their role was advisory) for nonmargarine foods and personal products (such as toothpaste) whose functions were to encourage transfer of products and brands between countries and to identify international brands. Only in 1966, after much internal dissension, were the coordinators given executive power and profit responsibility in a handful of Western European countries, and only in the 1970s, after a rigorous investigation by McKinsey, did conflicting jurisdictions between coordinators, national managers, and others begin to be sorted out. Even in the 1980s, Unilever lacked a coherent European strategy; during that decade the U.S. business was integrated in managerial terms with the rest of the firm.[64]

During the 1970s it seemed that the postwar growth in FDI might have peaked. U.S. manufacturing firms in Europe did not grow much faster than the European economy overall, and on some measures world trade grew faster than world FDI.[65] During the 1980s, however, FDI flows grew rapidly and faster than world trade. There were major shifts in the sources and destination of multinational investment from the 1970s. With respect to sources, the major continental European countries and Japan resumed outward investment – partly as their competitive advantages had grown and partly in response to the new protectionism. As a result, the U.S. share of total outward FDI stock fell from 50 percent in 1967 to 26 percent in 1990.

The resumption of Japanese FDI from the early 1970s was particularly striking as Japanese automobile and electronics firms responded to the relaxation of their government's controls on outward FDI, rising domestic labor costs, the revaluation of the yen after 1972, and the growth of U.S., and later European, protectionism to exploit their competitive advantages by

64. John Dunning, *Multinational Enterprises and the Global Economy* (London: Addison–Wesley, 1993), 16.
65. Martin Kenney and Richard Florida, *Beyond Mass Production* (New York: Oxford University Press, 1993); Tetsuo Abo, ed., *Hybrid Factory* (New York: Oxford University Press, 1994).

producing abroad rather than exploring. The upshot was a substantial flow of Japanese manufacturing investment into, first, the United States, and then into Europe. Japanese firms built virtually a new automobile industry in the United States during the 1980s[66] and made similar large-scale investments in parts of Western Europe in the 1980s: in some countries, industries that had almost disappeared under local ownership, such as automobiles and electronics, were reestablished under Japanese ownership.

The other big change from the 1970s was the growth of the United States as a host economy. In the postwar period, the United States dominated world outward FDI, but, in the late 1960s, it held less than 10 percent of world inward (i.e., being invested in the United States) FDI stock; thereafter, the U.S. role as a host economy, expanded dramatically and, between 1975 and 1980, accounted for about one-quarter of all world inflows and, during the 1980s, for over 40 percent. By 1990, inward FDI stock in the United States was as large as U.S. outward stock abroad.[67] Relatively foreign MNEs remained less important in the United States than other large host economies. At the end of the 1980s, for example, the foreign affiliate share of employment in the United States was less than 4 percent, whereas in major European host economies the equivalent proportion was often already over 20 percent.[68]

The 1980s experienced an almost worldwide shift to more open policies toward MNEs – a shift with multiple causes, including the spread of market-oriented policies, the failure of state planning and closed trading models, the undermining of exchange controls by the Euromarkets, and fallout from the world debt crisis. The consequences were radical and included the reopening of almost all developing and former (or still) Communist countries to MNEs. In the developed market economies, there was a noteworthy liberalization of restrictions on service sector FDI. The EU's Single Market program, launched in the mid-1980s, was specifically targeted at opening European markets to service sector FDI. By the 1990s the service sector accounted for more than 50 percent of the stock of world FDI.

Curiously, the geographical distribution of world FDI was comparatively unaffected by this changed policy environment. It remained skewed by the end of that decade. In 1990, the world's largest host economies were the United States (with 23% of total world inward FDI stock), the United

---

66. Robert E. Lipsey, "Foreign Direct Investment in the United States: Changes over Three Decades," in *Foreign Direct Investment*, ed. Kenneth A. Froot (Chicago: University of Chicago Press, 1994).
67. United Nations, *World Investment Report 1992* (New York: United Nations, 1992), annex table 8.
68. P. Patel and K. Pavitt, "Large Firms in the Production of the World's Technology: An Important Case of Non-Globalization," *Journal of International Business Studies* 22 (1991).

Kingdom (13%), and Germany and Canada (7% each). Canada had twice as much FDI as the entire continent of Africa and six times more than Japan, where government barriers to inward FDI had been dismantled beginning in the 1970s but where few foreign firms ventured. There was about as much inward FDI in the United Kingdom in 1990 as in Latin America, Russia, India, and China combined. The societal implications for the developing economies that received little FDI were considerable, for they became ever more excluded from the flows of innovation and technology, which by this period were largely concentrated in a few hundred large MNEs responsible for three-quarters of industrial R & D and for more than two-thirds of patents spread in foreign markets.[69]

Although, by 1990, the entire developing world accounted for less than 20 percent of world FDI stock, a few developing economies had remained or become substantial hosts. Singapore's extremely fast growth from the mid-1960s was almost entirely driven by foreign MNEs, and its 1990 share of world FDI stock – 2 percent – was about the same as that of all of Africa and three times that of Japan. Among other major Asian hosts (Indonesia, Malaysia, and Thailand), foreign MNEs invested heavily – especially in electronics. Most remarkable of all was China's reemergence as a host economy after a major policy change in 1979. During the 1980s, overseas Chinese firms in particular invested heavily in China; its share of world FDI stock rose from zero in 1980 to nearly 1 percent in 1990. During the following decade, a surge in inward FDI was to transform China into one of the world's leading host economies. In Latin America, multinational investment was heavily concentrated in a few countries led by Brazil and Mexico, which, although they had driven out foreign firms from resources and utilities in the postwar period, had sought to attract them in manufacturing industries such as automobiles as part of import substitution strategies.[70]

The world outside the triad of North America, Western Europe, and Japan remained singularly unimportant as a source of multinational investment. However, starting in the 1970s several firms from Asian newly industrialized countries (NICs), Taiwan and Korea especially, began to invest abroad – often first in neighboring countries and later in the United States and Europe. Between 1986 and 1990, nearly 2 percent of world outward FDI flows originated in Taiwan.[71] The nature of the competencies and the

69. Helen Shapiro, *Engines of Growth: The State and Transnational Auto Companies in Brazil* (Cambridge: Cambridge University Press, 1994).
70. Roger van Hoesel, *Beyond Export-Led Growth: The Emergence of New Multinational Enterprises from Korea and Taiwan* (Ph.D. diss., Erasmus University, Rotterdam, 1997).
71. Sanjaya Lall, *The New Multinationals: The Spread of Third World Enterprises* (New York: Wiley & Sons, 1983); L. T. Wells, *Third World Multinationals: The Rise of Foreign Investment from Developing Countries* (Cambridge, MA: MIT Press, 1983).

sustainability of such "Third World" MNEs have been under discussion since their discovery by researchers.[72] The Asian financial crisis of 1997–98 raised new issues about this especially in regard to overseas Chinese multinational conglomerates such as Thailand's CP group, whose organizational structure and business culture were ill suited to building sustained competitive advantages – at least in manufacturing.[73]

The nature of international business itself changed in the last decades of the century. During the late 19th century, as the world economy globalized, firms had often invested abroad using "network" structures of organization such as the clusters of "free-standing" firms identified by Mira Wilkins (see Chapter 2 in this volume) or the diversified "business groups" found around European trading companies.[74] However, as the pace of internationalization slowed, the boundaries of firms became more solid. The decades between the 1950s and the 1970s became the era of the classic MNE, when large integrated corporations appeared as the dominant organization form in international business. The large industrial enterprises of the United States were at the leading edge of all the new technologies of this period, and in much of Europe – although not Japan – large integrated corporations replaced earlier types of firms.[75] These firms conducted virtually all value-added activities within themselves. In the 1950s and 1960s, Unilever, for example, not only manufactured detergents, margarine, soup, ice cream, toothpaste, shampoos, and chemicals in numerous countries but also owned the plantations on which palm oil was produced, the ships that conveyed it to its factories, retail shops, fishing fleets to catch the fish sold in its shops, and extensive packaging, paper, and transport businesses that serviced all its other businesses.

As the pace of internationalization intensified, the boundaries of MNEs began to change; they abandoned the vertical and horizontal diversification seen in Unilever and focused instead on "core" products manufactured in turn outside the firm or in alliance with others. A key development was the growth of "outsourcing" – the start of a trend that, by the end of the 1990s, seemed to be transforming automobile assemblers such as Ford into multinational service firms that did little manufacturing themselves.

72. R. A. Brown, "Overseas Chinese Investments in China – Patterns of Growth, Diversification and Finance: The Case of Charoen Pokphand," *The China Quarterly* 155 (1998); Pavida Pananond and Carl P. Zeithaml, "The International Expansion Process of MNEs from Developing Countries: A Case Study of Thailand's CP Group," *Asia Pacific Journal of Management* 15 (1998).
73. Mira Wilkins and Harm G. Schröter, eds., *The Free-Standing Company in the World Economy* (Oxford: Oxford University Press, 1998); Jones, *Merchants*.
74. Alfred D. Chandler, "The United States: Engines of Economic Growth in the Capital-Intensive and Knowledge-Intensive Industries," in *Big Business and the Wealth of Nations*, ed. Alfred D. Chandler, Franco Amatori, and Takashi Hikino (Cambridge: Cambridge University Press, 1997).
75. Robert Reich, *The Work of Nations* (New York: Vintage Books, 1992).

Integrated production systems increasingly meant that labels such as "Made in America" were becoming meaningless because products to be sold were assembled from parts actually produced in other countries. By the 1980s, large U.S. MNEs such as IBM, which had once sought desperately to control its proprietary technology and brands and had given rise to much of the theory of the multinational enterprise in the process, were voluntarily developing and sharing their technologies with other firms through strategic alliances. The same trend toward, in Dunning's terminology, "alliance capitalism" was found in services such as airlines.

As a result the MNEs, at the end of the 1980s, acquired a different character. Some authors regarded them as stateless "global webs."[76] The reality, however, was less clear-cut. The "webs" were fragile, the strategic alliances were transient phenomena in most cases, and the national origins and ownership of large MNEs were highly visible despite all of the hyperbole surrounding globalization. Boards of directors of the largest MNEs continued to be overwhelmingly of home-country origin even if the globalization of capital markets led to wider dispersal of the ownership of corporations' equity. The globalization of key functions like R & D was also limited. Both Japanese and U.S. MNEs continued to conduct most of their R & D at home, although the MNEs of several small European countries such as the Netherlands and Switzerland, as well as the United Kingdom, had by now decentralized innovation to a much greater degree. In general, firms operating in industries with higher technological opportunities, such as computers, automobiles, and aeronautics, continued to conduct most of their R & D at home.

From the 1950s onward a new global economy began to be constructed as MNE service firms started international dissemination of management practices, cultural values, and lifestyles – as well as the building of a new trading and financial infrastructure – and as multinational banks and trading companies moved money, commodities, and information around the world on an unprecedented scale. By the 1990s, multinational service firms were the largest and most dynamic components of the new global economy albeit with a distinct convergence between services and manufacturing. Multinational manufacturers, starting in the 1960s, had begun to take advantage of new technological opportunities and regional integration to reorganize production systems, first integrating regionally and subsequently on a worldwide basis, and, beginning in the 1970s, Japanese and continental

---

76. Y. S. Hu, "Global or Stateless Firms Are National Firms with International Operations," *California Management Review* 34 (1992).

European firms again resumed FDI on a substantial scale while the United States grew as the world's largest host economy. But, under the pressure of fast internationalization, the boundaries of manufacturing and service firms had become blurred as they arranged for production and sought competitive advantages through alliances with other firms.

By the end of the 1980s, however, globalization was more a concept than a reality, and it is not evident that the level of international integration was greater than in the early 20th century. Global firms remained, in practice, national in many fundamental respects, whereas the huge flows of investment – and more important, knowledge and information – within MNEs largely bypassed the majority of the world's population in Latin America, Africa, Asia, and Eastern Europe.

4

Innovative Multinational Forms

Japan as a Case Study

SEI YONEKURA AND SARA MCKINNEY

Multinational enterprises have played a crucial role throughout Japanese economic history since the Meiji Restoration of the late 19th century. Although the evolution of several Japanese multinational enterprises in the last decades of the 20th century parallels the American multinational development experience, in early Japanese multinational organization certain innovative forms and unconventional business strategies deviated from some common Western practices and traditional multinational development theories. The Japanese effectively "changed the rules of the game." They played a key role in revitalizing Japanese companies and industries and contributed to economic progress of host countries abroad. Japan exhibited the "fastest sustained rate of industrial production, GNP, and per capita income over the last century."[1] During that century Japan became a prominent and powerful home country for successful multinational corporations.

The innovative multinational enterprises that effectively "broke the mold" rose in response to the unique historical conditions of the environment they faced, including the industrial composition of the domestic economy, the nature of the domestic market, and associated opportunities.

JAPAN'S EARLIEST MULTINATIONALS: *SOGO SHOSHA*

General trading companies in Japan, known as *sogo shosha* (defined simply as "a firm that trades all kinds of goods with all nations of the world,"[2]) are a Japanese organizational invention and among the earliest and perhaps most prominent multinational organizations in Japanese business history in scale

---

1. M. Y. Yoshino and T. B. Lifson, *The Invisible Link: Japan's Sogo Shosha and the Organization of Trade* (Boston: MIT Press 1986), 7.
2. Shin'ichi Yonekawa and Hideki Yoshihara, eds., *Business History of General Trading Companies* (Tokyo: University of Tokyo Press, 1987), 1

of physical size and in the range of businesses and commercial activities. These large trade and development companies arose in response to Japan's economic and trade environment of the 1860s not only to undertake import and export but also to assist Japanese manufacturers with overseas investment and joint ventures.[3]

Alfred Chandler, Jr., has questioned whether early trading companies should even be termed multinational enterprises. Uncertainty, constraints, and time delays did characterize their communications – particularly in the early development of British, Dutch, and East Indian trading companies – whereas modern multinational organizations, on the other hand, coordinate and control large quantities of transactions through innovations in communications technology and transportation.[4] Mira Wilkins, in contrast, argues that early trading houses did possess many attributes of the modern multinational firm. To some degree, early Japanese trading firms, like typical modern trading firms, operated in foreign markets and coordinated various operations and activities within the single enterprise and beyond the trade function alone. Wilkins suggests that, unlike the early East Indian firms, the *sogo shosha* survived into the 20th century and even into the 21st century. Japanese trading companies continue to represent viable economic units important not only within the domestic market but in world markets as well. In 1984, for example, the nine largest Japanese *sogo shosha* together generated sales of $378 billion,[5] handling between 45 and 50 percent of all Japanese imports and exports. Mitsui Bussan, Mitsubishi Shoji, and Sumitomo, three of the largest firms, maintain expansive networks of offices worldwide.

The first Japanese *sogo shosha* were established after the forced opening of Japanese ports with the arrival in 1853 of U.S. Commodore Matthew Perry and his fleet of "black ships," as the Japanese called Western ships. The opening of ports in Kanagawa (now Yokohama), Nagasaki, and Hakodate by "Western nations in keen pursuit of their mercantile policies"[6] marked the beginning of the organized development of Japan's foreign trade. Japan's more than 220-year isolation from the outside world had ended. In the development of foreign trade that followed, Japanese trading companies performed three key roles: importing necessary raw materials, exporting Japanese goods, and procuring industrial development technologies.[7] These

3. Ibid., 1–3. Yukio Togano, *Sogo Shosha no Keieishi-teki Kenkyu* (A historical business study on *sogo shosha*) (Tokyo: Toyo-keizai Shinposha, 1977).
4. See Mira Wilkins, *The Growth of Multinationals* (London: Edward Elgar, 1991), 219.
5. Lyn S. Amine, S. Tamer Cavusgil, and Robert I. Weinstein, "Japanese Sogo Shosha and the U.S. Export Trading Companies," *Academy of Marketing Science* 14 (1984): 21–32.
6. Yoshino and Lifson, *The Invisible Link*, 10.
7. Amine, Cavusgil, and Weinstein, "Japanese Sogo Shosha," 21–32.

companies established offices abroad to serve as the sales force for Japanese manufactured goods.[8] They moved quickly into new markets, developed market opportunities, and effectively coordinated expansive operations and diverse lines of merchandise – traditional commodities like soybean, grain, aluminum, steel, and petrochemicals, which dominate their overseas trade even today. Without their activities Japanese economic development could not have occurred.[9]

The form into which trading companies evolved in Japan is distinctly different from that encountered in England and America, where most trading firms developed into specialized, industry-specific enterprises. Japanese trading firms, *sogo shosha*, on the other hand, developed into highly general trading organizations, managing extremely diverse portfolios of various merchandise lines and servicing expansive geographical areas. Before the First World War, Japanese general trading companies were noted for handling "chicken feed to warships" and, during their peak in the 1970s, were commonly referred to as dealers of "noodles to missiles," effectively capturing the typical diversity of their product ranges.

The Japanese home environment shaped the Japanese firms' distinctive organizational forms through heavy dependence on importation of raw materials in the absence of natural resources in Japan itself and on use of export to afford these imports. Resource limitations thus prompted development of a national infrastructure geared toward trade. In addition, Japan had to import modern technology and machinery to assist industrialization, and its typically small-sized producers lacked both capital and trade expertise. The general trading firms, therefore, played an integral role in the prewar and the postwar Japanese economies.

THE ROLE OF *SOGO SHOSHA* IN PREWAR JAPAN

The prewar Japanese *sogo shosha* was essentially the pioneer of Japanese multinational organizations. Quite unlike the American experience, in which manufacturing organizations, having established themselves within the large home market first, then used this experience in business management to establish operations abroad, in Japan macroeconomic constraints and hurdles led instead to the emergence of a separate trade service network. This network was, and continues to be, managed independently from domestic producers and manufacturers.

8. W. G. Ohuchi, *Theory: How American Business Can Meet the Japanese Challenge* (New York: Avon Books, 1981), 5.
9. Wilkins, *The Growth of Multinationals*, 224.

Compared with Europe and America, Japan was a latecomer to industrialization. Following the 1868 Meiji Restoration, which signaled the close of Japan's lengthy self-imposed isolation, the country became acutely aware that to ensure its independence it would need to industrialize quickly and catch up with the more advanced West. This became a crucial national goal. The Meiji leadership saw industrialization as a prerequisite for modern military strength. They recognized the importance of learning from more industrially advanced countries and the importance of foreign trade as a means of acquiring the foreign currency necessary to purchase modern weaponry and machinery and to hire foreign advisers.[10] The effort to catch up with the more advanced West thus led to Japan's heavy reliance on foreign trade, and the importation of raw materials and semifinished goods was a consequence of the lack of a rich supply of natural resources. Imports, in turn, enabled the export of value-added finished goods, and exports generated the much-needed foreign currencies that paid for the imports.

Before this development the terms of trade had been typically disadvantageous to the Japanese, who faced both exorbitant commissions and unjust practices. Their lack of export competence in managing foreign trade led to blatant exploitation by foreign traders, which became a principal stimulus for the emergence of Japanese *sogo shosha*. The characteristically small size of domestic production firms in Japan meant that they essentially lacked the necessary capabilities and resources to manage international trade activities themselves – an inability that stemmed from both lack of capital and, perhaps more importantly, of trade know-how resulting from Japan's prolonged isolation and related linguistic barriers.

In what has been termed an example of organized entrepreneurship, the Meiji government and *zaibatsu* (industrial group) now sought to develop direct overseas trade actively in close collaboration between government and private enterprise. In pursuit of foreign exchange through exportation of coal, the government called upon the assistance of Mitsui, granting them exclusive rights to export all coal produced by the state-run Miike mines. The Mitsui *zaibatsu* was, thus, essentially the first organization commissioned by the government to undertake export. The coal and rice trades pioneered Japan's initial government-assisted foreign market connections and their growth and were the foundation upon which Japanese foreign trade and the *soga shosha* grew.

Wilkins argues that Japan's highly homogeneous population gave the Japanese little experience in dealing with other cultures' different customs,

---

10. Yoshino and Lifson, *The Invisible Link*, 11.

norms, and languages. Japan lacked knowledge of the economic, political, cultural, and legal environments of each foreign market and of the various types of business institutions abroad.[11] It thus relied on trade intermediaries – *sogo shosha* – who possessed the knowledge and expertise to bridge that gap. Japanese manufacturers, therefore, enlisted the services of the Japanese general trading companies, the *sogo shosha*, unlike their North American counterparts who participated directly in export activity themselves.

The *sogo shosha* specialized in information gathering and in transactional intermediation services and became a key conduit for distribution of a broad range of Japanese products,[12] providing networks, trade law expertise, and advice on customs. Their extensive information networks reduced risk for the small and medium-sized Japanese enterprises, matching supply and demand and arranging transactions. The advantage of such a dedicated trade organization for manufacturing firms is apparent when their importing or exporting has not grown to a level within any one foreign market that would warrant maintenance of their own overseas sales office.[13] The trading firms formed the core structural link between such Japanese producers and their overseas markets.

The *sogo shosha* were destined from the beginning to handle a diverse selection of merchandise and to serve numerous and varied geographic areas. This diversity not only reduced risk by distributing it across a variety of trades but also enabled economies of scale and scope, which were especially important in a country of small and medium-sized businesses in which human resources with knowledge of foreign trade were limited and an information gap caused by language barriers and by limited capital existed. Once the *soga shosha* had the necessary infrastructure in place, it made logical sense to exploit their range of resources and expertise in personnel, capital, and sales and distribution infrastructure across multiple product lines. Once the initial networks linking Japan with its principal export markets had been established, the addition of further offices represented only marginal costs. Such diversity was a fundamental point of difference between Japanese multinational trading companies and the British, Dutch, American, and East Indian trading firms, which typically specialized either by industry or geographic market.

The *sogo shosha* also performed an important function as procurement agents, identifying and importing raw materials, products, process

---

11. Ibid., 10.
12. Yoshihiko Tsurumi, *The Japanese Are Coming: A Multinational Interaction of Firms and Politics* (New York: Ballinger Publishing Company, 1976), 131.
13. Ibid., 132.

technologies, and machinery for Japanese firms. According to Tsurumi, more than half of all technologies licensed to Japan were channeled through Japanese trading companies.[14] So, too, they demonstrated an ability to identify and organize multiparty deals; in a form of third-country deals, branch offices abroad came to trade among themselves as well as with foreign third parties. Because of the *zaibatsu* connections it was not unusual for Japanese trading firms to arrange finance in the form of trade credit facilities, direct loans, and foreign exchange services for both customers and suppliers.[15]

Mitsui Bussan and Mitsubishi Shoji, two of the largest and most prominent Japanese general trading companies in the prewar period, neatly fit the model of the Japanese *sogo shosha*. Mitsui, the older of the two and the one that is usually considered the prototype of the *sogo shosha*, was officially established as the trading arm of the House of Mitsui in 1876; the company arose from a merger between Senshu-sha and Mitsui Kokusan-kata, a domestic trading establishment.[16] With the backing of the Mitsui *zaibatsu* industrial group, it grew rapidly to became the pioneer and forerunner of Japanese trading companies. As its charter stated, it endeavored to "... export overseas surplus products of the imperial Land and to import products needed at home, and thereby to engage in intercourse with the ten thousand countries of the Universe."[17]

Mitsui entered into the world of foreign trade after it was granted exclusive rights to market Japanese rice and coal. Japan's first rice export had been entrusted to the English rice merchant Walsh, Hall and Co. in 1872, but the second batch of rice was sold through the domestic product department of Mitsui 4 years later, though Mitsui did call on the British merchant E. B. Watson to undertake the actual exporting.[18] Foreign traders continued to manage such Japanese trade even in 1880, when Japanese merchants controlled less than 10 percent of Japanese trade. By 1900, they managed about 38 percent.[19]

Mitsui Bussan began its international expansion by use of commissioned agents for each key import market and then moved to establish its own sales offices, staffing them with its own employees. It set up a London office in

14. Amine et al., "Japanese Sogo Shosha," 23.   15. Yoshino and Lifson, *The Invisible Link*, 11.
16. H. Kawabe, "Overseas Activities and Their Organization," in *General Trading Companies: A Comparative and Historical Study*, ed. Shin'ichi Yonekawa (Tokyo: United Nations University Press, 1990), 171.
17. Yonekawa and Yoshihara, eds., *Business History*, 37.
18. K. Maeda, "General Trading Companies in Pre-War Japan: A Sketch," in *General Trading Companies*, ed. Yonekawa, chapter 5.
19. Seiichiro Yonekura, "The Emergence of the Prototype of Enterprise Group Capitalism: The Case of Mitsui," *Hitotsubashi Journal of Commerce and Management* 20 (1985): 63–104.

1877 after the Japanese Ministry of Finance commissioned it to handle all rice exports from Japan to Europe, and branches were soon opened in Paris (1878) and New York (1879) followed by Lyon and Milan. It was the true beginning of Mitsui Bussan's multinationalism. Its presence in the London market, additionally, provided an important connection for importation of machinery and woolen cloth for use by the Japanese army. Mitsui Bussan's Paris office was set up to sell raw silk manufactured in government-related silk reeling mills in Japan and from manufacturing operations in neighboring Asian countries.

A similar scenario describes Mitsui's exclusive involvement in the export of state-owned Miike coal to China, the key market for these exports. This direct exportation led, in 1877, to the opening of an agency in Shanghai. Mitsui later acquired the mine itself from the Japanese government at a favorable price, and it served as a significant source of income over decades to come. Mitsui's involvement in the coal trade stimulated establishment of its own shipping business, which, in turn, was used for additional imports and exports. Mitsui also undertook financing of export activities of Japanese producers, acting as a "foreign exchange bank with the use of government funds from 1877–1880 when the Yokohama Specie Bank was established."[20]

The cotton industry provided Mitsui with a further key growth opportunity, setting the pattern for the *sogo shosha* and its role in Japan's economic development. Mitsui Bussan made several important contributions to development of this traditional modern industry in Japan, beginning as a sales agent that imported raw cotton and exported value-added manufactured cotton products such as yarn and fabrics. The company imported spinning machinery and technology from England through its London office (opened initially to facilitate rice exports), assisting and promoting the modernization of the industry in general. Mitsui Bussan set up the Osaka Spinning Company, which began the practice of trading company participation in production. Like later *sogo shosha*, Bussan became an organizer and coordinator of the industry, organizing small and medium-sized manufacturers involved in cotton spinning and standardizing products by size and quality for export to enhance the international competitive power of Japanese goods.

In efforts to exploit and build upon their developing network, Mitsui handled diverse goods in pursuit of economies of scale. Just as the London office, which was opened for the export of rice, later imported woolen

---

20. Wilkins, *The Growth of Multinationals*, 236.

cloth for the army, so Mitsui's first overseas branch, established in Shanghai in 1877 to sell Japanese coal in China,[21] came to be used to procure raw cotton and then to promote and distribute cotton yarn and cotton fabric exports within the Chinese market.

Mitsui Bussan's first foreign investments were typically in Asia with branches opened in Shanghai, Hong Kong, and Singapore for coal trade and then leveraged to establish Japanese cotton yarn and fabric exports.

Mitsui Bussan had originated from government-commissioned transactions but grew also to manage importation and exportation of goods for private enterprises, helping to harness these private enterprises to the "national goal of industrialization."[22] By 1907 it was handling more than 120 varieties of goods through 40 foreign branches and offices across Asia, America, and Europe. At that time its business totaled 18.6 percent of Japan's exports and 20.7 percent of its imports.[23]

Sogo shosha as a whole actively sought new foreign market opportunities and aggressively pursued the geographic expansion of their sales and marketing networks. Even as early as 1881, 14 Japanese trading companies had offices in New York,[24] although many of these disappeared once the government's policy of export subsidiaries ceased. China became a key focus for Japanese foreign investment and trade during the pre–First World War period. Japan's success in the Sino-Japanese War (1894–95) and Russo-Japanese War (1904–05) in particular led to an expansion in overseas operations by opening up Korea, China, and Manchuria, each of which was a substantial and lucrative market for Japanese products. The trading companies dispatched personnel to these markets and opened branch offices to penetrate each market. Entry into China also offered Japanese manufacturers, with the assistance of *sogo shosha* like Mitsui, the chance to undertake production activities such as spinning factories abroad. *Sogo shosha* played a role not only in transactional intermediation but also in foreign direct investment prompted by an effort to access, develop, and secure key natural resources and trade compensations or to achieve manufacturing efficiencies through lower labor and land costs. In 1902, for example, the Shanghai branch of Mitsui Bussan absorbed a Chinese spinning factory, Xingtai, renamed the "Shanghai Cotton Manufacturing, Ltd.," and then operated and actively developed it. In 1907 Mitsui began a joint venture in

21. Hidemasa Morikawa, *Zaibatsu: The Rise and Fall of Family Enterprise Groups in Japan* (Tokyo: University of Tokyo Press, 1992).
22. Yonekawa and Yoshihara, eds., *Business History*, 30.
23. Wilkins, *The Growth of Multinationals*, 237.
24. Kawabe, "Overseas Activities and Their Organization," 173.

Talien with Santai Oil Mills, Ltd., as part of a strategy to increase soy cake production.[25]

General trading companies like Mitsui by then had begun to trade among third countries through increasingly comprehensive sales office networks abroad. Toward the latter half of 1895, Mitsui started to export Chinese goods to Europe and America and managed importation of American railway equipment and lumber and some European goods in China – especially through its own Shanghai branch.

Mitsubishi Shoji, the second largest of the prewar general trading companies, evolved from Mitsubishi's involvement in copper and coal industries. It became a stock company in 1918 and followed a pattern of development through vertical integration that largely paralleled the earlier experience of Mitsui Bussan, which had begun in shipping, with acquisition of its first ships in 1875. Like Mitsui Bussan, it also then moved into mining with the encouragement of the government. Its trading arm Mitsubishi Shoji emerged in response to a need to develop a marketing unit to handle the outputs of its mining ventures. Then Mitsubishi moved into heavy and chemical industries, shipbuilding, and manufacturing.

Mitsubishi Shoji *zaibatsu* membership, like that of Mitsui Bussan, placed it in the favorable position of sole agency status for handling of the diverse commodities and the goods produced and required by the businesses of the Mitsubishi *zaibatsu*. It enjoyed the backing of the *zaibatsu*'s capital resources to finance direct investments and joint ventures abroad. Typically, it also successfully introduced advanced Western technologies and production techniques, facilitating technology transfers to the benefit of Mitsubishi *zaibatsu* members. During the First World War, Mitsubishi Shoji evolved into a major *sogo shosha* because of its strong position in the heavy industries. In the short space of the 4 years between 1915 and 1918 it opened 18 sales offices from Sydney, Shanghai, and Hong Kong to London and New York. The range of merchandise handled also broadened substantially.[26]

The war had a profound impact on foreign trade, causing an economic boom in Japan. Cessation of exports from European countries prompted rapid development of Japan's own industries, and Japanese exports were in high demand.[27] Orders rolled in for military supplies from European nations and from Japan's Asian neighbors looking for substitutes for European manufactured goods no longer available. The result was a greater focus in Japan on heavy and chemical industries, on synthetic fertilizer, and other

25. Yoshino and Lifson, *The Invisible Link*.
26. Kawabe, "Overseas Activities and Their Organization."
27. Tsurumi, *The Japanese Are Coming*, 134.

chemical industries. Both the merchandise ranges handled by *sogo shosha* and the overseas locations they served expanded. It was around this period also that Japanese trading companies actively pursued strategies of rigorous direct investment, and Japanese colonies and underdeveloped regions became the primary focus of investments designed to secure and develop sources for natural resources.

During the prewar period, Japanese *sogo shosha* essentially managed more than half of Japan's trade activity. The proportion handled by trading companies like Mitsui Bussan and Mitsubishi Shoji grew dramatically from 15.5 to 51.1 percent in exports and from 19.1 to 63.8 percent in imports from 1891 to 1911. Mitsui, the dominant prewar *sogo shosha*, accounted for as much as 15 percent of Japan's exports and 21 percent of its imports by 1940.[28] Although *sogo shosha* alone cannot solely be credited for the growth and management of Japan's escalating trade volumes during the period graphed, it is, however, widely recognized that the weight of Japan's foreign trade was largely borne by general trading companies.[29]

Japanese *sogo shosha*, the pioneers of Japanese multinationalism, lacked the capital and volume necessary to specialize in one industry as American and British trading firms had characteristically done. British trading companies, in comparison, lacked the power the Japanese *sogo shosha* wielded within industries and also did not import or provide financial services. In the case of Europe and America, it was the manufacturers themselves who took on the task of complex industrial export. In Japan, the unique pattern of *sogo shosha* can, in retrospect, be seen to be logical from the outset given the conditions and status of Japan at the time. A similar pattern of development is evident in the postwar economic recovery of Japan.

POST–SECOND WORLD WAR DEVELOPMENT AND THE ROLE OF *SOGO SHOSHA*

Tsurumi[30] argues that the general trading company, in contrast to a specialized company, is largely a post–World War II phenomenon. He asserts that, although Mitsui Bussan and Mitsubishi grew to the status of general trading firms, the large majority of smaller trade houses – particularly those in the textile industries – tended to be industry specific in their scope. The business of C. Itoh, for example, was dominated by textiles, but their

28. Yonekawa and Yoshihara, eds., *Business History*, 2.
29. Tsurumi, *The Japanese Are Coming.*
30. Yonekura, "Emergence of the Prototype of Enterprise Group Capitalism," 63–104.

activities within the industry itself were extremely diverse moreover, their trading activities began to broaden substantially during the 1930s following the Great Depression. Likewise, the activities of Iwai, originally a small importer of English manufactured goods, diversified throughout the late 1920s and 1930s by the distribution of goods on behalf of the government-owned Nippon Steel. Iwai moved into importation of medicines, fertilizers, and chemicals across its branches in Sydney, Melbourne, London, and Bombay and its nine branches in China.[31]

During the Second World War, many Japanese business activities abroad came to a halt and foreign trade volumes plummeted, but the speed with which foreign trade expanded following the war resembled the earlier pattern of development in the course of the Meiji Restoration. Japan's strategy for economic recovery reflected several continuities from the prewar period.

Japan inevitably became involved in the postwar global market when it was granted permission in 1947 to resume participation in international trade. *Sogo shosha* pursued economies of scope in efforts to recover from the damage of the war through development of foreign trade, but a strong anti-*zaibatsu* sentiment following the war led to their forced dissolution. Mitsui Bussan and Mitsubishi Shoji were dissolved into numerous smaller companies under order of the Allied Powers in 1947, but in less than a decade both reemerged as general trading firms.

Japan's *sogo shosha* in this postwar period effectively developed Japanese international trade activity just as they had more than 50 years earlier. The strategy pursued by these postwar *sogo shosha* was the same as that pursued since the Meiji period of the late 1800s, and Japan's postwar economic miracle was built on the solid foundation of the economic development that began during the Meiji Restoration as well as on the successful experience in international trade that accumulated through institutions like the *sogo shosha*.

Japan's post–Second World War recovery represented Japan's second economic opening to the West. Japan was again faced with the need to modernize rapidly to catch up with the West. The emergence of Japanese multinationals after the war initially took the form of reestablishing of the sales offices of the major trading companies in key commercial centers following the strategy pioneered in the early Meiji period. Thus, efforts in the 1950s were directed toward reviving Japan's position as an exporter of finished goods and securing overseas resources. Following the *sogo shosha* model,

31. Yoshino and Lifson, *The Invisible Link*, 20.

trading firms sought to export and promote Japanese manufactured goods and to secure crucial imports in the form of natural resources and modern technologies. These firms drew upon the strategy of vigorous importation of advanced technologies through the use of international information and sales networks managed by *sogo shosha*.

Once again Japanese trading companies rose to serve as sales and procurement agents for many Japanese manufacturers who lacked the experience or resources necessary to participate directly in business transactions abroad.[32] The logic behind prewar *sogo shosha* was applied here as well. Japanese general trading companies assisted the multinationalization in manufacturing of several small- to medium-sized Japanese enterprises that rushed to establish production units in neighboring countries. Many such ventures were a response to labor shortages of the mid-1960s in Japan itself and the competitiveness of labor-intensive products manufactured in surrounding Asian regions. Trading companies offered both managerial and financial expertise and at times participated in joint ventures with Japanese manufacturers or local firms. In many instances it was the trading company itself that took the initiative to introduce and attract Japanese manufacturers to the prospect of manufacturing operations abroad.

The number of joint ventures escalated until the oil crisis that began in 1973 when a cartel of oil-producing companies raised the price of crude oil from $200 a barrel to $300 by the late 1970s. This event highlighted Japan's heavy reliance on the natural resources of other countries. Many of these joint ventures centered around projects that sought to develop such resources in typically underdeveloped nations. In particular, after 1955 there was a recognized need to secure stable sources of raw materials for the growing metal industries. General trading firms by this time had both overseas operations and much trade expertise. The typically limited capital resources of Japanese manufacturing firms for use in international expansion led *sogo shosha* once again to perform important roles as system and industry organizers, managing large-scale development projects that called for the involvement of several business organizations – often in a *zaibatsu*-type arrangement. Drawing on their extensive networks abroad and trade know-how, *sogo shosha* coordinated the formation of such groups and the establishment of international agreements as well as the contributions of each member organization whether managerial, technological, or, for example, labor related. This practice highlights the tendency of Japanese enterprises to pursue multinationalization as a group, linking trading companies,

32. Morikawa, *Zaibatsu*, xv.

manufacturers, and local parties abroad. Manufacturing operations were also established in developing Asian and South American countries to tap into the comparatively lower labor and land costs these regions offered.

Sogo shosha vigorously endeavored to place themselves at the core of groups of firms domestically in order to involve themselves in, and to carry out, other related businesses such as transportation, warehousing, insurance, and financing. Their core function, however, remained essentially the same as at their establishment: to internalize diverse functions fostering the effective integration and management of all of the disparate elements involved in the flow of goods such as importation and introduction of new process technologies, importation of raw materials, and production, distribution, and promotion of finished goods.

The probusiness attitude of the Japanese government during this postwar period helped to promote a favorable industrial climate. *Sogo shosha* reached their peak in the 1970s in terms of their sheer numbers within Japan and wide-ranging product lines. By the middle to late 1970s Japanese *sogo shosha* numbered in the thousands, and the total sales of the Big Ten alone collectively accounted for nearly 30 percent of Japan's Gross National Product (GNP).[33] Two factors can be seen to explain this peak: a lack of capital and a dearth of human resources skilled in international trade practices within Japanese manufacturing firms in the 1950s during Japan's postwar recovery.

Japan's postwar economic development and phenomenal growth were accompanied by rapid structural change. Perhaps the most notable from the perspective of Japanese general trading companies was the shift from the low-productivity, light manufacturing industries, such as cotton textiles, on which the prewar economy had been based to high-productivity growth industries such as heavy and chemical industries, and, later, electronics and automobiles. Technology-based exports like electronics, cameras, and motorcycles, which began to appear during the 1960s, are associated also with a move by manufacturing enterprises to establish their own sales and customer service networks overseas – particularly in the United States.

The trend toward some direct export activity by selected Japanese manufacturing firms in this period in some instances gradually reduced the role of the *sogo shosha* as export facilitators. In the case of consumer electronics and automobiles, the role of the *sogo shosha* was particularly limited. Japanese manufacturers, such as Matsushita, with differentiated, branded products that required substantial marketing support largely outgrew the services of

---

33. T. Ozawa, *Multinationalism, Japanese Style: The Political Economy of Outward Depency* (Princeton: Princeton University Press, 1979), 30.

trading company intermediaries and branched out to establish their own offices and subsidiaries abroad – particularly within key overseas markets. Sony and Hitachi, for example, built their own extensive international distribution networks in their foreign markets.[34] In the case of Sony, this was true from the outset. Some manufacturers, however, chose to continue to be represented by *sogo shosha* in more peripheral export markets not considered to warrant their full marketing attention. Toyota was a case in point. Although Toyota has established its own marketing networks in the American market, Mitsui Bussan handles the selling of Toyota models in the Canadian market through Mitsui's fully owned subsidiary Canadian Motors Inc. (CMI).[35]

These Japanese multinationals, which appeared in postwar Japanese industries like electronics, resemble American multinationals like GM and Ford by following a typical pattern: first, development of a sales office abroad and then establishment of knockdown manufacturing facilities overseas. Matsushita's activities in Asia and Europe followed this common model. However, a notable characteristic of postwar Japanese multinational development is the initial reliance of many manufacturers on *sogo shosha* because of the convenience.

Tsurumi[36] describes the need for providing after-sales service networks as a key impetus for Japanese manufacturers of specialized consumer products, particularly of electronics and automobiles, to establish their own sales offices in key export markets. Such after-sales service requires expertise trading companies themselves typically were unable to provide; hence, some manufacturers began to station their own sales personnel and service engineers abroad. Once export volume reached a size sufficient to support operation of a sales subsidiary, these manufacturers took over the entire marketing function that had been the responsibility of a trading company.

This trend toward direct exporting – combined with the fact that much of the business of general trading companies remained centered around Japan's low-growth and declining industries – and the rise of various kinds of enterprises offering similar though more competitive services have served to prompt innovation and strategic change among *sogo shosha*. Amine et al.[37] describe the most critical of the innovations witnessed as the move from a reactive stance to what they term "proactive trading." Although third party trade was initiated in the prewar period, its postwar increase served to offset

---

34. L. G. Franko, *The Threat of Japanese Multinationals – How the West Can Respond* (Norwich: IRM, 1983), 64.
35. Tsurumi, *The Japanese Are Coming*, 144.   36. Ibid., 144–48.
37. Amine et al., "Japanese Sogo Shosha," 21–32.

the decline of Japanese trade that the *sogo shosha* handled. They took on the role of intermediary between two companies within foreign markets. Amine et al. describe the postwar development of the *sogo shosha* as being characterized by an evolution from an importing and exporting focus to global corporations.

Japanese general trading companies were the first group of Japanese firms to make overseas investments in the form of global marketing networks.[38] They have played a key role in both the evolving Japanese and world economies, moving beyond importing and exporting goods and services to perform important roles as organizers and coordinators of industries through the formation of business groups to manage and facilitate sorting and standardization functions and investments. In stark contrast to American trading businesses, which typically sought economies through specialization, Japanese trading companies invested resources in diversification from the very early stages of Japan's industrialization in pursuit of economies of scope rather than scale.

In both the latter half of the 19th century and in the period of recovery during the 1950s after Japan's defeat in the Second World War, the development of *sogo shosha* followed a similar pattern for essentially the same reasons: Japan's need to industrialize and modernize required importation of technology, and the heavy reliance of the Japanese economy on foreign trade, based on lack of natural resources, necessitated importation of raw materials, which, in turn, required earning of foreign currency through export activity.

These Japanese general trading companies do not neatly fit conventional categories of multinational business activities. They have not only been transaction intermediaries but also bankers, venture capitalists, miners, and manufacturers. These companies have functioned as coordinators rather than controllers of business activity, channeling information, capital resources, raw materials, and finished goods into a comprehensive "system of activity." Their involvement in commercial activities has been both upstream and downstream, ranging from raw material extraction to market development and exchange transactions with end users. Unlike British and American trading firms, Japanese trading companies grew rather than disappeared. During the process of industrialization, they were an innovative multinational form that made a vital and highly substantial contribution to Japan's economic growth in reconstructing the postwar economy and nurturing its international competitiveness and success.

---

38. Ozawa, *Multinationalism, Japanese Style*, 30.

POSTWAR MULTINATIONALISM IN THE MANUFACTURING SECTOR

The postwar manufacturing sector in Japan was a key source of multinational activity and, in particular, of foreign direct investment in Japanese business history. Many Japanese manufacturers in the electronics and automobile industries tended to follow a more traditional linear model of growth than the *soga shosha*, beginning activities within the domestic market before launching operations overseas. Manufacturing firms within electronics and automobiles, which faced a fiercely competitive home market, generally sought growth in the form of increased sales, and, in turn, profits, by entering overseas markets through export activity. Many, for example Sony and Hitachi, then went on to invest heavily in sales networks and later in production facilities abroad through direct investment. Such small, innovative Japanese electronics firms made a considerable contribution to the postwar development of multinationals in Japan.

Although several Japanese manufacturers did make some foreign direct investments (FDI) in the early 1960s, not until the 1970s did major Japanese manufacturers become involved in substantial investments abroad. In 1971, Japan's total FDI was 288 billion yen, increasing to 2,030 billion yen in 1982 and 9,000 billion yen in 1989.[39] A major portion of such investments came from the manufacturing sector, which, in 1971, totaled 97.2 billion yen (33.8 % of the total FDI), reaching 524 billion yen (25.8 %) in 1981 and 2,330 billion yen (25.9 %) in 1989.[40]

Japanese FDI was geographically concentrated: 30 to 40 percent within Asian countries but only 10 to 20 percent in North America. In the 1980s, this pattern reversed; investments in Asia fell to 20 to 30 percent, whereas the North American share rose to as much as 40 to 60 percent. This new pattern was partly the result of the 1985 Plaza Accord when the G7 countries reached a consensus on appreciation of the yen. That decision led to appreciation of the Japanese yen by 30 to 40 percent. The appreciation requirement to use local products in manufacturing led to the rapid acceleration in Japanese FDI in the United States. As a result, in 1986 the Japanese FDI in the United States reached as high as 66 percent. Such investments were made predominantly to secure production facilities overseas and to enable Japanese manufacturers to operate closer to their target markets as well as, in some instances, to minimize the impact of tariff walls on their

39. Okura-sho (Ministry of Finance), *Zaisei kinyu tokei geppo tai naigai minkan toshi tokushu* (A special report on domestic and foreign direct investment statistics) (Tokyo: Ministry of Finance, 1983, 1993, 2000).
40. Ministry of Finance, *Monthly Report on Finance: Domestic and Foreign Private Direct Investments* (Tokyo: Ministry of Finance, 1983, 1993, 2000).

businesses. The extent of these investments illustrates the strong dependence of many Japanese manufacturing firms on overseas markets and resources in the postwar period, which parallels the prewar development of Japanese economic activity.

In the 1970s textile, petrochemical, and steel industries accounted for 20 to 30 percent of the total FDI made by the Japanese manufacturing sector, whereas the electronics and automobile industries were responsible for a mere 10 to 20 percent. However, after the oil shock of 1973, these latter industries soon grew to prominence, causing oil prices to soar and more than quadrupling the cost of oil in Japan. The consumer price index rose by around 10 to 20 percent. As a consequence, the oil crisis eroded the international competitiveness of the Japanese textile, petrochemical, and steel industries – industries that had been highly competitive in the early 1970s.

The textile industry, in particular, was highly labor intensive; the petrochemical and steel industries, on the other hand, were energy intensive, and soaring energy and labor costs after the oil crisis eroded the price competitiveness of both labor- and energy-intensive industries. Conversely, electronics and machinery, including automobiles, in the middle between the two extremes, were less labor- and energy-intensive than the more traditional Japanese industries on which much prewar and early postwar economic development had been built.[41] In their place, the electronics and automobile industries rose quickly as competitive export industries. The emergence of innovative postwar production, termed just-in-time (JIT), further served to propel the international competitive power of the Japanese electronics and automobile industries during the 1980s.

Within the Japanese electronics industry, Matsushita Electric Corporation was the first to make inroads into the U.S. market. As early as September 1959, it opened a sales subsidiary, the Matsushita Electric Corporation of America, to promote sales of its home appliances. It also expanded production facilities with the establishment of Matsushita Electric Taiwan and National Thai Co. in 1962 followed by Matsushita Electric Malaysia in 1965. Matsushita National Mexican S.A. and Matsushita Electric East Africa (Tanzania) followed in quick succession in 1966. Not until the 1970s, however, did Matsushita begin manufacture of its goods in more advanced countries like the United States and in Europe.

Hitachi followed a similar pattern of multinational development with the opening of its American sales subsidiary in November 1959, although it

41. Juro Hashimoto, *Nihon keizai-ron* (Japanese economy) (Kyoto: Mineruba, 1991).

undertook no production activities there until the late 1970s. In the 1960s, however, Hitachi aggressively developed knockdown production facilities in Taiwan – specifically, Taiwan Hitachi Co., Takao Hitachi Electronics, Taiwan Hitachi Television, and Taiwan Hitachi CRT. Toward the beginning of the 1970s Hitachi began to expand in a similar fashion into other Southeast Asian countries such as Thailand, Singapore, Malaysia, the Philippines, and India. Not until the latter half of the 1970s did Hitachi launch into European and American markets.

The establishment of NEC Taiwan Communications Industries in 1959 represented Nippon Electric Company's (NEC) first foray in FDI. This Taiwan-based facility, together with NEC de Mexico S.A., which had been established in 1969, formed the overseas production and sales subsidiaries of NEC. NEC America Incorporated, established in 1963, undertook marketing activities to support and promote its telecommunications and home appliance products within the United States. NEC Singapore Pte. Ltd. and NEC Malaysia Sdn. Bhd. were established in 1976 soon after as production facilities. NEC also became involved in two joint ventures in the 1970s, leading to formation of Samsung Vacuum Tube in Korea and Digital Communications Company in the United States.

In a pattern of development similar to that of the Japanese electronics manufacturers (i.e., establishing a sales subsidiary overseas), Fujitsu California Inc., set up in September 1968, represented the beginning of the globalization of Fujitsu Limited, Japan's largest computer company. Soon after, in the 1970s, Fujitsu Singapore Pte. Ltd., FACOM Korea Ltd., FACOM Philippines Inc., and Fujitsu Espana S.A. were added to its growing list of overseas sales and production subsidiaries. A fundamental difference between Fujitsu and the Japanese manufacturers Sony, Hitachi, and NEC is its activity within the U.S. market. Unlike these other manufacturers, which established their own facilities, Fujitsu invested capital within the U.S. organization Amdahl Co. to oversee its production and sales activities in the United States.

Each of these large Japanese electronics organizations conformed to a similar pattern of multinationalization, for each began as a player within the Japanese domestic market. Then, as competition intensified during the 1960s they began to seek growth overseas specifically through manufacturing in developing Asian countries and by developing of sales subsidiaries in the United States or Europe. During the 1970s, these subsidiaries gradually penetrated the U.S. and European markets with growing intensity; they formed seedbeds for the late 1970s growth in FDI.

The multinationalization of Sony differed markedly from the rest. In February 1960, Sony, a tiny startup company established after the Second

World War, set up its first overseas production facility, Sony Corporation of America. By 1974 it had hired more than 1,521 employees and had expanded its annual production capacity to about 250 thousand color televisions and about 90 thousand units of audio and stereo equipment. When these figures are compared with Japanese domestic production capacities, the extent of the U.S. operations becomes highly apparent.

Sony, with strong intentions to sell its manufactured goods in the United States, expanded its overseas manufacturing capacities aggressively to achieve this aim. The decision to pursue and penetrate the U.S. market actively was a relatively risky one because, for example, although the penetration of black and white television sets in Japan exceeded 95 percent by 1968, color televisions had only reached 26.5 percent by 1970. Furthermore, even though audio equipment such as stereo players and tape recorders had begun to appear on the market around this time, few had seemed to notice their potential for the future – particularly in the U.S. market.

The FDI of these organizations in the United States, as noted, was greatly accelerated by the rapid appreciation of the yen in the 1980s, and, as a consequence, these large corporations in the Japanese electronics industry expanded their local production abroad. This led in turn to a move to establish specialized research and development (R & D) laboratories in the United States and Europe. The greater the quantity of goods sold in these markets, the more important the knowledge of local needs and tastes in design became. To this end, NEC established the NEC Systems Laboratory Inc. in 1972 and Matsushita similarly opened Microelectronics Technology Corp. in 1977.

Although the pattern of multinationalization in the Japanese automobile industry[42] largely parallels that of the Japanese manufacture of electronics, FDI by automobile manufacturers began somewhat earlier. Toyota and Nissan, the two major Japanese automobile companies, began to participate in FDI activities in North America as early as the 1950s, although all overseas operations at this stage were simple sales subsidiaries. In 1957, Toyota established Toyota Motor Sales U.S.A. Inc., and, soon after, in 1960, Nissan introduced Nissan Motor Corporation in the United States to promote and distribute their automobiles. The establishment of manufacturing operations overseas by each followed soon after in the 1960s, beginning in Asia and expanding in other developing countries in the 1960s and 1970s.

---

42. The FDI data of the Japanese automobile companies are all from *Kaigai kigyo shinnshutu soran* (An annual review on the foreign direct investment).

NUMMI (New United Motor Manufacturing Inc.) represented the start of Toyota's serious participation in manufacturing activity in the United States. NUMMI, essentially a joint venture between GM and Toyota, that was successful and well received in the United States drew on GM employees and facilities to produce, for example, the Toyota Corolla, which was known in the United States as the Chevy Nova. On the basis of this experience, Toyota decided to establish a somewhat larger scale facility in Kentucky, the Toyota Motor Manufacturing Kentucky Inc. (TMMK), which grew, in the 1980s, to become one of the most competitive manufacturing facilities.

Nissan made its own first foray into large-scale production in the United States slightly ahead of Toyota, opening its first manufacturing facility in 1980. By 1982 it had invested $375 million. Both Nissan and Toyota continued to increase their U.S. production capacities throughout the 1980s.

Honda's pattern of multinational development was in contrast to that followed by Toyota and Nissan. Similar to Sony's strategy, Honda aggressively targeted the U.S. market from the outset. A comparison of the market share of each of these three Japanese automobile producers highlights Honda's daring decision to move into the United States; in 1970, within Japan, Toyota's market share was 39 percent, Nissan's was 32.6 percent, and Honda's was 1.7 percent. By 1975 these shares had shown little movement with 38.8, 31.6, and 4.8 percent, followed by 37.3, 29.1, and 4.3 percent, respectively, in 1980. By the 1980s Honda remained a tiny automobile company by Japanese standards, with little more than a 4-percent market share. Its innovative strategy led to its rapid multinationalization, as the next section demonstrates.

JAPANESE "FREE-STANDING ORGANIZATIONS" AND
THE HONDA MOTOR COMPANY

Mira Wilkins coined the term "free-standing organization" for a form of multinational enterprise, which is historically an important type of British FDI (see Chapter 2) in this volume defined as "a firm set up in one country for the purpose of doing business outside that country."[43] This is in contrast to the more familiar and conventional strategies of multinational enterprises of the present day, which begin their business operations in the home market and then move abroad. Conventional logic assumes that the

---

43. Mira Wilkins, "The Free-Standing Economy Revisited," in *The Free-Standing Company in the World Economy, 1830–1996*, ed. Mira Wilkins and Harm G. Schröter (New York: Oxford University Press, 1998), 3.

multinationalization of firms is achieved by leveraging and building on core competencies and competitive advantages by establishing branches abroad.

According to Wilkins, a defining characteristic of a free-standing organization is the establishment of a "new 'free-standing' unit in the home (headquarters) country with the immediate intention of operating outside that headquarters nation." Such overseas units are considered free standing because their international business has not directly evolved and grown out of an ongoing business operating in the home market. They are not created to internalize overseas operations in management and control within their existing business activities.[44] They therefore deviate from the linear evolution model based on the traditional theory of multinational enterprise development encountered in common practice in which organizations begin in the domestic market and build and develop this market on the basis of some form of competitive advantage such as a superior technology or specialized production, management, or marketing knowledge. The desire to capitalize on this competency in pursuit of further growth, it is generally believed, is what essentially drives a firm to become multinational. Similarly, the search for raw material sources is believed to begin in the home country, after which such resources are sought abroad. In doing so, firms expand offshore, evolving from headquarters within the home market on the basis of significant (domestic) market experience. The U.S. experience, in particular, suggests that multinational enterprises begin as a local organization, then become national, and finally, international. American multinational enterprises, such as GM and Ford, are examples of firms that followed the logical, linear, evolutionary model.

The international experience of several Japanese organizations does reflect the classic American model of multinational development as, for example, in the cotton industry. It moved from being a domestic industry and market to make foreign direct investments in spinning facilities in China; however, various other models, including quite revolutionary ones, are at play that "change the rules of the game" within an industry. Japanese business history suggests the use of structures that resemble free-standing organizations. Honda Motor Company and the *keiretsu* (groups of allied business enterprises) are two key Japanese examples of such multinational behavior, through free-standing organization each of these was able to pursue, and take advantage of, opportunities abroad. Such a strategy, which is essentially a form of strategic maneuvering, facilitated the development of markets abroad while minimizing or avoiding trade friction. It provided a means

44. Ibid., 5.

by which businesses could monitor key markets and draw on a host country's technological or natural resources. Honda, for example, recognized the potential of a foothold in the United States through North American–based operations, despite its "rookie" status within the Japanese automobile industry. It became the launching pad for Honda as an important multinational enterprise and stimulated the successful development of the Japanese automobile industry as a whole.

Honda, now one of the leading global organizations, has more than 130 production facilities across 52 nations supplying Honda products.[45] It was a latecomer to the Japanese automobile industry. Not until the late 1960s did Honda launch into production of automobiles, by which time eight Japanese automakers were firmly established within the domestic market. Driven by a policy of manufacturing in the heart of their customer base to build on a strategy that emphasized self-reliance through locally based production, Honda has led the Japanese, and the global auto industry as well, through an unconventional form of multinational enterprise – a form of global corporation Honda pioneered within the auto industry. It is a form widely imitated since then by others.

Honda's historical entry into the automobile industry, a highly hurried affair, was propelled by the concern that the Japanese Ministry of Trade and Industry (MITI) might seek to deter the arrival of new entrants into the Japanese small automobile industry.[46] MITI feared that many small automobile manufacturers that were unable to tap into economies of scale might greatly undermine international competitiveness in Japan. Around this time also, trade relations between the United States and Japan were becoming somewhat strained. Automobile exports to the U.S. and Canadian markets rose dramatically during the 1970s; the share of the U.S. market held by Japanese automobile producers alone rose from 4 percent in 1970 to 23 percent by 1980.[47] Protectionist demands peaked in 1981 with the U.S. establishment of the Voluntary Restraint Agreement to impose restrictions on the number of Japanese automobile imports. The founding of Honda of America, a stand-alone Honda Motor Company production base in the United States, was, therefore, an innovative response to the market conditions Honda faced both at home and abroad. It provided a way to meet increasing protectionism of various world markets – in this case the

45. D. Nelson, R. Mayo, and P. Moody, eds., *Powered by Honda: Developing Excellence in the Global Enterprise* (New York: John Wiley & Sons, Inc., 1998), 47.
46. A. Mair, *Honda's Global Local Corporation* (London: Macmillan, 1994).
47. Ibid., 73.

United States – and provided a strategy suited to Honda's "market-driven" approach.

Honda of America had begun production of two-wheelers in September 1978 in Marysville, Ohio. It was an acclaimed world leader in motorcycles and in a range of power products from lawn mowers to outboard motors with a strong competitive advantage in the home and international markets. Honda did not, however, have experience in car design and manufacture. But in November 1982 a Honda Accord rolled off a production line adjacent to their motorcycle plant. Honda became the first Japanese car maker to produce passenger cars in North America.

The initial decision by Honda to produce in the United States was met with rampant predictions of failure from industry analysts and commentators as well as from Honda's competitors, who said they considered the move too great a risk. Given the oil crisis of the 1970s, the devalued yen, the comparatively high U.S. labor costs, and the hostility of the Big Three – Ford, GM, and Chrysler at that time – Honda's move was widely believed to be ludicrous and doomed to failure. Honda rose to meet the challenge.

In a sense, Honda's North American strategy represented a form of counterlogic that contrasted with typical contemporary strategies by manufacturers to move offshore to secure lower labor costs or to places with fewer restrictions on production and thus to build a solid position within their home market through competitive advantage. Instead, Honda set up production plants within an advanced Western market, where, given its inexperience in the industry, it did not necessarily have a clear competitive advantage over local manufacturers. It was a strategic maneuver prompted by the sheer importance of the U.S. market and that country's growing protectionism, and represented a way to participate actively within the market without creating significant trade friction. In addition, Soichiro Honda, the founder of Honda, was strongly convinced that cars must be produced as close as possible to the end users, and, for this reason, it was considered logical for Honda to produce cars in the United States if it wished to sell cars successfully within that market.[48] Honda therefore became the first Japanese automaker to undertake locally based production – a policy decision that represented the beginning of a new era in Japanese auto manufacturing.

Although Honda's Marysville, Ohio, automobile assembly plant was not its first foray into the manufacture of motor vehicles – the production line was modeled on its facilities in Sayama, Japan – Honda's American operations do appear to satisfy Wilkins's definition of a free-standing organization.

48. Soichiro Honda, *Ete ni ho wo agete* (Sail away to the wind).

Based from the outset on a strategy of self-reliance, Honda of America represents a free-standing organization in the sense that its host country activities can be seen to "stand on their own."[49]

The history of Honda Motor Company dates back to 1946 with the founding of the Honda Technical Research Institute of Soichiro Honda and the production, in 1947, of the A-type bicycle engine, Honda's first commercial product.[50] The first Honda motorcycle, the 98-cc two-cycle Dream, rolled off the Japanese production line 2 years later. The export of the "Cub F" model to Taiwan in 1952 marked the beginning of Honda's overseas motorcycle sales activities. Exports of the Dream to the Philippines followed later that year and the "Shun-oh" was introduced to America in 1954. The opening of American Honda Motor in Los Angeles marked the beginning of Honda's active pursuit of growth through development of foreign markets for motorcycles. Not until 1965 did Honda's auto production begin at its Sayama plant followed by its Suzuka factory in 1967. These initial automobile production bases supported Honda's modest foray into the automobile industry but, as described earlier, its position as a small latecomer to the Japanese automotive industry was threatened by MITI's desire to "reorganize" the industry in efforts to improve its competitive standing in the international arena. Despite the lack of a clearly discernible comparative advantage in the home market – other than perhaps its reputation as a reliable and leading manufacturer of motorcycles – Honda boldly launched into American-based automobile production in 1982. Its strong brand position in the motorcycle market is not believed to have afforded it much of an advantage in building its U.S. automobile production and marketing activities in market that was then characteristically cost- rather than highly brand-conscious. Honda had to prove its ability to produce high-quality, low-priced automobiles upon its arrival in the market. Thus, Honda of America began car production with no clear advantage in either the domestic or the international arena – a process that runs counter to explanations of multinationalization offered by conventional theory.

Honda's international success, which was essentially spearheaded by the bold development of its independent American production base, has become a key model not only for Japanese but American and European automobile manufacturers as well. Toyota, internationally renowned in recent decades as a successful automobile manufacturer, closely modeled its own American manufacturing plants on Honda's American operations. Chrysler's

---

49. Wilkins, "The Free-Standing Company Revisited."
50. A brief history of Honda was extracted from "Honda Way."

own restructuring efforts, too, were based on detailed analyses of Honda, and Honda's North American managers were called on to assist BMW in establishing its own new "transplant."[51] Honda has, in fact, been described as having formed an "innovation pole" – an important source for examples of successful management practices and problem-solving philosophies.[52]

Throughout the middle to late 1980s, a wave of Japanese producers effectively followed Honda's lead. By 1984, both Nissan and Toyota had established assembly plants in North America. Mazda, Mitsubishi, Subaru, Isuzu, and Suzuki followed in quick succession toward the end of the 1980s. This led to a surge of multinational manufacturing, which then spread to Europe. In creating the model Japanese multinational manufacturing enterprise, Honda also effectively exported its Japanese-style cost structure and management practices – first to all of North America and later to Europe through implementation of just-in-time (JIT) relations and total quality control (TQC) practices with domestic suppliers.

International success in Japanese automobile manufacturing was, therefore, stimulated and led by a fledgling participant from within the domestic market. Honda effectively pioneered the multinational path and was followed closely by its more conservative Japanese competitors, transforming the Japanese automobile industry into one internationally renowned for strength and success. In this respect, Honda may be described as the most innovative of the Japanese multinational automobile manufacturers. It effectively quieted foreign and Japanese skeptics who were convinced that Japanese manufacturers would not have the confidence to venture outside of Japan and to build operations abroad lest they fail to repeat the successes they achieved within their home market.[53] Honda also differed from its Japanese rivals in receiving no help whatsoever from MITI and no strong *keiretsu* involvement. In these respects, too, it has deviated notably from the established models followed by Japanese car producers.

Corley's identification of two conceptual types of multinational enterprises – the use of branches and subsidiaries and the use of overseas companies established to operate solely or largely outside of the borders of the home country – suggests that specific home country considerations provide key clues to why certain modes of multinational enterprise development are chosen by particular firms.[54] Ozawa argues that Honda's foray into

51. Mair, *Honda's Global Local Corporation*, 3.   52. Ibid., 340.
53. Ibid., 4.
54. T. A. B. Corley, "The Free-Standing Company in Theory and Practice," in *The Free-Standing Company*, ed. Wilkins and Schröter.

American-based automobile production was motivated not only by the desire to enter the American market directly to pursue growth without trade friction but also by an aim to expand its share of a Japanese market dominated by incumbents like Toyota and Nissan.[55] In other words, Honda's being able to establish itself within Japan as a notable automobile manufacturer was believed to hinge, to a degree, on its success in overseas markets – particularly in the United States. Honda is a key example of the ability of some Japanese firms to transform both their own operations and the industry as a whole through strategic organizational innovation.

No examination of Japanese economic development can afford to overlook the role of Japanese general trading companies. Unconventional, multinational organizational forms such as the unique Japanese innovation *soga shosha* have been crucial in stimulating Japanese industrialization and economic growth. So, too, Japanese versions of free-standing organizations have played a key role in revitalizing Japanese industries – most notably the automobile industry.

The rise of Japanese multinationals was a product of Japan's heavily trade-dependent economy and the dynamic, adaptive process of responding to changes in the international economic environment. The Japanese economy depended heavily on foreign markets for both import and export activities in the light of Japan's necessary reliance on importation of raw materials, its rising land and domestic postwar labor costs, and the growing protectionism against Japanese goods in world markets. Japan's innovative multinationalism can be seen as a response to economic needs as well as to the new requirements of foreign markets. *Soga shosha*, stemming from the desire to gain control over foreign resources and recognition of the sheer importance of international trade to Japanese economic growth and industrialization, represented the spearhead of Japanese multinationalism. Honda's approach to multinationalism, equally innovative, followed a growth strategy that ran counter to the traditional linear model of multinational development. Evolving into what Mira Wilkins has termed a free-standing organization, Honda developed operations in the United States that placed it within its most important market, thus leapfrogging over competing Japanese care manufacturers.

These organizational innovations stretched beyond Japan to make significant contributions internationally such as through FDI and the introduction of Japanese production techniques like JIT and TQC and management techniques to America and to Europe.

---

55. Ozawa, *Multinationalism, Japanese Style*, 248.

Although many innovative Japanese enterprises, such as *soga shosha* and Honda, differ somewhat from the familiar linear pattern of multinational enterprise development and growth, several Japanese enterprises do conform to this traditional model as in multinational development of many Japanese electronics manufacturers. This suggests that models of development, the traditional linear model and the free-standing organization, for example, are not necessarily a dichotomy but provide complementary multinational growth strategies. The *soga shosha*, that uniquely Japanese innovation, evolved from a near hybrid of the two models.

PART TWO

Cultural and Social Implications of Multinationals

5

The Social Impacts of Multinational Corporations

An Outline of the Issues with a Focus on Workers

NEVA GOODWIN

Multinational corporations (MNCs) are in many ways the world's most powerful economic actors. As of 2000 there were only 44 nations in the world whose gross domestic product (GDP) was larger than the value-added of any single MNC.[1] Twenty-nine corporations are included in the list of the world's 100 largest economies. ExxonMobil (number 45 on the list) outranks Pakistan (number 46); General Motors (number 47) is larger than Peru, Algeria, New Zealand, the Czech Republic, and the United Arab Emirates – the next six on the list.

In making such comparisons it is important to remember that corporations, compared with nations, focus on a smaller number of goals, which, by many accounts, they pursue more effectively. It is not only the size of MNCs but their orientation and effectiveness that make it critical to understand how the interests of MNCs align with – and where they diverge from – the interests of the rest of society. This chapter will examine, in particular, the ways in which MNCs affect the life experience of workers: those that they employ directly and workers who are significantly affected by spillover effects of these firms.

Here we consider the last three decades of the 20th century. This was a period of particular significance for new global history, for a great spurt of "multinationalization" began and continued throughout these 30 years.

---

1. United Nations Conference on Trade And Development, 1998. *World Investment Report, 1998* (New York: UNCTAD). Following the methodology explained by Brian Roach in Chapter 1 of this volume (see the section headed THE SIZE OF MNCs: DIFFERENT WAYS OF ASSESSING SIZE), this comparison uses value-added as the basis for comparing the size of a corporation with the GDP of a nation. It is interesting to note that six out of the eight largest corporations are either energy or automotive companies.

THE ISSUE OF COMPETITION

A specter is haunting the globe – the specter of perfect competition. Our most prestigious economists have invited this specter to dwell among us. It is welcomed by some people: those who identify themselves primarily as consumers and are aware of the economic theory that shows how competition imposes cost-minimization on producers, lowering consumer prices. However, arrayed against this coalition of economic theorists and people conscious of their roles as consumers is what I would call a "pan-human conspiracy," including virtually everyone who plays some kind of role as a producer. This includes a wide spectrum from the highest paid executive to the lowest paid worker. Executives know in their hearts that their own good fortune derives not from competition but from shelter against it, and workers are beginning to suspect that their own ill fortune is somehow connected to competitive forces associated with globalization.

The belief embedded in neoclassical economic theory – that the ideally efficient world would be achieved if competition were "perfect" – stems from a time, early in the last century, when economic theory was divided between the neoclassicists and the Marxists. The neoclassicists adopted the consumer's point of view as the sole position from which to judge what was desirable,[2] whereas the Marxists took the equally truncated and insufficient point of view of the worker. Most human beings are, of course, both worker and consumer, but it is as workers and producers that they hate competition.

Karl Marx, in one of his more charitable moments, said, in effect, that capitalists cannot help being so horrible to employees: it is the system – above all, the forces of competition that drive the system – that makes capitalists behave as they do. To be sure, said Marx, "I paint the capitalist and the landlord in no sense *couleur de rose*."[3] He did not propose, we should assume, that they mean well. But the capitalist does not have to mean badly for the workers to be treated badly. The system makes them do it.

This line of reasoning reappears remarkably often in the words of defenders of capitalism as well as in the words of its critics. Milton Friedman would agree with the general principle that competition is a force that, properly unleashed, narrows the choices of a firm to a single pair: minimize costs or go out of business. The protesters at Seattle in the fall of 1999 and

2. This is a piece of economic ideology this author has criticized in several places, including Neva R. Goodwin, Frank Ackerman, and David Kiron, eds., *The Consumer Society* (Washington, DC: Island Press, 1996).
3. Karl Marx, "Capital: Volume 1." In *The Marx-Engels Reader*, second edition, edited by Robert C. Tucker (New York: W.W. Norton & Co., 1978), 297.

other increasingly vocal critics of international trade policy proceed on some similar assumptions. Although a variety of goals and beliefs are represented by different members of this new antiglobalization coalition, they share a deep concern about the force of transboundary competition. In a variation on the theme, a Filipino worker says "AOL is bringing us the knowledge and the resources we need to compete, and if we don't compete we perish."[4]

The standard economic view is that the alternative to perfect competition is market power based on industry concentration, which creates oligopolistic or monopolistic situations. The concentration ratios that are more or less officially accepted as proof of a noncompetitive situation are, however, hard to interpret as corporate boundaries shift with mergers and acquisitions and blur with strategic partnerships. In addition, data are hard to acquire for global concentration ratios, and the meaning of national concentration ratios becomes increasingly unclear in a global world. Nevertheless, the old idea of concentration still has some meaning. When, for example, four MNCs in an industry account for more than half of global sales (as is the case with the soft drinks industry[5]), it seems more than reasonable to surmise that these corporations possess enormous power.

Business history makes it clear that one of the first things for which corporations use their power is to erect shelters against the forces of competition. This is possible in a complex world in which market power (the ability to set prices rather than taking all prices as given by the forces of supply and demand operating in a competitive setting) is closely allied with political power but does not always have the same effect. MNCs seek economic power to gain market share; in this endeavor they compete, often fiercely, against other MNCs (as well as against smaller firms). However, they share common political – even cultural – interests. They are jointly dedicated to a steady increase in purchases – especially of their own products – but most recognize that they have a common cause in promoting consumerism in general. They also have common motive to maintain a world safe for MNCs; that is, to maintain – even as technological and other circumstances change – the advantages that allow MNCs to escape the whip of perfect competition.

Although, at many points MNCs do have to deal with the reality of local and, especially, global competition, their history is filled with successful

4. Romer Recabar, "an AOL techie," quoted by Thomas L. Friedman in "Under the Volcano," *New York Times*, September 29, 2000.
5. *The Encyclopedia of Global Industries* (1999). See Chapter 1 of this volume for additional data on global concentration ratios.

attempts to find shelter from these forces. The methods of achieving shelter – too many to list here in full – include political influence (through campaign donations, lobbying, or out-and-out bribes); intrafirm dealings (including self-generated investment capital, which provides some shelter from the external capital markets); and all the usual ways of reducing price-based competition from establishing of brand-name loyalty among consumers to monopolizing a market.

This list does not mean that competition has disappeared. Economic theory has identified market forces that promote competitiveness. Most forcefully, it is normally true that a firm that cannot produce profits will fail or be taken over by another firm. This fact creates a broad set of requirements that sometimes filter down to a very specific requirement: "do this or you will fail." More often there is leeway; a firm might have to reduce the take of top management or find ways to reduce the total wage bill going to the rank-and-file laborers, but it might not have to do both. The requirements laid down by the forces of competition are often weaker than the pan-human conspiracy that creates a great force in favor of sheltering against it. As a broad generality to use as our starting point, we could say that, given the existence of these opposing forces, the economic actors who have more power are able to claim more of the shelter, leaving weaker players to deal with the greater part of the merciless winds of competition.

ECONOMIC DEVELOPMENT – THE THING THAT TAKES TIME

In a firm that does not have shelter from competition, what kinds of strategies are likely to seem rational to a corporation – we'll call it "Minimill" – that is small in comparison with the size of its market? We can expect that Minimill will limit its strategic thinking to how to compete against other firms in the same industry whose sales or purchases have the potential to limit its own options. Its strategy team probably does not think of affecting the nature of the whole market into which it sells or the nature of the markets from which it draws its inputs (labor raw materials, or manufactured inputs purchased from suppliers).

Minimill's modest behavior is in sharp contrast to firms with a global reach that have larger ambitions and the resources to carry them out. One of the most obvious moves of the larger MNCs is to alter the demand side of the market by greatly expanding an existing need or even by creating a wholly new demand. Thus, Nestlé's created a demand for infant formula in the Third World. And General Motors, by buying and dismantling urban transit systems in U.S. cities, created a need for private transport, that is, cars and trucks.[6] The "beauty industries" create accelerating insecurity about personal appearance and with it the desire for myriad products that supposedly help consumers to achieve inhuman standards of youth and beauty.

More relevant here, however, are the strategic options for influencing the larger environment – we will use the term "regime" – in which a firm operates. Thus, with respect to the supply regime, a multinational corporation – call it "Maximill" – will be large enough in its market to affect, in diverse ways, the quality and quantity of the inputs that it needs.

For example, Maximill draws its middle managers and shop-floor workers from the communities in which the firm has located its plants. Competitive forces urge that MNCs locate where there is an adequate source of labor at the world's lowest rates. It is also rational for them to offer wages sufficiently above what the workers could otherwise earn so that there will be many eager applicants for jobs and relatively low turnover, thus limiting the cost of acculturization required to turn inexperienced recruits into disciplined, punctual workers. But a large firm need not simply take as given the quality of its inputs. Beyond offering incentives to stay with the firm and learn by doing, Maximill might also find it in its interest to affect the learning environment in communities where it plans to stay so that even new recruits will posess more of the knowledge and skills Maximill needs than they would without the firm's intervention.

Third World settings offering cheap labor often lack adequate infrastructure like ports, roads, and telephone lines. In such cases the Maximill strategy may be to get local governments to supply as much of this missing infrastructure as possible by telling each government that it is competing for Maximill's presence against a large number of other possible sites. The fear of losing a large source of anticipated income, including relatively well-paid jobs (and, possibly, bribes), sometimes induces city, regional, or national governments to spend significant resources to create what a corporation wants. Resources from foreign aid agencies and the energies of local people may also be directed toward the MNC's infrastructure and human capital needs.

Maximill may, in turn, purchase manufactured inputs from a large number of suppliers of various sizes who compete fiercely to maintain their sales to Maximill. To increase the competitive pressure, Maximill searches the World Wide Web for lower-priced inputs from all over the world. The effect is to turn local suppliers into dedicated cost minimizers – especially

---

6. Walter Adams and James W. Brock, "Bigness and Social Efficiency: A Case Study of the U.S. Auto Industry." In *Corporations and Society: Power and responsibility*, edited by Warren J. Samuels and Arthur S. Miller (New York: Greenwood Press, 1987).

in more developed areas of the world where suppliers had previously enjoyed more relaxed conditions that permitted the payment of wages higher than the minimum necessary. As the wages outside of Maximill's gates are driven down in the pressure to produce low-cost inputs for the huge MNC, Maximill increases its relative attractiveness as a high-wage employer.

Maximill may thus create a multitude of economic costs and benefits with spillover effects that extend well beyond its own sphere. Among the negative effects it can create are these:

- Harm to local people in the present or future from environmental costs externalized by the MNC.
- Diversion of scarce resources to the infrastructure Maximill needs if these displace other infrastructure projects that would have more beneficial effects – for example, meeting basic human needs or encouraging appropriate technologies.
- Added insecurity in the local economy if a large number of workers become dependent on Maximill for jobs (for example, migrating from rural areas or failing to learn indigenous skills), and if there is a possibility that the company will suddenly move its plant to another location.
- Reduced quality and pay of jobs in the cost-minimizing supply firms as a consequence of Maximill's strategy of inducing competition.

Positive effects might include the following:

- Acculturization, on-the-job training, and formal training of Maximill's workers if they are as a result better able to get other jobs or gain in their sense of self-worth and hence also boost their familial bargaining power. (This is especially relevant when the employees are young women who otherwise have little power to affect the course of their own lives.)
- Increased cash flow in the region as a result of the expenditures and transfers of pay by Maximill employees.
- "Backward linkages" to supply firms that could not exist without Maximill's demand for their products.
- Other developments in the region may be enhanced by the infrastructure built because of Maximill's incentives or resources.

It is impossible to come up with an overall bottom line of costs versus benefits for the effects of MNCs on resources for development. In different settings the various elements would be more or less important. On the one hand, powerful economic actors have few external constraints on their ability to externalize costs. On the other hand, the larger an economic entity is in relation to the environment (social, physical, and economic) in which it operates – and the more the entity identifies future conditions as relevant to its self-interest – the more it will internalize costs and benefits into its own goals.

Charles Wilson famously remarked, "What is good for the country is good for General Motors and what's good for General Motors is good for the country."[7] Wilson's statement was made to the Senate Armed Forces Committee in 1952 during the cynical GM campaign of buying and dismantling urban transit systems with the goal of stimulating private transportation – a campaign that gravely undermined public transportation in the United States with consequences for patterns of urban and suburban design that continue to hold the U.S. economy hostage to fossil fuels. Such clear conflicts between public and corporate interest are warnings that any statement of convergence made by a corporate representative should be examined with great skepticism. However, it may be appropriate to pay attention when the same point is made from the other side. The Harvard Business School's Michael Porter, for example, increasingly looks more like a spokesman for civil society than an apologist for industry as he explains what has become known as "the Porter hypothesis": that what is good for the environment is good for business.[8]

This issue has been broadened by development economist David Seckler to the context of regimes for investment. When, as mentioned earlier in this section, a powerful firm sets out to affect the relevant supply regime, it may choose to strategize globally but may not feel a need to think in a very long time frame. Investment is a different matter, requiring not only long-range thinking but the ability to think about how a present investment may change the environment – the regime – in which future activities and future investments will be made.

… [B]lind pursuit of comparative trade advantages in the present economic regime, which is determined by the basic social and technical conditions of the economy, can create comparative disadvantage in future economic regimes. To avoid this fate, firms and nations may have to invest in areas of comparative disadvantage in the present regime to develop comparative advantage in future economic regimes. While economists sometimes refer to this problem in terms of the difference between "static" and "dynamic" comparative advantages, it is a much more difficult problem than these words imply. It is problem of structural change in economic systems, of regime switches.[9]

7. General Motors CEO Charles Wilson, testimony before the Senate Armed Forces Committee, 1952.
8. See, for example, Michael E. Porter and Claas van der Linde, "Toward a New Conception of the Environment-Competitiveness Relationship," *Journal of Economic Perspectives* 9 (1995): 97–118.
9. David Seckler, "Economic Regimes, Strategic Investments, and Entrepreneurial Enterprises: Notes toward a Theory of Economic Development." In *As If the Future Mattered*, edited by Neva R. Goodwin (Ann Arbor: The University of Michigan Press, 1996), 133.

The point is that an entity concerned with future growth and development[10] may sometimes have to take actions that do not pass a normal benefit-to-cost analysis. Thus, for example, Maximill, operating a major plant in "Pettiplace," may benefit in the short run from externalizing some of its production costs by ignoring the harmful effects on water quality in the city of Pettiplace. However, if Maximill grows, or good water resources decline, to the point at which water pollution makes the firm's own operations more expensive, part of this negative effect will be returned to its internal cost calculations. A new benefit-to-cost analysis might show that the firm may benefit from paying to prevent this pollution at the source. If Maximill keeps its plant in Pettiplace for a long time, a true analysis might show that the health effects of water pollution on its pool of present and potential employees are significant enough to include in Maximill's cost function.

At the same time, some positive externalities could also turn out, when viewed from the perspective of a sufficiently long time frame, to return enough benefit that they could be expected to be included partly in Maximill's own cost accounting (thus, in fact, ceasing to be externalities). A good example, mentioned earlier, is the education level of the Pettiplace population. Any resources put into local schools or into formal and informal skills training at the plant may after a decade or more upgrade the qualifications of potential employees, raising the quality of the goods and services offered to Maximill by its local suppliers and raising the quality – and raising or lowering the cost – of its own production.

Higher wages can lead to another positive effect that can, in turn, benefit Maximill. If its workers are paid well enough, they can purchase not only other goods and services but also Maximill's own products (just as Henry Ford intended his workers to earn enough to be able to own Model Ts). These examples may combine or expand to Seckler's development regime effect. Elaborating on the statement quoted earlier, Seckler notes that

> . . . in addition to tactical investments within the present regime . . . public and private sector entrepreneurs also have to make investments in development processes, in *paths of action*, that are intended to create or to enable them to achieve strategic advantages and avoid strategic disadvantages in future economic regimes. Investment in research and development and in education are but two of the most notable kinds of such investments. Others are in institutional change, whether at the level of the structural adjustment policies of nations or managerial reforms of corporations.[11]

---

10. In the short run firms are more likely to use the term "growth"; as their time horizon lengthens, they are likely, for the reasons explained in the text, to think in terms that converge with the word "development" as understood by relatively "altruistic" agents such as governments, aid agencies, or NGOs.

11. Seckler, op. cit., 155.

In the past, if we looked for an actor who was pursuing paths of action that would create economic regimes more favorable to overall development, we would ordinarily look to national and international economic policymakers. Because the nongovernmental, for-profit entities – most notably the MNCs – are now among the world's largest economic entities they could (though they will not necessarily) adopt as part of their own strategic goals the economic health of regions in which they operate. If the whole economy of Pettiplace develops because of Maximill's contributions to infrastructure as well as the inflows of purchasing power stemming from Maximill's higher-than-average wage policy, then the company can benefit from the creation of a new market of consumers as well as from an increasingly sophisticated and well-prepared workforce.

Over time, in the broad arena of economic development (which can be relevant for rich countries that seek economic betterment as well as for poor countries), corporate operations acquire relationships with many stakeholders in addition to their own workers: neighbors, customers, suppliers, creditors, regulators, lawmakers and other representatives and institutions of government, and, of course stockholders. It is noteworthy that the trends of the 1980s and 1990s toward ever shorter periods for holding stocks seem to have weakened relationships with stockholders at the same time that a variety of other stakeholder movements were strengthening their relationships.

Although the short-term response to pressures for cost minimization may ignore relationships, in the longer term firms may suffer if their actions outrage any group of their stakeholders. More broadly yet, as MNCs gain ever more power to shape their environment they need to be aware of the concept of economic regimes – that is, situations that make it more or less likely that future investments will be able to make a reasonable return. Monsanto's forced divestment from genetic engineering (in the late 1990s) was a classic case of a corporation that ignored its stakeholders and consequently destroyed the environment of relationships for future investment in what it had expected to be a highly profitable area.

A better understanding of the ways in which MNCs (especially the largest ones) create and divert resources for development will depend on a fuller understanding of their long-run strategies. In particular,

- To what extent do they identify their own interest with economic regimes of increased overall development?
- How do they balance their competing interest in, on the one hand, minimizing input costs, and, on the other creating affluent consumer societies?

There is a danger that MNCs will increasingly adopt an answer to the second question that might seem an easy balance between production and demand, but that could damage social fabrics in ways that, in the very long run, may operate against everyone's interests. This dangerous response contains three prescriptions: support for economic policies that concentrate purchasing power in the hands of the rich, policies that focus on producing for that high-end demand, and strategies that minimize the wages of workers, thus writing them off as significant consumers.

It is important to note that, although such strategic decisions have not been determined by immutable forces like The Force of Competition, these forces do play a role. Still, the actual decisions are made by human beings who most often accept whatever is the prevailing wisdom (or fashion of thought) on these matters. The exceptions are the rare leaders in industry who ask, and answer, larger questions, such as

- What is rational?
- What is right?
- How much does it matter what is right, and how should this weigh against current definitions of rationality?
- What levels of costs is it unacceptable to expect the outside society to bear?
- What is the appropriate definition of success for a firm and for its CEO?
- How long a time frame should be used to measure success?

GOOD AND BAD JOBS

In the 1970s there was an interest that has now largely, but not entirely, subsided, in a theory of dual labor markets. That theory was described as dividing, by an invisible wall, a primary sector, where the good jobs were, from a secondary sector, where the bad jobs were. This was always too simplistic a description, but it does point to certain realities worth considering.

One such reality is the most commonly mentioned differences between sectors of good (primary) and bad (secondary) jobs: Good jobs have good pay, including benefits – medical insurance, pensions, and so on; they provide decent working conditions, job security, and opportunities for career advancement; they often permit the worker a degree of autonomy and choice on how the work is done. Bad jobs, on the other hand, have low pay, scant or no benefits, frequently unpleasant work environments (hot or cold, noisy, dirty), and little or no job security; they have few or no opportunities to develop skills that will allow a move to a better job and little or no auto-nomy at work.[12]

In the 1960s and 1970s there seemed to be a distribution pattern of good and bad jobs. A primary sector consisted of huge firms (often those who, by historical accident, got there first) offering good jobs. These used capital-intensive technologies and were spread out geographically and diversified in activity. In a secondary sector of bad jobs were small firms[13] with rela-tively little financial or built capital that hired workers with little training or education and typically operated in locations of much general poverty.

Where were the MNCs in this pattern? Clearly they had the size and the technological and geographical attributes of the primary sector. Their jobs have generally been seen as better than similar jobs for comparably qualified workers in other local firms. However, at the end of the 1960s a very abrupt (when seen in retrospect) change occurred. To Bennett Harrison and Barry Bluestone the 1970s were the time of The Great U-Turn – a turn away from the gradual reduction in inequality that had occurred in much of the world from the Second World War on. The Great U-Turn is said to have introduced, in the last quarter of the twentieth century, a period of rising inequality in the United States[14] and, to varying degrees, also in other developed nations and between nations as well. With the general decline

12. For a review of dual labor market theory, see William T. Dickens and Kevin Lang, "Labor Market Segmentation Theory: Reconsidering the Evidence." In *Labor Economics: Problems in Analyzing Labor Markets*, edited by William Darity, Jr. (Boston: Kluwer Academic Publishers, 1993).

13. Often a "small firm" is defined as one hiring fewer than 50 people, whereas a "large firm" has 500+ employees. There is obviously room for a middle ground that is important in its own right but is not part of the idealized story of dualism. Remember, also, that depictions of primary and secondary sector firms are always to be taken as polar types, not a perfect picture of the real world. For example, some big firms may not have market power in a situation in which many big firms compete fiercely against one another; similarly, the only barbershop in a small town may have considerable monopoly power.

14. The United States is a special case; the inequality figures that will be cited for the it are much greater than for other industrialized nations. See, for example, Charles Derber, *Corporation Nation: How Corporations Are Taking Over Our Lives and What We Can Do about It* (New York: St. Martin's Press, 1998):

    With the 1990s came a second hint of a new Gilded Age: the revalation that the United States had become the most unequal country in the developed world – with the gap between rich and poor growing disturbingly vast. By the mid-nineties, not only was the gap the largest in fifty years, but as the United Nations reported, "the United States is slipping into a category of countries – among them Brazil, Britain, and Guatemala – where the gap is the worst around the Globe."

    See also Richard B. Freeman and Lawrence F. Katz, "Rising Wage Inequality: The United States versus Other Advanced Countries." In *Working Under Different Rules*, edited by Richard B. Freeman (New York: Russell Sage Foundation, 1993). In the 1990s the rest of the world has shown a tendency to follow the patterns of economic behavior pioneered by the United States; what we see here today may be what we see in the rest of the world in the near future – unless there is some kind of global revulsion over these trends.

in industrial employment leading to the "shrinking middle" of the income distribution, the stage was set for the anxious decade of the 1970s and for the mean decade of the 1980s. Not all of the gains of the previous quarter century were lost – notably, throughout much of the world the relative and absolute position of women continued to improve. However, at the global level,

the poorest 20% of the world's people saw their share of global income decline from 2.3% to 1.4% in the past 30 years. Meanwhile the share of the richest 20% rose from 70% to 85%. That doubled the ratio of the shares of the richest and the poorest – from 30:1 to 61:1.... The gap in per capita income between the industrial and developing worlds tripled, from $5,700 in 1960 to $15,400 in 1993.[15]

The last three decades of the century in the United States appear to have been a prolonged "shake-out" period (one presumably not yet over) in which the economic and political power of large MNCs has increased as the size of these behemoths has grown in relation to the countervailing powers of government[16] because the lines along which that power and associated resources are shared appear to have changed. The complexity of the impact on workers is exemplified by a 2002 *Forbes* magazine report on Wal-Mart.

"Wal-Mart's Supercenters are able to underprice their supermarket competitors about 15%... in part because they are more efficient but also because the discount giant uses nonunion labor. Wal-Mart matches the union pay rate in union markets, but the averate wage at Wal-Mart nationally [in the U.S.] is less than $10 an hour before bonuses."[17] This has led to poor morale and dozens of lawsuits accusing Wal-Mart of engaging in antiunion activities and forcing workers to put in unpaid overtime. At the same time, Wal-Mart is seen as offering ample opportunites for advancement. Wal-Mart has evidently picked its fights carefully: low pay is no longer the one that will cost it most in finding employees (as of 2002 the firm was estimating a need to add some 800,000 employees over the next 5 years in the United States alone) because rival firms such as Kmart and Target have also gone the low-wage route.

This marks a dramatic change as compared with the quarter-century after the Second World War when American corporations faced little

---

15. UNDP (United Nations Development Programme). *Human Development Report 1996* (New York: Oxford University Press, 1996), 2.
16. It is worth noting that the power of third sector (nongovernmental, not-for-profit) organizations may well have increased as fast as, or faster than, the power of the for-profit sector. By some measures (e.g., gross expenditures), the third sector is still relatively miniscule, but the numbers of people involved, in one way or another, may indeed be a significant counterweight to the other two sectors.
17. *Time Magazine*, January 5, 2003.

international competition. Wartime destruction in Europe and Asia left the United States with few economic rivals. In the United States, the raw forces of competition, including the cost-minimization effects on workers as production inputs, had been somewhat tamed by legislation on job safety, working hours, and grievance procedures; by socially accepted norms that grew up with the presumption of these protections; and by the continuing (though gradually declining) role of unions as watchdogs over these protections.

By the 1970s, however, with reconstruction in Europe and Japan leading to renewed global competition, many American companies began to lose markets to lower-cost foreign producers. Reduced trade barriers along with increasing corporate sophistication in international trade were widely perceived as squeezing out some of the excess revenues associated with market power especially, but not uniquely, in U.S.-based firms. So, too, computerized technologies deeply affected production methods in most industries (not only in those identified as information industries). Changing production techniques in the new globalized climate of competition seemed to call for new management theories, providing two contrasting ways in which business could respond to the new environment – a cooperative model and a competitive model.[18]

The *cooperative model* suggests an effort to retain the existing workforce and wage levels while retraining workers for new skills if necessary and at the same time seeking ways to produce higher quality goods and services and to make the company's operations more efficient and more responsive to market demand. Some economists call this cooperative option the "high road" to competitiveness. That approach appears to be especially relevant to highly mechanized, integrated, and continuous flow processes. The cooperative model of management stresses the ways in which productivity depends more on the effective interaction of many people than on the motivation and effort of single individuals. Although, under some circumstances, threats

---

18. See Robert A. Buchele and Jens Christiansen, "Industrial Relations and Productivity Growth: A Comparative Perspective." *International Contributions to Labor Studies* 2 (1992): 77–97; Robert W. Drago and Richard Perlman "Supervision and High Wages as Competing Incentives: A Basis for Labor Segmentation Theory." In *Microeconomic Issues in Labour Economics: New Approaches*, edited by Robert Drago and Richard Perlman (New York: Harvester Wheatsheaf, 1989); Applebaum, Eileen, and Batt, *The New American Workplace* (Ithaca, NY: Industrial Labor Relations Press, 1995).

Note that management theories are given an unusual amount of attention in this chapter. If we believed that the behavior of MNCs and other firms could all be explained as rational responses to inexorable competition, this emphasis would be out of place. However management theories can be creative – not just responsive – in situations in which even the most "rational" actors do not have full information with which to respond to competition; in which competition is far from perfect, leaving a large area of slack where there is room for experimentation with less-than-perfect systems; and in which the human factors of faddishness and the desire for peer approval can play a significant role.

may be effective in maintaining a reasonably high level of individual effort, they do not work as well in getting people to use the imagination and creativity that support teamwork in complex activities. For the cooperative model to work, workers must feel they have a stake in the long-run success of the firm. Job security and profit-sharing measures, in turn, motivate workers to find ways to improve the organization of production.

By contrast, in the United States of the 1970s and 1980s, most large, multinational companies took the "low road" based on the *competitive model of management*.[19] That model prescribed firing many workers, cutting wages, subcontracting work to smaller low-cost firms, and demanding a faster pace of work from those employees who were retained. In such a model, when labor relations are already conflict ridden or antagonistic, threats are management's strongest motivators. Thus, the threat that an MNC will move operations may be a stick that will force workers to work harder, for less pay, or under worse conditions than they would otherwise do. In this case, productivity will suffer when workers' power rises compared with the power of management; for example, when workers gain more workplace rights or when the general level of unemployment goes down. In firms that have adopted a cooperative management model, on the other hand, workers' power is less threatening or not threatening at all.

In the United States in the 1970s, the emphasis on minimizing the cost of paying workers was relatively new for large corporations that had been enjoying the ability to compete on grounds other than price alone. Economists such as Gordon, Harrison, and Bluestone have suggested that U.S. MNCs had several choices in how to respond to increased global competition; cutting the cost of the workforce was just one of the options they could have pursued. To the environmentally aware, another option can be inferred from how long firms resisted reducing costs of a different set of inputs: energy and materials. A focus on inefficiency in these costs remained relatively unfashionable during most of that decade; only in the later 1970s did the ever louder voices of environmentalists, and their growing alliance with consumer power, begin to make cracks in this resistance.

Porter and others have emphasized "win-win" environmental improvements as opportunities for firms to reduce production costs by minimizing or reusing "waste" products that should not be discharged into the

19. For a review of these management alternatives, see Frank Ackerman, "New Directions in Labor Economics: Overview Essay," in *The Changing Nature of Work*, edited by Frank Ackerman, Neva R. Goodwin, Laurie Dougherty, and Kevin Gallagher (Washington, DC: Island Press, 1998); Frank Ackerman, David Kiron, Neva R. Goodwin, Jonathan M. Harris, and Kevin Gallagher, eds. *Human Well-Being and Economic Goals*. (Washington, DC: Island Press, 2000).

environment. That these opportunities still exist today, though less commonly than before, is evidence against the simple economistic assumption that competition will drive firms to adopt all possible cost-effective efficiency measures. Global competition, it appears, is sufficient to drive firms to adopt some cost-cutting measures; it has not yet become strong enough to create a rush for all possible efficiencies.

The now lamented middle-class jobs – the jobs whose loss created the growing hole in American society's protective middle-income ozone layer – were typified by Detroit's highly unionized blue-collar jobs. The "downsizing" of these jobs came as U.S. firms chose a cost-minimizing, low-road strategy. Why did they make such a choice? Jerome Himmelstein, for one, says of the response of major U.S. corporations to the economic slowdown of the 1970s that they mobilized their political muscle, devoting it to conservative, antiegalitarian causes – most importantly a multipronged attack on the efficacy of labor unions.[20] In Himmelstein's view, in certain situations corporations do not see a dramatic opposition between profits and wages. So, for example, under economic circumstances like those that existed in the period from the Second World War to the early 1970s, both wages and profits rise together. However, when macroeconomic growth slows, corporations lean toward a conservative ideology that regards wage increases, government benefits, and government regulation as enemies to profits.[21]

---

20. Jerome L. Himmelstein, "The Mobilization of Corporate Conservatism," in *To the Right: The Transformation of American Conservatism* (Berkeley: University of California Press, 1991), 129–164.

21. The case for the image of a "golden age" and a "great U-turn" for workers in the United States may be made by comparing the trajectory of *total final corporate profits* (defined here as total net corporate income less total net taxes [total taxes minus tax credits]) with changes over time in *average production wages*. (All data below are assembled from various annual editions of the Statistical Abstract of the United States rendered in constant 2002 dollars.)

- Real average hourly earnings climbed steadily from $9.91 in 1945 to $16.30 in 1973.
- Total final corporate profits (henceforth "profits") were fairly flat from 1945 to 1960, averaging $142.25 billion per year in those years.
- Profits trended strongly upward from $136 billion in 1960 to $527 billion in 1979 except for a sharp drop in 1968 with recovery beginning in 1971.

These data suggest that workers were the primary beneficiaries of productivity gains in the 1950s whereas workers and owners shared the gains from 1960 to 1973.

- Wages declined steadily from $16.30/hr in 1973 to a low of $13.66/hr in 1993 – a decline of 16 percent from peak to trough.
- Wages began to rise slowly in 1994 and were at $14.58 by 2000 – a gain of 6.7 percent but still well below the 1973 peak.
- During the decade of the 1980s, profits fluctuated several times with a mean of $330.6 billion per year.
- Profits climbed steadily from $387 billion in 1990 to $812 billion in 1997 and then softened into the 700 billions.

It should be noted that the existence of a choice of management theories is not, in itself, disproof of an hypothesis of competitive profit maximizing as the overriding motivation in corporations. Thus, each of the two approaches described above, cooperative and competitive, can be understood as a partial response to the basic requirement of the competitive model: that all firms maximize profits by simultaneously minimizing costs and maximizing revenues. One approach, the competitive, emphasizes costs, whereas the other, the cooperative, emphasizes revenues; however, each firm obviously has to pay attention to both. High-road cooperative approaches are supported by "efficiency wage" theories, which suggest that it may be worthwhile for MNCs (and other employers) to adopt a strategy in which the increased input cost of high wages is justified by the increased productivity of workers who feel attached to the company:[22] "improved performance . . . requires the reinforcement of internal, firm-specific attempts to build a committed, loyal workforce capable of agile and intelligent response to evolving technologies and fast-moving global economic forces."[23] It is an open question whether this strategy can work well when it depends on the wage level alone without including some other relationships such as worker morale or the loyalty that comes with job security. Indeed, if all employers planned to offer efficiency wages, they could not succeed because the efficiency wage, by definition, needs to be higher than average, which would be an impossibility for all employers. However, attachment, loyalty, and trust, are not – like relative wages – part of a zero-sum game.

The bias of most economists who study industrial relations is on the side of the revenue-maximizing "high-road" approach because this option appears to contribute more to the economic growth and development of the economy as a whole than does the cost-minimizing alternative. It also promises greater social equality and cohesion. It is impossible, of course, to say how the course of history would have been different if U.S. MNCs had leaned more than they have to this option. However, if we accept Gordon's conclusion that MNCs in other countries were more likely to take the "high road," we can examine their outcomes for evidence of what happens when

In summary once again, workers and owners both lost ground in the 1980s, with the losses to workers beginning sooner – in the early 1970s – and lost relatively more ground for longer. In the 1990s corporate profits grew enormously – far surpassing any previous level – whereas wages recovered only part of what they had lost in the 1970s and 1980s.

22. See, for example, Drago and Perlman, op. cit., and Akerlof, and Yellen, "The Fair Wage-Effort Hypothesis and Unemployment," *Quarterly Journal of Economics* 105 (May 1990): 255–283.

23. Laurie Dougherty, "Restructuring Employment: Flexibility versus Security: Overview Essay." In *The Changing Nature of Work*, edited by Frank Ackerman, Neva R. Goodwin, Laurie Dougherty, and Kevin Gallagher (Washington, DC: Island Press, 1998).

that road is chosen or supported by the national government.[24] Political liberals would probably speculate that the dangerous increase in income inequality and, especially, in wealth inequality over the last three decades would not have occurred had MNCs chosen the "high-road" approach. Political conservatives, on the other hand, would probably emphasize the competitive edge U.S.-based MNCs managed to regain and might suggest that the United States would have been in a weaker position if its businesses had taken a different road.

Alternative histories aside, globalization, changing technology, and fashions of thought about management gave even the most oligopolistic firms a rationale for downgrading many good jobs. In the 1970s and 1980s, as ever more primary sector firms "went global" (became MNCs), they increasingly responded to competitive forces, and the association between big firms and good and secure jobs began to break down at every level and in every part of the world. (The change was perhaps most dramatic in Japan, where the difference between primary and secondary sector firms and jobs had been especially striking.[25])

Dual labor market theory earlier discerned "internal labor markets" through which large, sheltered firms developed and compensated workers as they climbed the internal career ladder.[26] But MNCs are now increasingly incorporating a variety of labor relationships such as outsourcing and reliance on a growing proportion of temporary, self-employed, and part-time workers. A study by Katherine Abraham covering the years 1972–1986 has shown increasing use of such market-mediated work arrangements at the same time that the previously established trend toward stronger employer – employee attachments has slowed down. Abraham suggests that the principal reasons for this shift have been the desire of employers for greater staffing flexibility,

---

24. A detailed analysis is given in David M. Gordon, Thomas E. Weisskopf, and Samuel Bowles, "Power, Accumulation, and Crisis: The Rise and Demise of the Postwar Social Structure of Accumulation," in Victor D. Lippit, ed. *Radical Political Economy: Explorations in Alternate Economic Analysis* (Armonk, NY: M.E. Sharpe, 1996), 226–244.

    See especially Figure 3.3, which plots the percentage of employment that is managerial and administrative (1980 data) against the percent change in real manufacturing wages (1973–89) for 12 developed countries. The United States had the highest managerial percentage and the lowest growth in manufacturing wages, which suggests that corporations in the United States are most likely to take the "low-road" approach. Gordon concludes that firms in some countries, including Germany, Japan, and Sweden, tend to take the "high road" whereas firms in countries such as the United States and Canada take the low road.

25. See, for example, James R. Lincoln and Yoshifumi Nakata, "The Transformation of the Japanese Employment System: Nature, Depth, and Origins," *Work and Occupations* 24 (February 1997): 33–55.

26. Peter B. Doeringer and Michael J. Piore, *Labor Markets and Manpower Analysis* (Lexington, MA: Heath, 1971).

a need for specialized skills and services in a time of rapidly changing (market and technological) conditions, and a search for wage flexibility to permit a firm "to take advantage of low market wage rates for certain types of work without violating internal equity constraints."[27]

The total number of workers formally employed in MNCs has risen over time, but the increase has been far less than might have been predicted given the growth in number, size, and profits of the MNCs themselves. Employment data for all MNCs are not available, but a constructed comparison of several aspects of growth in the 50 largest MNCs from 1983 to 2001 shows that, although revenues increased 179 percent and assets increased 686 percent during this time, the number of employees of the top 50 MNCs increased by only 21 percent.

At the same time, there is a striking difference between the total wage bill for rank-and-file workers and the compensation of top management. During the 1980s and 1990s much downsizing was justified by CEOs' claims that they were facing such fierce and inexorable competition that they had no other choice. In fact, however, although CEOs were cutting out workers and reducing workers' wages they were not turning all of the funds "saved" into profits. A substantial amount went instead into skyrocketing compensation for CEOs and other top management. In April 1999, *Business Week* noted that five best-compensated U.S. executives received, collectively, a total of $1.2 billion:

Despite the anecdotal connection, no academic has proven that higher pay creates higher performance. While self-interest is, as Adam Smith observed centuries ago, a great motivator, the link between pay and any objective standard of performance has been all but severed in today's system. The options windfall is as likely to reward the barely passable as the truly great; moreover, it's rewarding virtually one and all in amounts that are expanding almost exponentially.... In using options, companies today are in effect outsourcing the oversize compensation to the stock market.[28]

Huge compensation increases went not only to CEOs but to their seconds-in-command – up 37 percent in 1998 to an average of $7.6 million a year – at the same time that blue-collar pay was increasing at an annual rate of only 2.7 percent and white-collar workers' pay by 3.9 percent. Rep. Martin Olav Sabo (D-Minn.) was quoted as saying, "We have a significant gap that has been growing between the top and the bottom for 25 years." Every year since 1991 Sabo sponsored a bill that would abolish corporate tax

---

27. Katherine G. Abraham, "Restructuring the Employment Relationship: The Growth of Market-Mediated Work Arrangements." In *New Directions in the Labor Market*, edited by Katherine G. Abraham and Robert B. McKensie (Cambridge, MA: MIT Press, 1990), 96.
28. Jennifer Reingold and Ronald Grover, "Executive Pay," *Business Week*, April 19, 1999.

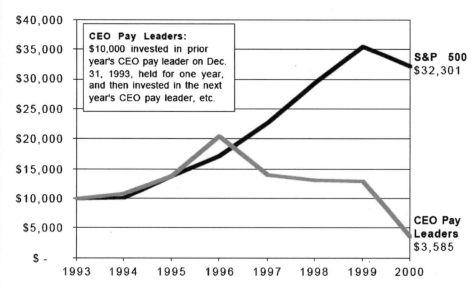

Figure 5-1. CEO Pay Leaders versus S&P 500, 1993–2000 (Value as of Dec. 31 of each year)
Source: "The Bigger They Come, The Harder They Fall" by Scott Klinger; published by
United for a Fair Economy, April 6, 2001.

deductions for any company whose CEO's salary is more than 25 times that
of the lowest-paid worker at the firm.[29]

Especially interesting data in a 1999 survey of executive compensation
by *Business Week* conducted in conjunction with the market research firm
Standard & Poor's Compusat indicated that the average U.S. laborer's weekly
pay in 1998 was 12 percent below the 1973 level (adjusted for inflation)
despite a 33 percent increase in worker productivity in that same period, whereas
the CEOs of the companies selected for that survey experienced an average
36-percent pay hike.

The standard model of competitive firm behavior predicts that wages and
salaries will directly reflect the incremental revenue (the "marginal revenue
product") attributable to each earner from the production workers up to
and including the CEO. If the workers in that period were not being compensated for their own rising productivity, we might at least conclude that
CEO salaries especially reflected superior leadership. After all, during the
year in question, the Standard & Poor's 500-stock index rose 26.7 percent.
Yet the rise in stock price was not responsible for the rise in the pay of
the executives covered by this particular study because it represented a sub-
group of the S&P 500 – a group of underperforming companies whose 1998
earnings actually fell by an average of 1.4 percent. Figure 5.1 was compiled

29. Jennifer Reingold and Fred Jespersen, "Executive Pay," *Business Week*, April 17, 2000.

by United for a Fair Economy and shows how one's portfolio would have performed if, starting in 1993, one's investment strategy had been to invest $1,000 in each of the 10 companies that had the highest-paid CEOs – and then, at the beginning of the next year, to have taken one's funds and reinvested them again in the 10 companies with the highest-paid CEOs – continuing thusly until 2000. This strategy would have resulted in a portfolio worth $3,585 – about one-tenth of the rise in value of the S&P 500 over that time.

These data point to several dramatic trends especially apparent in the United States but emerging also in other countries that follow U.S. business patterns. One such trend is the growing pay gap between ordinary workers and the top corporate earners. Another is the loss of lower and middle-level management jobs – a loss that contributes to a hollowing out of the income profile. A third is the rising profits of MNCs. The question of where those rising profits are going follows from this. (See below.)

Given that workers in MNCs generally receive higher pay than workers in comparable jobs in purely local firms,[30] the question arises of whether the growing size and importance of MNCs will increase, or could increase, the proportion of good (primary sector type) jobs in the world as a whole.

A sobering first response to this question is a reminder that the percentage of the world's workers employed by MNCs is small; it is hard to calculate but generally thought to be no more than between 1 and 2 percent.[31] Not all MNC employees are treated like primary sector workers; therefore, we need to ask how the secondary sector of smaller firms is affected by events in the primary sector of larger firms. Does the rising tide of prosperity – if, indeed, that tide *is* rising for workers with full-time, formal jobs in sheltered industries – lift conditions for those in the secondary sector?

On the one hand, MNCs have been subjecting their suppliers to fierce competitive pressure for cost minimization. Yet, increasingly close supply chain relationships are emerging in response to numerous pressures from other sources. Thus, environmental groups have successfully persuaded firms like Home Depot to insist that all their suppliers of wood products accept certification for sustainable harvesting practices. Similarly, pressures from human rights and labor groups have caused Nike to become the world's first MNC to make public the location of all of its Third World subcontractors. This is of particular interest because that disclosure is clearly the result of

---

30. See, for example, *The Economist*, January 8, 2000, pp. 46–7, "Foreign Friends."
31. See Chapter 1 in which it is estimated that the 500 largest firms provide about 1.6% of the world's formal jobs.

the bad name Nike acquired as an employer (even though only, as Nike has protested, through subcontractors) of woefully underpaid workers, including many children. Although Nike's move does not, in itself, change this, it opens the floodgates to pressures that can be brought to bear for better working conditions in such Third World factories.

The growth in size and number of MNCs might have been expected to marginalize small and medium-sized firms. However, even in industries that offer significant cost advantages to large firms, a large enterprise cannot operate without partners and requires a network of related and supporting activities (e.g., contracting out specialized production and design tasks, supplying inputs, etc.). So, too, large firms depend on smaller, less stable, firms to absorb the fluctuations in market demand that occur in all markets. Thus, globalization has brought MNCs into an increasingly complex web of relationships with a variety of other firms from those of comparable size and power to tiny and informal firms. These relationships, ironically, often depend on personal relationships of trust and shared experience as when high-placed managers play golf or attend the Davos gatherings together (see Chapter 6 in this volume). At other times these interactions depend on an introduction by a trusted mutual acquaintance or on a working relationship that has built up over time between, for instance, a member of the MNC's management team and a creditor or a supplier.

This is a picture full of contradictions, many of which can be traced back to the strain between competition-induced cost minimizing versus competition-dodging relationship building. The contradictions are, perhaps, most obvious in relationships between MNCs and their suppliers. The tendency of MNCs to exert downward pressure on the latter's wages may be the clue to understanding a new and much more subtle kind of dual labor market. Now, firms with the power to create shelter for themselves use that power to maintain a small trove of good jobs – from the technician with special skills to the CEO. At the same time, these firms respond to external pressures by trying to reduce a selected group of other input costs – those emphasized by current management theories. Since the 1970s the input costs on which these theories have focused have been the lower tier of the company's own workers and the inputs purchased from other firms – that is, the MNC's suppliers.

The supply chain effects of public pressure (as mentioned earlier in this section with respect to Home Depot and Nike) have not yet reduced MNC wage pressures on suppliers, but such an outcome does remain a future possibility. For now, however, cost minimization pressures and popular trends are often causing MNCs to act in ways that, in effect, pit all the world's workers against one another in a competition for jobs.[32] This stark modern reality can have the effect of putting a divisive wedge between groups who might otherwise be allies: for example, workers within a given region, workers from one region versus workers from another, or workers who belong to different ethnic groups.

Dual labor market theory has never completely gone away, but, as has been suggested, the world it attempts to describe is far more complex and more fractally divided than the world of the 1960s and early 1970s. Yet the difference between "good jobs" and "bad jobs" continues to be as significant as it was when this theory was first developed. This, or some other theory, must account for the fact that wages and working conditions often seem to be determined by job characteristics unrelated to output of the actual jobholder – an observation that conflicts with the standard economic expectation of wages equal to the marginal revenue product of the worker.

The neoclassical economic position maintains that more competition is always better than less because it favors consumers by maximizing their choices and minimizing prices. Labor market dualism has always looked different to various observers depending on whether they identify with consumers or with workers – or, if the latter, whether they identify with those who have, or seek, primary sector (good) jobs or with those who appear stuck in the secondary sector. Dual labor market theory painted a picture in which primary sector firms diverted some of the potential consumers' surplus to both workers and owners, justifying the unpleasant characteristics of the secondary competitive sector as the necessary price for maximizing consumer choice.

In recent decades, the pan-human conspiracy to which I have referred – in which all producers the world over have reason to conspire against the force of competition – seems to have lost traction because high profits appear to be increasingly separated from good wages and working conditions. The hypothesis offered in this chapter is that the new, increasingly globalized form of competition of the 1970s and subsequently still permitted much shelter within which excess revenues could be generated, but it was accompanied by owners' and top-level managers' capture of an increasing share of these revenues at the expense of the workers. However, the inequality that has

---

32. Compare Sarah Anderson and John Cavanagh, *Field Guide to the Global Economy* (Washington, DC: Institute for Policy Studies, 2000), 43: "An extensive study of organizing drives at U.S. manufacturing firms by Cornell University found that in 62 percent of the cases, management fought the union by threatening to shut down the plant and move production to a lower-wage area." The study referenced is Kate Bronfenbrenner, *Final Report: The Effects of Plant Closings or Threat of Plant Closing on the Rights of Workers to Organize*; Cornell University, New York State School of Industrial and Labor Relations, 30 September 1996.

grown over the last quarter of a century in the United States and elsewhere seriously weakens any claim corporations could make that a future of ever larger, more concentrated firms would be one of an expanding primary sector that ultimately might cover all workers. Most broadly, if by "primary sector" we mean to include all working situations that can produce good jobs, we now have to accept that things have changed. Whereas it used to be possible to identify the primary sector with large firms, it is now much less clear where protection against competitive cost cutting can carve out space for good jobs.

PROFITS AND SURPLUS — POTENTIAL AND ACTUAL

The economist Herbert Simon has proposed a provacative thought experiment. Imagine that an alien from Mars were to take a photo of Earth using a special camera. On photographs taken with this equipment, social structures organized along nonmarket lines would show up as solid green areas. Market connections of exchange would show up as red lines running between them. The photo would be dominated, Simon suggests, by green areas. "Organizations," according to Simon, "would be the dominant feature of the landscape."[33]

Organizations are structured networks of relationships. The conglomerate form, which came to fruition in the three decades that this chapter considers, carries to an extreme the creation of a world of relationships among suppliers, producers, managers, stockholders, advertisers, and distributors (not to mention lawyers, accountants, and regulators) who are connected not through a market but through a single firm.

A small firm may be conceived as a small island of cooperative organization within the surrounding sea of market competition. A large firm is a larger area of cooperative organization because it creates an area within which many more employees — perhaps hundreds or thousands — relate to one another not as atomistic individuals engaging in market transactions solely to advance their individual interests but around the (at least partially) shared goal of advancing the firm's interest.

An article in the OECD *Observer* notes that

"international trade within single firms accounts for around one-third of goods exports from both Japan and the United States, and a similar proportion of all US goods imports and one-quarter of all Japanese goods imports. Few data are available for other countries, but given the increasing importance of foreign direct

---

33. Herbert A. Simon, "Organizations and Markets," *Journal of Economic Perspectives* 5(2) (1991): 25–44.

investment, it is likely that the importance of this intra-firm trade has increased at the global level."[34]

Their conclusion from this fact is that the supposed benefits of increased competition – "that is, independent firms competing to keep prices low and quality high" – are not passed on to consumers. Instead, such firms pursue their own, not the consumer's interests.

The question is, What is the firm's interest? Mainstream theory in the United States says that it is, or should be, the owners', that is, the share-holders', interest in profit maximization. At the same time, the hypothesis of a pan-human conspiracy suggests that a major interest of any firm that has the power to pursue it (and MNCs are the outstanding exemplars of such power) is creation of shelter from competition. So long as the firm's interest is defined as profit maximization, shelter can be understood as simply a means to produce surplus revenues, which, in a sort of toothpaste-tube theory, are all squeezed out at the end of the production process in the form of profits. An alternative understanding of firms' deployment of resources – one proposed here – suggests ways to allocate what we define as surplus revenues.

A variety of economic theories have been based on alternative concepts and measures of surplus. The interpretation presented here starts out from the neoclassical definition of the necessary costs of doing business in the assumed context of perfect competition, including the market prices for raw materials and manufactured inputs, prevailing interest rate on money, and compensation of all employees at the lowest rates that can attract the desired skills. In competitive circumstances managers are assumed to try to pay as little as possible for each input. In an economy full of such compet-itive firms, input prices would be standardized; the lowest price one firm could get away with would be the same price paid by the next firm for the same quality of labor or other input. In the neoclassical economic model of perfect competition, with prices and costs both driven to the minimum, the use of all receipts taken in by the firm is absolutely determined and nothing is left over after paying for all necessary inputs to production. In this reasoning, "economic profits" are zero; however, "normal profits" – the return expected by owners (who would otherwise not supply their capital) – are included among the "minimum necessary costs of production" and are positive.

Diverging from this model of perfect competition, we instead assume the presence of various kinds and degrees of shelter so that not all costs are at their minimum nor are all selling prices competitively driven to their

34. <http://www.oecdobserver.org/news/fullstory.php/aid/850/The_global_business_.html>.

lowest point. This is the existing world in which similar products or similar inputs are often sold at a wide variety of different prices. We do, however, preserve the concept of necessary costs as a benchmark against which to define surplus.

Sheltered situations are rife with *potential surpluses*, which we define as *a firm's ability to earn revenues above the minimum required to cover its necessary costs*. Such potential surpluses may be allocated in several different ways at various points in the production process – sometimes before they appear as profit or even as revenue. For example, potential surplus could be used up in behavior that simply increases production costs, preventing some or all of the potential revenue from appearing as such. This can result in a not-so-uncommon situation in which a firm with market power charges higher prices for its products than a similar competitive firm charges, even while the firm with market power has no extra revenues but only higher production costs.

The following list of different ways in which potential surplus may be allocated will begin at the bottom of the toothpaste tube with some potential surplus used in production costs that are raised above the minimum possible. Thus,

1. Workers may appropriate some of the potential surplus by putting somewhat less than maximum effort into their jobs, creating more relaxed (or less than optimally efficient) working conditions.[35]
2. Managers may relax their own effort level, failing, for example, to shop around for the lowest prices for nonhuman inputs. When suppliers know that the producer is going to be relaxed, they may raise their own prices even up to the extremes cited as the 20-dollar nails or 600-dollar toilet seats supplied to military producers in the United States. (When a potential surplus is absorbed in such higher costs the manager might be receiving part of the potential revenue in the form of a bribe or relaxed vigilance.)

Other forms of surplus allocation of particular concern to workers and lower-level managers occur later in the production process (higher up in

---

35. Harvey Leibenstein was the economist who first emphasized this possibility, using the term "X-inefficiency" to describe the less-than-maximum-effort-level he regarded as the norm (Ralph Gentile and Harvey Leibenstein, "Microeconomics, X-Efficiency Theory and Policy: Cleaning the Lens," *Man, Environment, Space and Time* 1(1) (Fall 1979):1–26). Leibenstein's contribution has yet to be fully accommodated within an economic theory that describes labor as an input to production along with materials, machinery and so on. Economic efficiency is achieved when all inputs are employed in the correct relative proportions (determined as a function of their relative cost and relative contribution to production) and output is maximized per unit of input. When the latter condition is applied to the labor input, it is often taken to mean that effort level and attentiveness must be maximized at all times. It turns out, however, that maximum effort level is virtually impossible to define – let alone achieve – on a steady basis. Maximum effort may be exerted in bursts when the motivation is high (spurred by fear, avarice, or a sense of urgent mission), but even labor camps have not been able to maintain that maximum in a productive way over long periods.

the toothpaste tube) when the potential surplus has appeared as revenues but has not yet been identified as profits. For example, the potential surplus may be used for the following purposes:

3. To support more pleasant working conditions through the firm's possibly providing a cafeteria or day care center for workers or a car and driver for a manager;
4. To provide improved compensation for workers (higher wages or better benefits like health insurance or pension plans);
5. To hire more workers than necessary (past the point at which the wage of the additional worker is equal to the value added to the firm's output).

The preceding uses of potential surplus are most likely to appear when workers, lower-level managers, or both have a certain amount of power. Often that power resides in knowledge: if upper-level managers and owners do not know (but those lower down do know) that the firm has the potential to generate additional revenue, the upper levels may not realize that that potential is being used in these ways. Other sources of workers' power may include an effective labor union or scarce skills.

A different set of revenue diversions is more likely to emanate from top management manifested as follows:

6. Greater than necessary salary, bonuses, and other nonsalary income for the CEO and other top managers;
7. Expenditures directed to increasing the firm's size or to suppressing rivals in cases in which such strategies increase the CEO's status and power even if they are not strategies for maximizing profit;
8. Purchase of power that may be used in ways contrary to the public interest – for example, to fight legislation that mandates product or workplace safety.[36]

Seckler's concept of investing in paths of action (cited earlier) can sometimes be applied to entries 7 and 8 above, where such actions create strategic advantages for a firm. Such strategies may, however, incur large negative externalities with resources used in socially unproductive struggles over market share or in ways that subvert government regulation.

A benign diversion may occur if owners or managers instead show concern about the community in which the firm operates, or about some other social issues, by choosing to allocate some surplus revenue to the following:

9. Social goods, like environmental protection (beyond what is "rational," in cost terms, for the firm) or community amenities like art museums or health

36. Neva R. Goodwin, "Corporate Power: Why Does It Matter? Overview Essay." In *The Political Economy of Inequality*, edited by Frank Ackerman, Neva R. Goodwin, Laurie Dougherty, and Kevin Gallagher (Washington, DC: Island Press, 2000).

care. (Note that environmental protection can be supported by either actual or potential surplus; the latter is what is at issue when a portion of the potential surplus is not realized as revenue because it has been used to pay for more expensive, environmentally friendly production methods or technologies.)

Only after all of the foregoing nine possibilities have been accomplished, or bypassed, does the remaining surplus appear in the form economists define as

10. Profits, that is, above-normal returns to the owners of capital.

Most management theories promulgated in the last three decades of the twentieth century have advocated a version of the toothpaste-tube approach in which the presumed goal is to squeeze the maximum possible amount of surplus through the tube to bring it out at the top in the form of profit. This approach has been countered by two other trends. On the one hand, managers – sometimes by trial and error, sometimes through conscious instruction – keep rediscovering some version of "efficiency wage theory" that suggests a significant loss in worker commitment when the tube is squeezed too hard. On the other hand, more dramatically, CEOs have captured an increasing part of the surplus in their own compensation – sometimes offsetting significant portions of the cost savings achieved by firing thousands of workers or by reductions in these workers' benefits packages.[37]

When we look at workers in MNCs compared with those employed elsewhere, we see an advantaged group. When we look at MNC workers compared with workers in equivalent positions in similar firms of 40 years ago we see surprisingly little improvement. When we compare the changing situation of MNC workers with that of top management, we see a dramatic decline in the workers' share of the firms' good fortune. For example, as reported by the U.S.-based organizations, Institute for Policy Studies and United for a Fair Economy,

between 1990 and 1999, total CEO compensation grew by 535%, not adjusting for inflation. This far outstripped growth in the stock market (the S&P rose 297%) and in corporate profits (which rose 116%). Meanwhile production worker pay lagged far behind, rising only 32.3% (from $345.35 a week in 1990 to $456.78 a week in

37. United for a Fair Economy examined the *Business Week* list of the "top 10" corporations – those 10 corporations whose CEOs received the world's highest compensation packages during the particular year. "In each of the years between 1994 and 1999, at least 50% of the companies each year announced significant layoffs (more than 1,000 employees or 5% of the workforce) within three years of the CEO appearing on the *Business Week* top ten list" (Scott Klinger, "The Bigger They Come, The Harder They Fall"; published by United for a Fair Economy, April 6, 2001).

1999.) This boost in worker pay only barely outpaced inflation, as the Consumer Price Index grew 27.5% over the decade.[38]

On the basis of *Business Week*'s annual executive pay scorecard (1999), the average top executive in a major (multinational) U.S.-based corporation in 1998 received compensation of $10.6 million, including salaries, bonuses, and stock options that have been cashed in but not unrealized stock options.

Adding these gains [unrealized stock options] into the picture sends CEO compensation soaring high into nine-digit levels. In 1998, according to research by compensation expert Graef Crystal, five CEOs saw their wallets widen by more than 232 million [each] – the equivalent of $116,000 an hour.[39]

This compensation of top CEOs is nearly ten thousand times the hourly rate of the average production worker.

CONCLUDING COMMENTS AND ISSUES FOR FURTHER EXPLORATION

The discussion of "regimes" for investment and development earlier in this chapter suggested that corporations share a common interest in enlarging the pie that they will divide among themselves. The limit on the size of that pie is the total size of the global money economy understood as the total money value of final goods purchased in a single year. It is not, however, necessarily in the interest of the rest of society that the size of this total be maximized as, for example, if it were increased by creating a militarized world that produces and sells many guns, bombs, and defenses against them; or by creating highly inegalitarian economies dependent on luxury consumption; or by selling products whose advertising campaigns are designed to make people dissatisfied no matter how much they have; or by selling products that harm human health (which, in turn, requires additional expenditures on health products).

From the MNC point of view, the size of the total pie is not the only important consideration; there is also the issue of how it is to be shared among various groups: one set of categories would include (1) MNCs, (2) smaller firms and individual economic actors, (3) governments, and (4) not-for-profit NGOs. Among these groups the MNC share has clearly been growing in recent decades (see Chapter 1 in this volume). MNCs share an interest in promoting this trend as well as in enlarging the total global pie that sets the limit on the MNC share. Although this chapter does

38. *Executive Excess 2000*, August 30, 2000, 3.
39. *Too Much*, a newsletter published quarterly by United for a Fair Economy and the Council on International and Public Affairs; summer, 1999, 3.

not attempt to consider whether any intervention could effectively alter the relative growth of the MNC sector, one of its purposes has been to indicate some of the issues to be considered if one were to try to evaluate whether this growth is socially beneficial. These issues include the two just mentioned – the total size of the global money economy and how it is divided among the four groups of monetized economic actors listed just above.[40] A third issue, which was discussed in the preceeding section, is the within-firm division of the potential surplus accruing to each MNC.

The common economic identification of "the firm's interests" as identical with the owners' interests would suggest that the pie they want to maximize is actually the share of total global revenues that goes to profits as opposed to wages and rents. This contrasts with the 1970's image of dual labor markets in which the world was divided into a different "us and them" – the "us" identity provided by the simple holding of a job – any job – in a large corporation and the "them" identity by work in the secondary sector (as well as the jobless, working in the informal sector, or not at all).

If an entire economy possessed all of the characteristics of the primary sector, including a potential surplus that could benefit workers as well as owners, the debate would resolve itself on some fairly clear issues such as on the question, Which is more important: low consumer prices or good working conditions? But the present trend toward markets dominated by ever larger MNCs turns out, after all, not to lead toward an ever-growing area of shelter for workers from the brutalities of market competition. It does, indeed, provide some shelter from competition – and large potential surpluses are generated in that shelter – but even as these potential surpluses have grown their division among profits, wages, and economic rents[41] seems to have become more, not less, unequal.

Although we are thinking about what there is to divide and how it gets divided, we can hardly ignore the approach that focuses on the division of society's total revenues between owners and workers. This topic has been so strongly identified with Marxist theory that it has been almost entirely avoided by other economists to their loss. In any case, in the world of the twenty-first century the issue needs to be posed afresh with new categories to distinguish among different kinds of work and workers and the recognition that top management has become a special category of

40. Of course, not all of any economy is monetized; indeed, estimates of the amount of nonmonetized economic activity taking place in households, communities, and some parts of the NGO sector generally come up to between 20 percent and 30 percent for industrialized countries and more in the Third World.
41. The technical term "economic rents" refers to moneys accruing to the owner of a scarce resource such as the special skills imputed to some CEOs, pop singers, basketball players, or other stars.

its own. It is also necessary to recognize that corporate ownership is now distributed among institutional investors, private individuals, and others in ways that are dramatically different from any time before 1970. These issues cannot be followed further here except to say that the thrust of this chapter indicates an urgent need for a new look at the old question of how society's product is divided.

In the creation of new kinds of dualism – both in labor markets and in the distribution of resources around the world, within nations and within firms, and especially within firms that are MNCs, where so many kinds of power are concentrated – there is new urgency to the discussion of how firms allocate surplus revenues. The growing power of significant countervailing forces such as diverse emerging groups of stakeholders to impose regimes of transparency and accountability on MNCs will mediate the intentional or unintentional decisions of future MNCs on allocations of surplus. These decisions will be important determinants of their own social impact.

This chapter has disputed a simple view of globalization as simply un-regulated capitalism on a global scale. That capitalism is now operating on a global scale is certainly true, but if "unregulated" suggests that competition rules all, squeezing out room for cooperation or for any choices other than profit-maximizing ones, then there is a need for new approaches that can examine the realities of a rapidly changing world. Thus, we have reached the point of vanishing returns from focusing on the ideologically freighted assumption that perfectly competitive markets would be desirable – that is, if they were possible. Future observers of the economic scene will more prof-itably pursue a fresh consideration of the real options. Kelvin Lancaster and others made the point half a century ago that, when a presumed optimum is unattainable, it may be better to look in other directions than to assume that the next best alternative is to get as close as possible to the unattainable first choice. The new global history may provide guidance in considering the related basic question: Given the bundle of constraints and possibilities that confront this brave new globalized world, what goals should we pursue?

Rising GNP may, in some cases, be a desirable means but is not an end in itself. It is becoming ever more evident that the health of future societies will depend upon the degree to which institutional, cultural, legal, and other contexts shape corporate goals so as to converge with societal goals.[42] For this to occur, issues like security, satisfaction of basic needs, comfort and luxury,

---

42. See, for example, Neva R. Goodwin, "Civil Economy and Civilized Economics: Essentials for Sustainable Development," in *The Forerunner Volume* for the *Encyclopedia of Life Support Systems* (EOLSS Publishers Co. Ltd., Oxford, UK, 2001). Also available on the Global Development and Environment Institute Web site at <http://www.gdae.org> as Working Paper 01-01, January 2001.

and equity and fairness must be reconsidered. Are such elements basic to our societal goals? If so, what balance ought we to seek among them, and how can we balance the achievement of these goals in the present with the metagoal of sustaining them for the future? Are we creating structures and incentives that are likely to move us toward such a balance? What kind of society do we want, and, in that context, how can MNCs – among the most potent players on the world's stage – be motivated to operate in accord with, rather than in opposition to, those societal goals? Values, facts, and analysis are inextricably, and inevitably, intertwined. Success in studying and mapping a new global history will require cooperation among many academic disciplines as well as with individuals and groups outside of the academy. This chapter is one step in that direction.

6

A Global Elite?

BRUCE MAZLISH AND ELLIOTT R. MORSS[1]

It is both interesting and important to reflect upon whether any individuals or network of individuals and groups can be seen as running the world and, if so, who they are and what are they up to. Within the context of global economy we ask these questions: Is there a global elite? Who runs the multinational corporations (MNCs) and other global institutions? In what kind of historical perspective should any such global elite be seen and how can research answer these questions? Also, what normative questions, if any, should be applied to the behavior of any global elite whose existence has been confirmed?[2]

EARLY CONCEPTS OF AN ELITE CLASS

"Elite," according to a standard dictionary, denotes a "socially superior group." The word comes from the Latin *eligere*, which means "to choose." Thus, the elite is the "choice part" of the body politic. It can refer to a social group of any size or dimension: a high school can have an elite class and so can a nation. In identifying a global elite, it is useful and perhaps necessary, as Peter Dobkin Hall argues, "to go beyond examining traditional economic and political elites" of the sort studied by previous scholars. Although these elites (for instance, among members of the Trilateral Commission, the World Bank) continue, Hall says, "to exist and to exercise considerable influence, they are being challenged by new elites based on specialized policy and technological expertise whose actions are framed by . . . much more genuinely

---

1. The first part of this chapter up to the section "Hypotheses about the Global Elite" is principally the work of Bruce Mazlish; that section is the work of Elliott Morss; the remainder of the chapter is by the two authors jointly.
2. See, for example, C. Wright Mills, *The Power Elite* (Oxford: Oxford University Press, 1956); E. Digby Balzell and William Domhoff, *Who Rules America Now?* (New York: Simon & Schuster, 1983).

global (as opposed to merely international) perspectives."[3] Whether small or global, however, elite stands in contrast to equality. Further, the term "elitism" often is used not only to describe social stratification but to advocate or to oppose what it describes. Before one advocates or opposes, however, one must understand.

The aim of this chapter is to develop the notion of a global elite. The subject of elites has intrigued popular as well as scholarly writers over the years. In a 1936 book, *Politics: Who Gets What, When, How*, the political scientist Harold Lasswell declared that "the influential are those who get the most of what there is to get. . . . Those who get the most are *elite*; the rest are *mass*."[4] Lasswell and Daniel Lerner's later volume, *World Revolutionary Elites*, published in 1965, became a model of sorts for subsequent empirical research.

Prominent among the historical speculations on elites is, of course, the Marxist notion of a "ruling class." Marx himself never attempted to provide empirical content to his idea nor to engage in empirical research to prove it. To Marx, "ruling class" referred, broadly, to the bourgeoisie of his own time and also to earlier landed aristocracies. Most of his own attention, and that of his followers, was centered instead on the proletariat. In the 20th century, somewhat under the spell of Marx, the noted sociologist C. Wright Mills did attempt empirical studies of the ruling class – specifically, his landmark study of 1956, *The Power Elite*.

In a different tradition is the work of the Comte de Saint-Simon and his followers. In the aftermath of the French Revolution of 1789 and its overthrow of the existing social structure, Saint-Simon proposed to reorganize society on the basis of production. Productive individuals were to replace the nonproducing aristocrats of the ancien régime. Saint-Simon had no illusions about equality: "The community has often been compared to a pyramid. I admit that the nation should be composed as a pyramid . . . but I assert that from the base of the pyramid to its summit the layers should be composed of more and more precious materials."[5]

---

3. Personal letter from Peter Dobkin Hall to Bruce Mazlish, March 20, 2000.
4. Harold D. Lasswell, *Politics: Who Gets What, When, How* (New York: McGraw-Hill, 1936), 13. Anyone wishing a start on this literature would do well to consult Dankwart A. Rustow's synoptic review article, "The Study of Elites: Who's Who, When, and How," *World Politics* XVIII (1966), which deals with five other books on the general subject in addition to Harold D. Lasswell and David Lerner, *World Revolutionary Elites* (Cambridge: MIT Press, 1964). Further references to the subject are easily found in Rustow's article, which, though now outdated, is a classic, or in any university library catalog.
5. Henri Comte de Saint-Simon, "On Social Organization" (1825), in *Selected Writings*, ed. F. M. H. Markham (Oxford, England: Basil Blackwell, 1952), 79.

A few years before, Saint-Simon, in his journal *Organizer*, had proposed in place of the marshals, cardinals, and officers of the royal household, 50 each of France's top physicists, chemists, engineers, bankers, businessmen, and others. The total was 3,000.[6] This was a "power elite" that might be studied empirically. Saint-Simon, an aristocrat by birth, sought to divest himself and others like him of power and prestige by placing a business and a scientific-technological elite at the apex of the social pyramid. Bankers were high up on his list.

Earlier elites had been principally warriors, priests, or bureaucrats such as the mandarins of China or the aristocrats of medieval Europe. All such forms, the earlier and Saint-Simon's, have persisted to one degree or another into more modern times. What is most interesting for our purposes here is to note that an elite like the European aristocracy was transnational, that is, not bound by fixed territorial loyalties. As the social critic Lewis Lapham suggests, "the hierarchies of international capitalism resemble the feudal arrangements under which an Italian noble might swear fealty to a German prince, or a Norman duke declare himself the vassal of an English king."[7] "Until recently," Stephen J. Kobrin writes, "and especially in Europe, elites were transnational; the medieval nobility saw itself as European rather than national. Elites might have been linked to territories and titles certainly were grounded in place, but they were not territorial in the modern sense."[8] Saint-Simon's own emphasis on a new elite of producers emerging from the Industrial Revolution of the early 19th century can be seen as parallel to today's "producers," who operate in an "Information Revolution."

AN EMERGING GLOBAL ELITE

Just as there have been many kinds of elites in the past, so there are many kinds in the present: local, regional, and national. Is there also an emerging global elite and, if so, is it a consequence of, or the instigation of, the process of globalization itself? If the answer to both questions is affirmative, as we believe it is, further questions follow: Is such an elite homogeneous? Is it made up of distinct segments – such as business, media, military – and if so how do these segments relate to one another? More sustained research is needed to answer some of these questions. Here, we focus on the

---

6. "First Extract from the 'Organizer'" (1819), 72.
7. Lewis H. Lapham, "Leviathan in Trouble," *Harper's Magazine* (September 1988): 10; we use it as quoted in Stephen J. Kobrin's paper, "Back to the Future: Neomedievalism and the Postmodern Digital World Economy," *Journal of International Affairs* 51 (Spring 1998): 365.
8. Kobrin, "Back to the Future," 377.

multinational enterprises and their presumed elites while recognizing that a multinational corporation (MNC) elite will be connected to other elites as well.

The definition of MNC, and that of its aliases, such as transnational enterprise and international firm, imply that all are business enterprises that generate income from their activities in more than one country by producing goods, selling goods, selling services, and by making investments, both direct and in financial assets.[9] An extension of this definition is that "in its simplest form an MNC is merely a form or agent of foreign direct investment (FDI)." This may be too limiting a definition because some MNCs, such as McKinsey & Co., do not make foreign direct investments although they are part of the global "advice" industry that includes accounting and legal firms.

At the core of the New Global History inquiry is the assumption that the nation–state is being transcended in multiple ways – not that the nation–state is disappearing or even "withering away," as some have asserted, but that it is changing or reordering many of its functions in the light of a new global reality. This would mean that national elites will persist but increasingly interact with a developing global elite. Dual identities will frequently be the result. Of course, as Mary Yaeger suggests, the same individuals often move from a national to a global elite status.

We are catching glimpses of a deterritorialized status group that is in certain ways akin to the earlier aristocratic society of the European Middle Ages. Signs of the times appear in the self-description of himself as a "global citizen" offered by Thomas Middlehoff, former CEO of the Bertelsmann media and publishing conglomerate. "We are not a German company," he insists. "We are a real global company."[10] His firm increasingly recruits its young executives from leading American and Asian universities rather than from German or broader European sources alone; it uses English as the firm's common language.

In the same vein, when asked whether Microsoft is an American company, the No. 2 man in the company, Steve Ballmer, replied, "We like to think we are a company based in America that is a global company. In every country we are Microsoft. Not American. Microsoft. Microsoft Japan. Microsoft Italy."[11] Similarly, ABB (Asea Brown Boveri), the giant electrical

9. For an extensive discussion of the nature of the MNC or MNE, see Chapter 2 of this volume.

10. The quotes are from an interview with Middleshoff by Doreen Carvajal in the *New York Times*, October 19, 1998, C1. See also Daniel Johnson, "Springtime for Bertelsmann," *The New Yorker*, April 27 and May 4, 1998, 106.

11. Thomas L. Friedman, "Foreign Policy 3.1," *New York Times*, October 8, 1995.

engineering MNC, which originated in Sweden, moved its corporate head-quarters to Zurich. It employed a few years ago 18,000 workers in 40 coun-tries. Especially germane to our concerns is Boveri's management structure, which has been described as "a coordinating executive committee (with members from eight countries)" with "an elite cadre of 500 global man-agers" carefully selected by the CEO with "particular attention to the cul-tural sensitivity of its members, and to their spouses' willingness to move."[12] As expected, the company's language is English. The central question, how-ever, relates to neither personnel nor language but to who are the core decision-makers. These decision-makers will be an important part of the global elite.

Added to these trends is the growing insistence on global teams of innovators: "In technology, teams are tops," says one commentator. "And for the most innovative companies, U.S.-only teams are old hat. Global teams are the rage."[13] So is global education the rage with MIT forming al-liances with Singapore and Cambridge, England, and with business schools scheduling many of their classes in different parts of the globe, drawing their students from across the world.

A sobering consideration is that most MNCs – whether in the United States, Japan, or elsewhere – elect only nationals to their board of directors. The appointment of Nobuyuki Idei, Sony's chief executive, to the board of General Motors, made news. Nobuyuki Idei joined only a handful of other Asian executives who are serving on such boards; Du Pont and IBM, for example, have Asian executives on their boards. This parochial tendency itself need not, however, undermine the concept of an emerging global elite, for even if not on the same board, executives of the large MNCs interact in other forums. Their companies, too, are often in alliances both nationally and globally.

The overall direction seems clear. Increasingly, companies appear to be expanding globally and reorganizing themselves accordingly. Although there are retreats – Ford, for example, at one point moved back from its global structure to a more regional one – the overall trend toward global companies and elites appears fairly constant. Such global elites, like the companies they lead, increasingly see themselves as cosmopolitans, as global citizens, with an identity that embraces but that also transcends the nation-state and its restricted sense of territoriality.

---

12. *The Economist*, January 6, 1996, 56.
13. See G. Pascal Zachary, "The Rage for Global Teams," *Technology Review*, July/August 1998, 33, and The MIT Report, September 1999, 3.

A NEW GLOBAL ELITE'S IDENTITY AND BEHAVIOR

An inquiry into such a global elite, its identity and behavior, is an essential part of a new global history initiative.[14] If there is indeed an emerging global elite it is of great importance to understand its patterns of activity because of the immense power it exercises. Neither globalization nor the MNCs are faceless entities; their processes are powered by the individuals who make up the corporate corps. They can be studied and understood.

A global elite, for one thing, tends to have a global vision in contrast to the often insular views of national government leaders worried about local electability. Members of the global elite worry not about elections or dispensing pork to their home districts but about the sale of pork and other products and services across national boundaries. Their lobbying is principally about the World Trade Organization (WTO), or about, for instance, the expansion of NATO membership, which will open up new markets for arms sales in Eastern Europe.

It needs to be said, for another thing, that the global elite is overwhelmingly male, though this characteristic is hardly surprising. As Yeager has shown in her exhaustive study of *Women in Business*, in spite of the advances women have made, "it's still a man's world."[15] This is so on the national level, and, accordingly, on the global as well (see our discussion of Davos in what follows). Yet, advances are being made as is evident in the formation of women's networks such as the Financial Women's Association of New York, which has about 1,100 members. The composition of classes at the top business schools, in which women are now a significant percentage of the total, suggests how the national and global winds are blowing. It is clear that changes are in process in the composition of the global elite. One of the tasks of future research is to map that shift.

Another important consideration is the sites in which the global elite function. They are, of course, numerous, and among them are the MNCs themselves as well as consulting, accounting, and legal firms; business schools; international organizations like the World Bank and the

14. In some quarters there is opposition to elite studies of any kind. As one historian reminds us, "The case against the 'elitist' bias in historiography and for the restoration of the 'subjecthood' of non-elites as historical actors has been strongly argued, among others, by the 'subaltern'school' of South Asian historiography" (Leila Tarazi Fawaz, *An Occasion for War. Civil Conflict in Lebanon and Damascus in 1860* [Berkeley: University of California Press, 1994], 4). However, elite studies do not preclude nonelite studies; indeed, the two should go hand in hand while recognizing as well that subaltern school studies themselves are a reaction to the globalization process.

15. See especially Mary A. Yeager, "Introduction." *Women in Business* (Northampton, MA: Elgar, 1999); this work includes a splendid bibliography, "Just for Women: A Corporate Alumni Network," *New York Times*, October 27, 1999, C1 and C12.

International Monetary Fund; groups of leaders meeting in such venues as Davos, the Trilateral Commission, and Bilderberg; and also the various nongovernmental organizations known as NGOs. It is the crossovers and intersecting lines among these groups that make for an operative global elite.

The Trilateral Commission, according to Stephen Gill, was founded by the banker David Rockefeller "and a small group of wealthy and influential private citizens in 1972"; in 1990 it had "about 350 members, some of whom [held] key positions in at least 60 of the world's 100 largest corporations." The members of the Commission have included Robert McNamara, Henry Kissinger, Paul Volcker, Caspar Weinberger, and Giovanni Agnelli as well as German industrialists and several Japanese cabinet members and chairmen of major global companies. Drawing upon a range of elite intellectual, political, and economic networks – mostly from the United States, Europe, and Japan – and some occasional individuals from other parts of the globe, the Commission has sought "to promote a reconstructed capitalist world order, which is compatible with the forces of transnationalization" and to "develop a strategic consciousness and consensus amongst the ruling establishment of its member nations."[16] The Commission's power has been great, though not as great as conspiracy-minded thinkers maintain. It reached its apogee in the United States during the Carter administration – Zbigniew Brzezinski, President Carter's National Security Adviser, was a key figure in the formation of the Commission.

Gill has looked at the Trilateral Commission with a balanced but critical eye in the framework of Gramscian hegemony of transnational capital, that is, that the people generally have acceded to the power of a minority class of elite in response to their manipulation of social and political strategies to maintain that power. Further research, he writes, could seek to identify each of the small groups of these "wealthy and influential private citizens" and then to correlate their place in other networks. Gill, in a 1990 study of the Commission's members, concluded that it and the Council of Foreign Relations, Bilderberg, and other groups are consciously co-opting top intellectuals to shape a common perspective.[17]

Another node in the global elite network comprises the major law firms, most of them with headquarters in the United States. The second largest

16. Stephen Gill, "The Emerging Hegemony of Transnational Capital: Trilateralism and Global Order," in *World Leadership and Hegemony*, ed. David P. Rapkin (Boulder, CO: Lynne Rienner Publishers, 1990), 120, 121. Peter Johnson has been of enormous help in providing a list of Trilateral members during the 1970s. In the future we hope to analyze that list in the fashion we accord to the Davos membership list itself later in this paper.

17. Gill, *American Hegemony and the Trilateral Commission* (Cambridge: Cambridge University Press, 1991).

in revenue as of 1998, Baker & McKenzie of Chicago, had offices in 35 countries; its lawyers represent dozens of nationalities. It also has the distinction of having as its top partner a woman; of the nation's largest law firms only one other has a woman in such a post.[18] Because MNCs necessarily adapt to societies with diverse political, social, cultural, and legal systems, it is only natural that MNC lawyers will be drawn from diverse cultural backgrounds.[19] It would be useful to be able to identify the members of the top global law firms and analyze their backgrounds, education, and ethnic and national affiliations and determine how they are plugged into a global network.

In this same vein, Silicon Valley is a network with enormous ramifications. Of its more than 11,000 firms, one-fourth of them, we are told, are run by immigrants, and half of this leadership consists of young Chinese or Indian entrepreneurs represented in more or less equal parts. Research by Amrit Srinivasan has concluded that these entrepreneurs do not function as ethnic enclaves as such but with an identity of global players.[20]

Another prime site to be investigated is the world of management consultant firms – a type of firm pioneered by Arthur D. Little. The current leaders in that world include McKinsey, Boston Consulting Group, Bain & Co., A. T Kearney, and Booz-Allen. McKinsey is perhaps now the most notorious. We are told that it "makes a big point of not having a headquarters; it is supposed to be a global association of equal partners, not a top-down corporation – there are eighty offices in thirty-eight cities, and more staff abroad than in the United States"[21] – though the biggest office is in New York City. McKinsey is a yellow brick road to future corporate success; those who have traveled on it, now in a "network of famous alumni," include Louis Gerstner of IBM, Harvey Glubb of American Express, Jim Manzi, formerly of Lotus; and John Malone, the cable-television czar. No wonder that a quarter of the senior class at Harvard – 450 people – applied in the year 2000 for about 10 entry-level jobs at BCG, McKinsey's counterpart in the Boston area!

McKinsey, boasting that it is the largest nongovernmental employer of Rhodes and Marshall scholars on the planet – another elite group that

---

18. Melody Petersen, "Big Firms, Big Money," *New York Times*, October 9, 1999.
19. Alice Teichova, "Multinationals in Perspective," in *Multinational Enterprise in Historical Perspective*, ed. Alice Teichova, Maurice Levy-Leboyer, and Helga Nussbaum (Cambridge: Cambridge University Press, 1986), 368.
20. Amrit Srinivasan, "South Asians in Silicon Valley: Some Field Notes and Thoughts" (a lecture given at the South Asia Forum at MIT Seminar, Cambridge, MA, November 23, 1999).
21. Nicholas Lemann, "The Kids in the Conference Room," *The New Yorker*, October 18 and 25, 1999, 212. This article is a mine of information, and many of the further statements about McKinsey quoted herein come from this source.

would bear further investigation – clearly sees itself as beyond any national definition. Rajat Gupta, an Indian, as the head of McKinsey (he has now stepped down), symbolizes its chosen identity. McKinsey employees think of themselves as a meritocratic elite operating on a global stage. Former, and present, consultants – 8,500 or so of them – keep in touch via a Web site. It does make sense that a global elite network will maintain ties to one another via the computer network because the World Wide Web has partly given rise to the global elite network itself and subsequently has fostered its continued functioning as an elite.

A GLOBAL WAY OF LIFE

A member of the global elite does not only network through its institutions but also "culturally" by participation in a common global way of life. Just as national and local elites "club" together: in actual clubs – on golf links, at charity events, and so forth – so members of the global elite play a similar exclusive game but at a higher level.

In a 1988 *New Yorker* cartoon set in a restaurant, a waitress asks a customer, "Ranch, creamy Italian, French, or global?"[22] Our elite would know exactly which dressing to opt for to apply to their salad and would know what goes into it. The magazine *Leaders*, glossy and fat – its volume 20, number 4 issue, for example, comes to 370 pages – is saturated with advertisements of global firms. It cannot even be subscribed to; it is distributed gratis to a selected group of powerful leaders. A promotional letter claims "a *worldwide* audience that controls close to four trillion dollars in assets, goods and services. Our readers are either directly or indirectly responsible for controlling most of the world's natural resources and industrial production." This unabashed claim to global hegemony is underlined by the extent to which these selected leaders have benefited financially from their activities. The median net worth of *Leaders'* readership is cited as "approximately $6,000,000 (low estimate)."[23]

We are told that *Leaders* circulation includes the following among others:

- The major investors operating on behalf of labor, corporate, and government pension funds worldwide;
- Chairs, presidents, and members of the boards of the major multinational and global corporations;
- Chief financial officers of the leading MNCs worldwide; and

22. Cartoon, *The New Yorker*, September 28, 1998, 36.
23. The promotional letter from which these quotes are taken bears no date.

- Political and government leaders worldwide, including the decision-makers who buy large quantities of goods on behalf of their own countries.

What does *Leaders* offer this elite readership? A typical issue of the journal features several interviews with CEOs of major companies. Readers of *Leaders* need to know their peers. There is also a section on a particular spot on the globe, say Romania or the Sudan, with interviews with the president of the country, the president of its senate, the prime minister, the minister of finance, and so on. And then there is an illuminating section entitled "Leaders Style." In a typical issue, members of the global elite will learn about "On Being Well Shirted" (the guide being the managing director of Brioni of Rome) and about the right shoes, the right watches, and similar accoutrements as well as in which hotel to stay in any given spot on the globe, what to eat there, and how to entertain and be entertained – in short, how to live graciously and appropriately globally. It is not enough to have global wealth and power; one must also maintain a global life style.

HYPOTHESES ABOUT THE GLOBAL ELITE

To give the concept of a global elite more concreteness, we offer several hypotheses:

The first hypothesis is that there is not one but four global elites and that the first one derives its status from social and family backgrounds. This elite tends to come from the same geographic areas and attend the same schools, where it developed a network of individuals, almost all men, as noted earlier, with considerable power and influence. This elite may be in positions in government – for example, as diplomats – or in the private sector as senior corporate managers.

The second global elite we propose derives its power from developing and implementing profit-making ideas. It is not in its origins a homogeneous group. These "idea people" are the heads of Microsoft, Cisco Systems, and AOL, for example, and come from a wide variety of family and educational backgrounds.

The third global elite derives its status from a top position in a global organization. The President of the United States, the President of The World Bank, or the head of a major company would be examples of this elite. Voting electorates and headhunting firms as well as boards select candidates for many of these jobs. They choose from a pool already, to some degree, preselected by money, family, and experience; hence, this group shows a degree of homogeneity. However, because many obtained their elite positions via the political process of election or appointment, their individual backgrounds can be quite diverse.

The fourth elite is composed of the managers of global organizations. For the most part, they are graduates of Western business and technical schools; consequently, this group tends to be extremely homogeneous not only in education but in tastes, lifestyles, and career goals. This is a also a widely traveled group; to fulfill its management responsibilities, its members travel continually, flying business class, using their laptops en route, staying at the same hotels, using the same fitness centers, and eating at the same restaurants. They are the "worker bees" of global corporations.

Elites have traditionally been considered as groups of individuals; we believe there is merit in ascertaining whether there are elite industries as well. For elite industries, for example, being big is important. Still, bigness alone is not enough – manufacturing and industries that focus on natural resource extraction are no longer elite industries. We hypothesize that the new elite industries involve primarily information transfer, media, finance, and the supplying of advice. Information transfer includes all the Internet firms and the hardware companies that support them as well as telecommunications companies and the paper couriers. Media firms include the creators and providers of movies, television, and "real time" entertainment – that is to say, live entertainment, like sporting events. Finance includes insurance companies, investment companies, and organizations in banking and stock markets. The "advice" industry consists of lawyers, accountants, management consultants, and investment bankers.

ANALYSIS OF THE YEAR 2000 DAVOS LIST OF ELITES

It can be hypothesized that commissions and forums try to get members of these elites to attend their global meetings. Thus, the Trilateral Commission and the World Economic Forum gather annually, and one can only attend these meetings if invited. It is not easy to get an invitation. The Forum characterizes itself modestly as "the foremost global partnership of business, political, intellectual, and other leaders of society committed to improving the state of the world." Its president, Klaus Schwab, summarizes its guests as "the best minds" and its goals and approach as follows:

... we constitute a unique partnership of representatives from business and government. Our basic philosophy is that the great challenges facing humankind as we move into the next century can only be met through joint efforts on the part of government and business. But these efforts have to be stimulated by the best minds and have to be made transparent to the public. In short, what makes the Foundation unique is that we are a truly global community, a global partnership of business, government, academia, and the media.[24]

24. We wish to thank Professor Schwab and the World Economic Forum for providing us with the attendance list for the year 2000 meeting. The invitation list was offered to us on the understanding that we would not mention the names of any invitees and only present findings on groups. We did not receive lists of those who actually attended the meetings.

Every year, the approximately 2,000 global leaders who are invited to the Forum in Davos are offered more than 280 or so workshops or presentations over 6 days of meeting.

Because an analysis of such invitee lists could provide useful information on those who are regarded as today's global elites, we have studied the characteristics of the 2000 World Economic Forum's list of invitees. The list is not of members of the elites alone but also includes "facilitators." Many of the academic and media representatives were invited to the meetings as facilitators to publicize the event or "to stimulate the best minds."

We are also aware that the list of those invited must be seen in context. The Forum started and, no doubt, continues as a sincere attempt to bring together global elites, yet it also is an income-generating business that attracts persons who will pay "big bucks" to acquire global elite status, meet global elite, or just attend a good intellectual show. There is no way of ascertaining from the list itself who are the elite and who are the facilitators. Still the list shows us a good deal. Among those findings are the following:

1. Seven percent of invitees, judging from first names, are female, and 93 percent are male. At least insofar as the Davos list represents elites, the global elites are, as we know from other sources as well, still predominantly male.

2. When the invitees are identified by institutional affiliation we can distinguish those participants from corporate, government, nongovernmental (NGOs, including trade associations as well as other "cause" groups), and academic institutions (Table 6-1). We found that the largest number of invitees whose affiliation we could establish represent the private sector and the next largest the government. Academic and NGO representation combined was not quite 12 percent. More than half of the invitees from NGOs and corporations were their leaders, that is, CEO or president, whereas most government and academic invitees were not political or institutional leaders, that is, president or prime minister. It is notable that only 10.9 percent of invited academics were presidents. This can either mean that university professors rather than their presidents are elite members or that the academics were invited as "hired hands" – that is, to write papers and make presentations (see Table 6-1).

Table 6-1. *Davos Invitees (2000) by Institution and Leaders*

Institution	Invitees as Percentage of Total	Leaders of Groups as Percentage of Groups
Corporate	77.0	63.0
Government	11.3	27.2
Academic	6.5	10.9
NGO	5.2	89.4
TOTAL	100.0	56.9

Table 6-2. *Davos Invitees (2000) by Industry and Leaders*

Industry	Invitees as Percentage of Total	Leaders of Groups as Percentage of Groups
Manufacturing	16.5	69.5
Mining	5.1	80.8
Media	28.9	26.7
Finance	25.0	59.8
Hi-tech	13.1	73.3
Advice	9.3	42.4
Travel	2.3	76.1
TOTAL	100.0	45.8

3. The corporate invitees from industry whose industries we could identify came from manufacturing, mining, media, finance, hi-tech, advice services, and travel services. (In media we included both paper and electronic means of communication. In finance we included insurance, investment companies, and organizations in banking and stock markets. In hi-tech we included anything connected with computers and transmission of information. In advice services we included lawyers, accountants, and consulting organizations.)

Considering the Davos roster overall, we found evidence to suggest there are global elite industries as well as global elite individuals (see Table 6-2). At Davos, invitees from media, finance, hi-tech, and advice were represented in numbers that exceeded the value that their industries added to global production, whereas invitees from manufacturing were underrepresented in numbers less than the value their industries added to global production. Because of the overrepresentation of the first group and the underrepresentation of the second, it can be inferred that media, finance, hi-tech, and advice are now considered elite industries.

There is one possible exception to this statement. As noted earlier in this section, media representatives were invited to Davos to pubicize what went on rather than because they had elite status. Only 26.7 percent of media invitees were presidents or CEOs, suggesting that the intention was to invite the working press rather than the leaders of the media industry.

4. The Davos invitee list was also analyzed by country of invitees. See Table 6-3 for data on the number of invitees, population of countries, per capita GNP of countries, and invitees per million population of each country.

When the Davos invitee list was analyzed by country for three income categories – low-income (average less than $1,000), middle-income (between $1,000 and $10,000), and high-income (above $10,000) – there was no correlation between population size of the countries and the number of invitees: most invitees (78.5 percent) came from high-income countries even though the population of these countries is only 15 percent of the total population. On the other hand, the percentage of invitees from high-income countries is close to the percentage of global production taking place in high-income countries (78.3 percent; see Table 6-4).

Table 6-3. *Davos Invitees (2000) by Region or Country, Population, and GNP/P*

Country or Region	Population (Millions)	GNP/P (in U.S.$)	Number of Invitees	Invitees per Million Population
Africa				
Mauritius	1.2	3,700	1	0.9
Tunisia	9.0	2,050	1	0.1
Zambia	10.0	330	1	0.1
Zimbabwe	12.0	610	3	0.3
Cote d'Ivoire	14.0	700	3	0.2
Mozambique	17.0	210	1	0.1
Ghana	18.0	390	1	0.1
Morocco	28.0	1,250	4	0.1
Kenya	29.0	330	3	0.1
Algeria	30.0	1,550	5	0.2
Tanzania	32.0	210	1	0
South Africa	41.0	2,880	53	1.3
Nigeria	121.0	300	3	0
TOTAL	362.2	845	80	0.2
Asia and Pacific				
Singapore	3.0	30,060	10	3.3
New Zealand	4.0	14,700	1	0.3
Sri Lanka	19.0	810	2	0.1
Malaysia	22.0	3,600	3	0.1
Australia	36.0	8,970	38	1.1
Korea	46.0	7,970	7	0.2
Thailand	61.0	2,200	2	0
Philippines	75.0	1,050	9	0.1
Japan	126.0	32,380	39	0.3
Pakistan	132.0	480	2	0
Brunei	166.3	4,570	5	0
Indonesia	204.0	680	3	0
India	980.0	430	43	0
China	1,239.0	750	34	0
TOTAL	3,113.31	2,421	198	0.1
Latin America				
Uruguay	3.0	6,180	1	0.3
Costa Rica	4.0	2,780	1	0.3
Honduras	6.0	730	2	0.3
Bolivia	6.3	25,000	3	0.5
Bulgaria	8.0	25,000	2	0.3
Ecuador	12.0	1,530	4	0.3
Chile	15.0	4,810	5	0.3
Venezuela	23.0	3,500	8	0.4
Argentina	36.0	8,970	21	0.6

Table 6-3 (*continued*)

Country or Region	Population (Millions)	GNP/P (in U.S.$)	Number of Invitees	Invitees per Million Population
Colombia	41.0	2,600	9	0.2
Mexico	96.0	3,970	39	0.4
Brazil	166.0	4,570	27	0.2
TOTAL	416.3	5,121	122	0.3
Eurasia				
Estonia	1.0	3,390	1	1.0
Kyrgyz Republic	5.0	350	1	0.2
Bosnia	6.3	25,000	1	0.2
Hungary	10.0	4,510	7	0.7
Czech Republic	10.0	5,040	8	0.8
Kazahkstan	16.0	1,310	1	0.1
Poland	39.0	3,900	16	0.4
Turkey	63.0	3,160	13	0.2
Mongolia	96.0	3,970	1	0
Russia	147.0	2,300	39	0.3
Slovenia	2.0	9,760	4	2.0
TOTAL	395.3	3,463	92	0.2
Middle East				
Bahrain	0.6	7,660	3	4.7
Qatar	0.7	25,000	5	6.7
Cypress	0.8	700	1	1.3
Kuwait	2.0	25,000	5	2.5
Oman	2.3	25,000	2	0.9
United Arab Emirates	2.7	18,220	6	2.3
Lebanon	4.0	3,560	1	0.3
Jordan	5.0	1,520	2	0.4
Israel	6.0	15,940	15	2.5
Syria	15.0	1,020	1	0.1
Saudi Arabia	21.0	25,000	10	0.5
Egypt	61.0	1,290	11	0.2
Iran	62.0	1,770	4	0.1
TOTAL	183.1	5,608	66	0.4
North America				
Canada	31.0	20,020	54	1.7
United States	270.0	29,340	553	2.1
TOTAL	301.0	28,380	607	2.0
Western Europe				
Liechtenstein	0	43,570	2	62.5
Iceland	0.3	28,010	1	3.3
Luxembourg	0.4	43,570	6	14.1

(*continued*)

Table 6-3 (*continued*)

Country or Region	Population (Millions)	GNP/P (in U.S.$)	Number of Invitees	Invitees per Million Population
Norway	4.0	34,330	3	0.8
Ireland	4.0	18,340	3	0.8
Denmark	5.0	33,260	11	2.2
Finland	5.0	24,110	17	3.4
Switzerland	7.0	40,080	149	21.3
Austria	8.0	26,850	12	1.5
Sweden	9.0	25,620	19	2.1
Belgium	10.0	25,380	38	3.8
Portugal	10.0	10,690	11	1.1
Greece	11.0	11,650	6	0.6
Netherlands	16.0	24,760	37	2.3
Spain	39.0	14,080	17	0.4
Italy	58.0	20,250	27	0.5
United Kingdom	59.0	21,400	171	2.9
France	59.0	24,940	118	2.0
Germany	82.0	25,850	126	1.5
TOTAL	386.8	22,532	774	2.0
GRAND TOTALS	**5,157.96**	**5,744**	**1,939**	**0.4**

5.   To obtain a clearer picture of invitee selection by country, we conducted a country-specific analysis of invitees relative to the population of each country. We found no statistical correlation between a country's population and its number of invitees. Table 6-5 lists the countries with the largest number of invitees relative to their population. Quite clearly, invitees were not chosen on the basis of the population size of their countries.

A similar examination was made of invitees relative to their gross national product, and these results are presented in Table 6-6. The United States, the United Kingdom, and France were not on the list. Switzerland, with 111 invitees, was at the top – of course, Switzerland was the host country. South Africa was next. Six countries were African. It is also clear that the number of invitees was not highly correlated with GNP.

Table 6-4. *Davos Invitees (2000) by Income Category, Population, and Production of Country*

Income Category	Invitee (%)	Population (%)	Production (%)
Low–income	5.7	59.6	6.4
Middle–income	16.2	25.4	15.3
High–income	78.5	15.0	78.3
TOTAL	100.0	100.0	100.0

Table 6-5. *Davos Invitees (2000) by Country Population*

Country	Number of Invitees	Invitees per Million Population
Bermuda	4	63.5
Liechtenstein	2	62.5
Switzerland	111	15.9
Luxembourg	3	7.0
Bahrain	3	4.7
Qatar	3	4.0
Singapore	8	2.7
Kuwait	5	2.5
Finland	12	2.4
United Kingdom	125	2.1
Belgium	21	2.1
United Arab Emirates	5	1.9
Israel	10	1.7
Austria	30	1.6
Sweden	14	1.6
Netherlands	24	1.5
France	86	1.5
United States	393	1.5

Table 6-6. *Davos Invitees (2000) by Country GNP*

Country	Number of Invitees	Invitees per Billion GNP
Bermuda	4	2.5
Liechtenstein	2	1.4
Bahrain	3	0.6
Kyrgyzstan	1	0.6
Honduras	2	0.5
Switzerland	111	0.4
South Africa	43	0.4
Zambia	1	0.3
Estonia	1	0.3
Mozambique	1	0.3
Zimbabwe	2	0.3
Mauritius	1	0.2
Ecuador	4	0.2
Cote d'Ivoire	2	0.2
Qatar	3	0.2
Luxembourg	3	0.2
Ghana	1	0.1

Table 6-7. *Davos Invitees (2000) by Region, Population, and GNP/P*

Region	Population (Millions)	GNP/P (in U.S.$)	Number of Invitees	Invitees per Million Population
North America	301.1	28,380	607	2.0
Western Europe	386.8	22,532	774	2.0
Middle East	183.1	5,608	66	0.4
Latin America	416.3	5,121	122	0.3
Eurasia	395.3	3,463	92	0.2
Africa	362.2	845	80	0.2
Asia	3,113.31	2,421	198	0.1
TOTAL	5,157.96	5,744	1,939	0.4

6. It is interesting to note which countries show up on lists for Tables 6-4 and 6-5, that is, which countries have more invitees than both their population and GNP would warrant. Countries on both lists include Switzerland, Bermuda, Liechtenstein, Luxembourg, Bahrain, and Qatar. Switzerland, as noted, is probably overrepresented because the conference is based there. Bermuda, Liechtenstein, and Luxembourg are money centers, and Bahrain and Qatar generate significant sums from investment through oil exports.

7. As one might expect, the regions of North America and Europe had the largest number of invitees relative to their populations, and Asia and Africa were underrepresented (see Table 6-7).

If invitees to the Davos conference are the global elite, the preceding statistical analysis suggests who they are. The findings suggest further that global elites should not be thought of exclusively as individuals but also as industries and regions. Thus, agriculture and manufacturing now appear not to be elite, relatively speaking, whereas media, finance, hi-tech, and advice industries are. It is no surprise that North America and Western Europe are considered elite regions; Asia and Africa are not.

FUTURE DIRECTIONS FOR RESEARCH AND ANALYSIS

The analytical findings offer several new ideas and point in a direction for future research. Further research into the size and primary activities of the individual companies represented at the Conference ought to provide a high payoff. So, too, there are numerous research possibilities for a fuller understanding of the nature and constitution of a global elite. The Trilateral Commission, Davos, the top legal firms and management consultant groups, and the magazines directed to these groups are all possible sites for amassing rich empirical data. (The one group we have left out entirely is the military elite; for our purposes, trying to add them in was too daunting. Clearly, in future work some analysis of the military–industrial complex would be essential.) The results, we are sure, will demonstrate that parts of the elite are in conflict with other parts. Nuances and differences will appear but perhaps also a pattern of commonalities and unities of character and purpose. Research can provide a deeper sense of the dynamics involved and of the shifts that have occurred and are occurring in the composition of the global elite.

One of the more interesting books on what the author David Kowalewski calls the "Global Establishmentism" (though he does not go into the details on personnel) asserts that

> [N]etworks of private and personal elites, or "establishments," have been constructed in national political economies across the world. These national establishments, in turn, have become more transnational in their structure and processes. Increasingly, the establishments of the North have meshed with others across national boundaries, ratcheted their power up to the global level, and drawn the establishments of the South into their fold. In brief, *a single Global Establishment has emerged, which links the economic and political elites of developed capitalist countries and those of underdeveloped capitalist countries into a web of mutual benefit.*

MORAL QUESTIONS

To this assessment of fact, Kowalewski then adds the judgment that "*this integration, however, has been of dubious benefit to the nonestablished.*"[25] This charge, that the global elite serves its own interest and not that of the majority of populations in the world, is a common one. It is echoed by the comments of the former French Prime Minister Lionel Jospin that "we have to accept a networked world, but not a world dominated by networks, because then it would be dominated by private interests."[26] Often, the criticism takes the form of highlighting the disparities between countries of the North and countries of the South.[27] It cites, for example, the huge sums received by CEOs in the United States. It asks, What is the social contract equivalent to that which is often said to have existed in the 1930s in the United States between big business and the New Deal?[28]

---

25. David Kowalewski, *Global Establishment. The Political Economy of North/Asian Networks* (New York: St. Martin's Press, 1997), 3.
26. Quoted in the *New York Times*, November 22, 1999, A4.
27. Cf. Ivan Head, *On the Hinge of History: The Mutual Vulnerability of North and South* (Toronto: University of Toronto Press, 1991).
28. See, for example, the unpublished paper by Olivier Zunz, "A New Elite Faces a New Social Contract" (presented at the conference on Mapping the Multinationals, Pocantico Hills, NY, September 30–October 3, 1999).

In assessing, let alone judging, the power of the new global elite to shape its economic, political, social, and cultural world universe, we must learn more about these new masters of the globe. Information presently analyzed only touches on such key questions as the following: Who are the global elite? How are they constituted? What is their training? What are their values? How might those who are not members of that elite affect the way in which the elite exercise wealth and power over us? There are no manuals or guides (*Leaders* aside) for the members of this elite such as those circulated in the Middle Ages for the courtier and aristocrat on how to behave properly in manners and in moral behavior. Before we can even contemplate writing such tracts for the contemporary society we need to put faces on the global elite and map their physiognomies more accurately. This chapter has been intended as a step in that direction.

PART THREE

The Governance of Multinationals

7

Governing the Multinational Enterprise

The Emergence of the Global Shareowner

ROBERT A. G. MONKS

In the decade following the collapse of communism no ideological or practical obstacles stood in the way of the global spread of capitalism. Popular enthusiasm for electoral democracy and a market-based economy was so widespread as to permit large corporations to write their own rules of relationship to society. The category Corporate Governance emerged as the rubric under which various theories of the accountability of private power to public interest were developed.

Of a corporation's constituencies, only shareowners have the legitimate power to control their destiny. They profit to the extent of the surplus remaining after all commitments have been satisfied. Shareowners lose when some obligations to other constituencies cannot be discharged in full. Any class so situated should have both the responsibility for creating the "language of accountability" within which the enterprise functions and the authority to do so.

Shareholder activism developed rapidly during the 1990s. At the same time that shareholder involvement became more effective as a discipline to management, forces outside of the corporation loosely coupled under the nomenclature of nongovernmental organizations (NGOs) began strident public protest over the exercise of corporate power. This pattern of protest was manifested in the withdrawal of the Organization for Economic Cooperation and Development's (OECD) draft Multilateral Agreement on Investment (MAI) in the spring of 1998, the demonstrations in Seattle at the World Trade Organization meeting in the fall of 1999, at Davos in the winter of 2000, and in Washington, DC in the spring of 2000. During this period a new class of owners emerged who were informed, motivated, and capable of monitoring the functioning of even the largest transnational corporations.

Table 7-1. *Global Investors: A Profile of the Largest Pension Funds*

Rank	Fund	Country	Billion (in U.S. $)
1	Stichting Pensionfonds ABP	Netherlands	159.7
2	California Public Employees' Retirement	United States	133.5
3	Association of Local Public Service Personnel	Japan	101.3
4	New York State Common Retirement Fund	United States	99.7
5	General Motors Investment Management Corp.	United States	87.0
6	California State Teachers' Retirement	United States	82.6
7	Alimanna Pensionsfonden (Board 1, 2, & 3)	Sweden	80.1
8	Florida State Board of Administration	United States	77.5
9	National Public Service Personnel	Japan	75.6
10	New York State Teachers' Retirement System	United States	71.1
11	Texas Teacher Retirement	United States	69.5
12	Public School Personnel	Japan	67.1
13	Federal Retirement Thrift Investment Board	United States	64.5
14	New Jersey Division of Investment	United States	63.3
15	General Electric	United States	58.7

Out of the class of institutional investors as a whole, the public and private pension funds, a discrete subcategory we call the Emerging Global Shareowners accrued a significant share of the funds and thus of the power to influence policy. In pension systems created by government action in many countries – conspicuously in the United States, the United Kingdom, the Netherlands, and Japan – tax policies have induced individuals to place funds into trust for their retirement. We calculate that the 300 largest pension funds own 15.8 percent of those corporations on *Businessweek*'s roster of the 1,000 largest corporations in the world.[1] It is a percentage ownership large enough to empower the pension class with significant rights under the corporation laws of all industrialized countries (see Table 7-1).

HISTORY OF THE GLOBAL SHAREOWNER

The Global Shareowner is in the process of being recognized and defined. Although the pattern of foreign investment has been common in the West since the 17th century, the beginnings of a class of portfolio investors with world perspective probably came with the introduction of the modern pension system in the United States (Employee Retirement Income Security Act [ERISA] of 1974). This statute created an institutional framework that

---

1. The methodology used in deriving this result is described at length in my forthcoming book for Harvard Business School Press provisionally entitled *A History of Investment*.

provided assurance on questions of the scope of investment authority, custody, delegation, and liability sufficient to permit development of a global investment culture.

Following the Second World War, as American corporations spread their operations around the world, the Global Shareowner followed in embryonic form because these corporations were obligated to provide pension arrangements for their workers in other countries. These pension funds of multinational corporations and institutions were the earliest global investors. Because an elementary principle of pension investing is the desirability of matching liabilities and assets, when General Motors accrued pension liabilities for its Opel workers in Germany it had strong reason to finance pension promises with obligations designated in deutsche marks. Perhaps the most successful early example of this trend was the pension fund of the World Bank, which, under its legendary chief investment officer Hilda Ochoa, frequently ranked at the very top of the list of competitive performers. Success led to imitation.

During the second half of the 20th century, several institutional developments occurred that were critical to the evolution of the modern Global Shareowner: currency and investment restrictions were relaxed and then abandoned by the principal industrial countries, brokerage practices and costs became more efficient and less costly, global custody arrangements (no mean question when dealing with "bearer" securities) matured, the accounting and legal professions of various countries converged toward mutually understandable and compatible standards, and international organizations – in particular, the OECD – began discussion of core international investment "rights" based on the principle that all countries would treat investors, domestic and foreign, alike. At the same time, the burgeoning mutual fund business began to develop country-specific funds, permitting investors to enjoy the benefits of diversification once they had decided to allocate assets to a particular country. The spectacular success of The Japan Fund, selling at a premium over market, encouraged many imitators.

The special characteristics of pension funds such as the Global Shareowner are attributable in substantial part to a new industry of consultants – the Frank Russell companies of Tacoma, Washington is preeminent among them – because the structure of ERISA itself placed a premium on trustees' availing themselves of expert advice. An entire industry of consultants, backed up by the academic work of many of the most highly regarded economists, brought a new and higher level of sophistication to the investment process of pension funds. This sharpened focus, in turn, illuminated differences between general investment objectives and those suitable for "defined benefit" pension plans. Concepts too general for the investing world at large proved useful when applied to pension funds. Because fully funded pensions have a quite different perspective from institutions that focus on maximizing value, mathematical tools, in particular, were developed to evaluate risk and to demonstrate how diversification among economies lowered the risk of the portfolio itself. Investing in foreign countries became a permanent part of the discipline followed by pension trustees not on the basis of a given country's particular appeal but because the process of diversification lowered the risk level of the portfolio as a whole. Pension funds, as a result, can be expected to remain global investors for the foreseeable future.

Although the law itself makes no distinction among kinds of shareholders, relative size, both in assets and in number of participants, provides a strong argument that managers of pension funds should run the enterprise for the benefit of the pension beneficiaries. By formally identifying a coherent object for management duty, we begin to be able to articulate some of the fiduciary relationships – the obligation of owners to beneficiaries, for example – and to identify methods of meaningful enforcement.

The emergence of Global Shareowners as a new element in the evolution of the multinational corporation has provided a governance structure of empowered owners. The question remains of whether these owners can move effectively enough to forestall governments and NGOs from assuming a larger role in the governance of corporations.

CHARACTERISTICS OF GLOBAL SHAREOWNERS

Global Shareowners have characteristics that bear, in important ways, on the discharge of their "legendary function"[2] of monitoring. For example, the Global Shareowners are

- *Universal,* in the sense of owning all companies with shares traded on stock exchanges in all industries;
- *Long term* in holding period (indeed, the pattern of indexation suggests virtually permanent ownership);
- *Global* in outlook with increasingly similar expectations for financial performance and reporting in all countries and the ability to require consistent conduct;
- *Humane* in the sense that their beneficial owners make up a substantial portion of the population and have an explicit human interest in a clean, safe, and civil society as well as in adequate retirement income;

2. James Willard Hurst, *The Legitimacy of the Business Corporation in the Law of the United States, 1780–1970* (Charlottesville: University Press of Virginia, 1970). During the nineteenth century shareholders were essentially involved in the management of ventures and were thought ("legendary") thereby to ground the venture to human scale.

- *Legal* constructs with the scope of their responsibility subject to periodic definition by the legitimate lawmaker rather than flesh and blood human beings with the "thousand natural shocks that flesh is heir to."

OWNERS' RESPONSIBILITIES

Much has been written about the difficulties institutional investors face in the "free rider" problem, of problems of fiduciary prudence and of risk versus reward, of conflicting interests in other relationships with portfolio companies,[3] about the disinclination of the Global Shareowners to expose themselves to the risks of activism, and, not least, concerning current Global Shareowners' utter lack of qualification for the challenge of effective shareholder involvement. We should no longer ask whether institutional shareholders want the responsibility of ownership nor even whether, with their present staffing and configuration, they are suitable to exercise it. Our society cannot afford corporate owners who do not organize themselves to be responsible with the same tenacity and ingenuity they use to assert their own prerogatives. Ownership implies responsibility. Jonathan Charkham and Anne Simpson have made the following observations on responsibility in *Fair Shares: The Future of Shareholder Power and Accountability*:

Before we go further, we must repeat the reason why we believe an obligation is necessary. It is because the good working of the market-based system demands it for economic, social, and political reasons. The economic reason is that there needs to be a mechanism for controlling boards that do not work well so as to prevent unnecessary waste of resources; the social reason is that listed companies are a crucial and integral part of the fabric of a modern society and their success reduces alienation; the political reason is that the limited liability company has achieved its far-sighted originators' aims beyond their wildest dreams, of producing concentrations of power and resources, and that those who exercise these powers must be effectively accountable for the way they do so. The power and influence of the leaders of companies in domestic politics – and indeed internationally – are considerable.[4]

SHAREOWNER ACTIVISM AND VALUE

The pursuit of long-term value optimization requires appropriate attention to the interests of employees, customers, and society. McKinsey & Company has considered this question at considerable length in several recent articles.

---

3. The golden rule of pension fund activism is "Have your pension fund do unto me as you would have mine do unto you."
4. Jonathan Charkham and Anne Simpson, *Fair Shares, The Future of Shareholder Power & Accountability* (Oxford: Oxford University Press, 1999), 224.

One such article, on "The Virtuous Cycle of Shareholder Value Creation," concludes that

> shareholder value is still a controversial topic in Europe, but we believe that embracing it is an essential ingredient of any plan for European economic reform. There is overwhelming evidence to support the view that shareholder value should be the explicit goal of all corporations. A shareholder mindset benefits not only the shareholders themselves, but society at large, setting in motion the virtuous cycle of value creation, job creation and wealth creation.[5]

Shareholder activism can be shown to be profitable. That great investor from Omaha, Nebraska, Warren Buffett epitomizes the kind of monitoring shareholder whose involvement enhances the value of the whole enterprise. Buffett personally salvaged the rogue Salomon Brothers from the bankrupting implications of its illegal activities. He devised a satisfactory structure by which to be compensated for his efforts. Oftentimes – as in his involvement with Champion Paper, Salomon Brothers, or USAir – Buffett will negotiate participation with management through a special class of equity security, these convertible preferred stocks assuring Buffett both downside protection and income as well as upside gain. If he has a better deal than ordinary shareholders, they have a better deal than they had before Buffett's involvement. ("A rising tide lifts all the boats.") The market makes a calculation – the dilution caused by Buffett's preferred position discounted by the rise occasioned by his involvement – of pre- and post-Buffett common stock prices. Although, unhappily, one cannot create a world system based on the availability of an infinite supply of Warren Buffetts, his experience corroborates the worth of an effective monitoring shareholder.

The value and importance of shareholder activists is now recognized on a global basis as former U.S. Treasury Secretary Lawrence Summers said several years ago:

---

5. Jacques Bughin and Thomas E. Copeland, "The Virtuous Cycle of Shareholder Value Creation," *The McKinsey Quarterly* (1997): 156, 167. The European viewpoint is well articulated in a recent article in the *Daily Telegraph*:

> At the core of the debate is the idea that companies are accountable not just formally to their owners but also in less well-defined ways to a group of wider key stakeholders for their actions. This notion has been helped along by the rise in consumer activism as shown in the GM food controversy and, before that, by the Shell/Greenpeace dispute. At the same time the success of companies that proclaim their concern for the community in areas in which they operate, like the Body Shop, has suggested that there is widespread public support for the trend. . . . Today, the idea that a business exists only to serve its shareholders is not tenable. A company is judged not just on its balance sheet but to a growing extent on its corporate character. Does it serve the community in which it operates? Are its products ecologically sound? Does it pollute the environment? Does it do business with undemocratic regimes? (Alan Osborn, "Corporate Citizenship: Heeding the Voice of the Community," *Daily Telegraph*, July 27, 1999).

The priority in Europe, as many people in Europe have recognized, has to be on developing an appropriate domestic growth strategy. That means restructuring companies, allowing *empowered shareholders* to do the work of restructuring. It was these kinds of changes from the bottom up that I think contributed, along with deficit reduction, to the prosperity that we're enjoying in the United States.[6] [Emphasis added]

A company with informed and effectively involved owners is worth more than one without these assets.[7] Individual activists can make an adequate profit that justifies their initiative. Why then can we not sit back, note the ascending activist trend, and confidently expect the market to do its magic?

CONFLICT OF INTEREST

We cannot expect magic because the "market" itself is polluted by mixed messages from government. On the one hand, ERISA provides, in words as clear as language permits, that trustees must consider "exclusively" the interests of beneficiaries; on the other hand, the preponderance of ERISA fiduciaries have other commercial interests with portfolio companies and a pervasive concern not to act in a manner that will be viewed as threatening by CEOs on whose gifts depend the award of lucrative business. There is not a single example over the last 15 years in the United States[8] of shareholder activism or a shareholder resolution publicly identified with a private pension plan or one of its money managers other than the College Retirement Equity Fund (CREF). The U.S. Department of Labor's path-breaking pronouncements requiring trustee involvement are followed not by those it regulates but by others. Shareholder activism, therefore, is not an expression of the 30 percent of total ownership represented by pensions but rather of the 10 percent controlled by public pensions and by the occasional entrepreneur.

Public pension funds – particularly California Public Employees' Retirement (CalPERS) and State of Wisconsin Investment Board (SWIB) – have indeed ensured that important issues are raised, but the public plan system is not credible as the unique element in a constructive activist program. Although not subject to business pressures, public plans are strongly influenced by noncommercial considerations such as holocaust recovery from the Swiss banks for New York City and tobacco investment for New York

---

6. U.S. Treasury Secretary Lawrence Summers on CNBC, July 7, 1999.
7. See *inter alia* <http://www.lens-inc.com>.
8. An outstanding exception in the United Kingdom is the leadership of Hermes CEO Alastair Ross-Goobey in successfully challenging the excessive length of "rolling contracts."

State. Public plans are staffed by civil servants without experience in the business sector and therefore without credibility there, nor, as a political matter, are they in a position to follow through on initiatives. They can raise consciousness of problems, but their own internal political dynamics makes it virtually impossible for even the most committed public plan to allocate resources for lawyers, advertising, and specialists necessary for success in a confrontational context. So long as the private pension system – representing 20 percent of the total outstanding – is allowed to eschew activism and "boycott" the efforts of other shareholders, ownership-based governance will only be marginal. One is reminded of the wise aphorism attributed to a former Commissioner of the Securities and Exchange Commission (SEC). "If CalPERS didn't exist, The Business Roundtable would have to invent them." This cynical comment indicates that corporate hegemony is best served by the appearance of effective regulation and the reality of utter license. Although shareholder activism has been given much credit for increases in competitiveness in particular, the results must be suspect when really critical issues, like mode and executive compensation, are not addressed.

THE PROBLEM OF PROOF

If the language of the ERISA statute is so plain and the evidence of value added through activism so indisputable, why have disgruntled activists not found relief in court? And why has the U.S. Department of Labor not enforced the law? There are several reasons why not, and most of them are grounded in law. There is, for example, the question of proof. How can it be proven that the vote or failure to vote of a single shareholder has caused a specific amount of damage?

But the enforcement part need not be difficult or expensive. The President of the United States should, in a proper forum, articulate a policy that all fiduciaries, but particularly the pension funds governed by ERISA, must concern themselves with corporate practices – including but not limited to the treatment of workers and the environment – that affect the long-term value of companies whose stock they hold. The President should then direct the U.S. Department of Labor, which oversees ERISA compliance, to convene the fiduciaries of the country's largest ERISA-governed plans and ask them to document their policies for voting proxies and for influencing management decisions in the long-term interest of their participants. At this point, the funds should be required to demonstrate that inaction in these areas does not, in fact, destroy value for plan participants. No uninvolved plan sponsor, trustee, or investment manager would risk being put out of the pension business by ERISA provisions. It would not take long to see more assertive voting and proactive discussions about long-term sustainability among shareholders, CEOs, and directors.

One shareholder response that requires minimal commitment[9] is divestment from companies that market dangerous products. The New York State Common Fund has stopped new purchases of tobacco holdings and reduced such holdings to 0.5 percent of the fund total; Florida and Maryland have divested. Many other state and city pension funds are either freezing existing levels or partially divesting from tobacco holdings. Such divestment creates public attention that may be politically useful – it is noteworthy that the sole trustee of the New York State Common Fund is an elected official – but it is difficult to understand how transferring ownership from people who disapprove of tobacco to those who do not fosters a policy of abolition. Beyond this lies a serious question of conflict of interest. Ought the social agenda take precedence over the obligation of trustees to manage for the "exclusive" benefit of plan participants? The U.S. Department of Labor has consistently taken the position that such divestment of tobacco investments is illegal for private employee benefit plans under ERISA. Partly as a result of "outside pressure" (a 10-percent shareholder vote in 1997), the well-regarded Sara Lee Corp. sold its Doewe Egberts Van Nelle Tobacco unit to Britain's Imperial Tobacco in June 1998. Divestiture of stock or of an operating division does not, however, answer the basic question of how stockholder involvement can effectively influence a company's involvement in the political and government process.

CORPORATE POWER AND THE STATE

But what are the Global Shareowners to do when corporate power has gained too much influence over the political process and thereby called into question the legitimacy of the law? Such dramatic circumstances indicate the upward explosion of CEO pay and the use of corporate power to overwhelm monitors and regulators.

The Business Roundtable, an organization composed entirely of CEOs, organized an effective lobbying effort culminating in an actual vote by the U.S. Senate (88–9) on May 3, 1994, directing the hitherto impeccable and

---

9. The commitment may be minimal, but the dollars and cents impact on the beneficiaries may be quite large. Former New Jersey pension fund Chief Investment Officer Roland Machold estimated the costs of South African divestiture at more than a half billion dollars.

independent Financial Accounting Standards Board not to take into account as an expense the present value of executive stock options. As a result, the current level of executive compensation in the United States represents one of the largest – nonviolent – transfers of wealth from one class to another in recorded history. This combination of economic and political power in the pivotal area in which management's conflict of interest (i.e., how much do they pay themselves?) is most acute illustrates the need for constraint on corporate power. In light of the co-optation of government by business in several similar critical situations, there is plain need for accountability by some other entity – one capable of independence and influence. Because business has the power to dominate outside regulators – governmental and nongovernmental[10] – the ultimate restraint must come from within the corporation itself.

The word *corporation* is not mentioned in the U.S. Constitution. The Constitution provides explicit structure within which the power of the state is to be exercised; at the time of the Constitution's adoption this concerned the relationship of the state and the church. Church power, in consequence, was kept out of the ongoing political process by the first article of the Bill of Rights, which explicitly guarantees the separation of church and state. There has been no institutional recognition of the comparable problems presented by corporate power. If, when the Constitution was adopted, the most prominent nongovernmental institutional power in existence was the church, today that most prominent power is the corporation. Yet U.S. corporations have, for more than a century, been accorded precisely the same rights secured for individuals in the Bill of Rights but extended – again, exactly parallel with the rights of individuals – to political speech and contributions.[11] Rather like a separate and distinct system within the state, corporations have thus been treated like enlarged individuals. Baron Thurlow's[12] celebrated aphorism states that corporations "have no body to incarcerate and no soul to save," and yet the United States has chosen to pursue the human simile and pretend that criminal law provides an effective sanction against unacceptable corporate conduct. We have been slow to come to grips with the reality that we have created a dynamic form of life and energy in corporations that requires accommodation in a polity hitherto largely populated by flesh and blood citizens and that these corporations'

---

10. This hyperbole is based on situations like the tobacco industry's May 1998 "rolling" Congress with its $30 million advertising campaign. Although it risks being overstatement, I conclude that when all the corporate ingenuity is focused on a problem, only the shareholders have the raw power to require conduct that is contrary to management's wishes.
11. *Bellotti v. Bank of Boston, Buckley,* and so forth.
12. Once Lord Chancellor of England.

dynamic forces cannot be ignored – among them the momentum to grow and to maximize profits.

There has been no suggestion in the chartering grant by the state that the corporate creature is to have absolute license to "externalize" its functioning on to the state. Nor is there a concept of the computation and allocation of costs and benefits arising from corporations. It is of paramount importance to recognize as a goal the existence of corporations within a society that has full knowledge (or as full as possible) of the impact of those corporations and that also has the uncoerced capacity to enact laws defining the acceptable boundaries of coexistence.

In fostering an ideal framework, where will society find the power to achieve effective compliance? Among the various corporate constituencies,[13] shareholders do have the motive and the power to hold corporate managements effectively accountable. Milton Friedman has provided the orthodox definition of ownership responsibility: "Few trends could so thoroughly undermine the foundations of our free society as the acceptance by corporate officials of a social responsibility other than to make as much money for their stockholders as possible."[14] Only owners, he states, can decide whether and to what extent to defer profits. He requires that value maximization be accomplished "within the rules." In recent times, ownership has been reagglomerated into the hands of relatively few global shareowners.

There is another participant in the drama. Lawmaking in America is a complex and dynamic process with multiple levels of government – laws, proposed laws, regulations, and policies with the full force of government, especially when propounded by a prosecutor with authority to commence litigation. Washington, DC, may command the most attention, but the original proposed tobacco settlement in the spring of 1997 was pioneered by the attorneys general of several states. One of the wisest of these, Richard

---

13. David Korten, *The Responsibility of Business to the Whole*, posted on the Internet, June 19, 1998, <http://iisd1.iisd.ca/pcdf/1997/responsibility.htm–>:

> To ask the corporation to be responsible in some way to a broader set of stakeholders for meeting a variety of often vague and fragmented standards is to deny its nature as an institution designed to pursue a single clearly defined objective for a single interest constituency. It essentially means asking the corporate CEO to be responsible for making value choices on behalf of the corporation's shareholders, customers, and the society beyond profit maximization. Even if the law and the corporate board were to grant a CEO such discretion, what reason do we have to expect she will exercise it to the larger benefit of larger society. To whom and through what mechanisms is a corporate CEO accountable for the exercise of this discretion?

14. Milton Friedman, *Capitalism and Freedom* (Chicago: University of Chicago Press, 1962), 133.

Blumenthal of Connecticut, neatly proposed a model role for American lawmakers in worldwide corporate governance:

In the end, my feeling is that pressure will keep the industry at the table, but looking abroad, that same kind of pressure may not exist beyond the borders of our country. And so, I think in providing a model of how we can make a rogue industry obey the law change the law that it makes society healthful [*sic*]. We can provide an example for the countries of the world who do not have the legal systems that we do here that can vindicate those rights, and we can set a model of what free enterprise really ought to be, not just arbitrarily setting regulatory bounds, but really setting realistic goals that can be met so our society ultimately is the beneficiary and we can truly – as we have said as Attorneys General – save a generation of children who otherwise would become victims now at the rate of 3,000 a day of a lifetime of addiction and diseases that tobacco causes.[15]

Blumenthal poses a conundrum for the Global Shareowners, for it is they whom he addresses. They should not be able to take refuge in a mere transferring of tobacco operations from one society in which they are penalized to another in which they are not. Ultimately, they will have to make judgments that take the global economy itself into account because global shareowners with permanent and universal holdings have no interest in condoning lower standards in different countries. Global Shareowners will have to reconcile themselves to the vagaries of a commercial world in which they either essentially react to the shifts of public will become activists.

Government pressure itself is not self-executing, and, furthermore, Americans have little confidence in direct governmental intervention. The century-long experiments with public ownership of industry in certain countries have failed on many counts (e.g., the pollution standards in Eastern Europe). Global Shareholders will find this involvement a difficult and continuing process – one beset by errors and by the need to reverse and begin again. Nor is there is a formula for comfortable compliance with changing even fickle notions of appropriate corporate behavior. Persistent and respected efforts to restrain power when it threatens individual freedoms may be the only tolerable guiding star. The case of tobacco dramatically illustrates the effect of continuing pressures on corporations to operate within a framework of public acceptance.

POSITIVE CHANGE WITHIN THE SCOPE OF EXISTING LAWS

The absence of any specific mention in the U.S. Constitution of large corporations leaves us without a guide to choosing a public mode for their

---

15. Honorable Richard Blumenthal, Attorney General of the State of Connecticut, speaking at the 25th Anniversary of IRRC in Washington D.C., Spring 1997.

governance. The law regarding trusts may have promise in this regard, but a concept like this is applicable only to a minuscule portion of the population; moreover, GNP may not provide effective control over the publicly traded corporate sector. A strong U.S. president could take the position that adequate authority already exists under the laws that regulate the pension system, mutual funds, and bank trusts. Other possibilities for governance include explicit new laws with enforcement authority in the SEC, the Pension and Welfare Benefits Agency of the Department of Labor, or even in a new agency set up for that purpose.

The ideal equilibrium of the creative tension between management and ownership is unknown, but there should be no reluctance to accept more gradual progress. In the United Kingdom the Department of Trade and Industry has nudged institutional shareholders. Although institutions do not vote in political elections, there are other measures of sensitivity to ownership responsibilities. Enforcement of the existing trust laws may be a place to start to encourage a spacious concept of ownership that will transform corporations into more sensitive global citizens.

8

The Financial Revolutions of the Twentieth Century

ZHU JIA–MING AND ELLIOTT R. MORSS

In the search to understand the power and extent of multinational corporations, an important piece of the puzzle relates to what we call "financial revolutions"; seen in the context of global history, we seek to understand the process of globalization in historical perspective. In dealing with the financial revolutions involved in the dramatic growth of multinationals – especially in the second half of the 20th century – we are telling a story of how capital has been amassed and concentrated so as to finance the kinds of enterprises that characterize the global epoch itself. It is the story of how capital has been, and is, transferred from those who have it to those who have been creating the global enterprises.

In the wake of these revolutions, as the new Leviathans – the multinational corporations (MNCs) – grow in size and influence, so does the pressing need to hold them accountable in ways that go beyond a mere bottom line. That story of accountability has tended to focus on multinationals themselves and thus to neglect financial instruments and institutions initiated by the MNCs or by outside attempts to regulate them that would circumscribe or circumvent their actions.

Much attention has been given to how the information and transportation revolutions have contributed to the growth of MNCs, and how they have provided the necessary infrastructure for a global economy. But the financial revolutions, which have also received little attention, will have a significant impact on the form and rate of MNC growth over the next several decades. The best available comprehensive data on the importance of MNCs is inadequate because data on the financial services industry do not include banking MNCs (see Table 8-1). So, too, "gross product" is a very partial measure of the impact of the financial services industry. Nor do these data adequately measure the influence of MNCs. The influence of consulting firms, accountants, and other professional service organizations is

203

Table 8-1. *U.S. MNCs, 1997: Gross Product and Employment by Industry*

Industry	Gross Product (in billion U.S.$)	Employees (in thousands)
Manufacturing	1,081	12,843
Food	108	1,095
Chemicals	200	1,667
Metals	55	852
Machinery	149	1,839
Electrical	128	1,760
Transport	221	2,443
Other	221	3,187
Petroleum	230	660
Wholesale	69	1,166
Finance	107	1,290
Service	161	3,710
Other	443	6,723
TOTAL	2,091	26,392

Source: U.S. Department of Commerce, *Survey of Current Business, July 1999.*

far greater than these data would suggest. Although the size of these service organizations is not comparable with the largest MNCs, they are influential in the advice they provide to the largest MNCs. They are, moreover, not small: Deloitte Touche Tohmatsu, for example, a medium-sized accounting and consulting firm, has 85,000 employees in 132 countries and grosses $11 billion per year.[1]

In describing these financial revolutions, we limit our discussion of implications to the first decade of the 21st century because the accelerating pace of change makes it extremely difficult to see beyond the next 10 years.

FINANCIAL REVOLUTIONS OF THE TWENTIETH CENTURY

Over the last century the financial sector developed in sophistication and in ability to mobilize savings for a variety of purposes. The following financial revolutions emerged:

1. The institutional revolution.
2. The risk-adjustment industry.
3. Changing money mechanisms.
4. Changing criteria for a good investment.
5. Changing criteria for a strong currency.

1. *The Economist*, November 20, 1999, 86.

1. The Institutional Revolution

Before the beginning of the 20th century, new investments had been financed primarily from retained earnings. Then commercial banks came on the scene, taking money in as deposits and lending it out for investments. Toward the end of the century, in its last two decades, a dramatic expansion occurred in numbers and types of financial institutions – many of them MNCs. Whether the new financial institutions – including insurance companies, pension funds, stock brokers, investment banks, mutual funds, venture capitalists, and financial management companies – were to serve primarily as passive brokers with little impact on global developments or whether they could control the global economy was not apparent at their beginning.

Insurance Companies. Insurance companies, which take in fees and pay out only when events they are insuring against actually occur, amass a large asset base. A recent estimate is that insurance companies in developed countries had more than $7.5 trillion in assets in 1995,[2] and the average annual asset growth rate between 1990 and 1995 was 13 percent. At that same growth rate, insurance company assets in 2000 would have been $13.8 trillion. Insurance assets will continue to increase as insurance services expand in developing countries.

Pension Funds. The pension fund industry, in which funds are accumulated with payments occurring at retirement, has grown dramatically in recent years, and its growth is likely to continue. It is estimated that pension funds in developed ccountries had accumulated $5.2 trillion in assets in 1995 and that, between 1990 and 1995, they grew at an average annual rate of 11.0 percent.[3] By 1999, total global pension fund assets were estimated to have been $13 trillion.[4]

Stock Markets and Brokers, Mutual Funds, and Investment Brokers. At the beginning of the 20th century, there were only two things to do with accumulated funds to earn an income: make a direct investment or loan the funds out, but since stock markets came into their own,[5] and despite a few major downturns (especially the U.S. stock market collapse of the end of the 1920s and the resulting global depression), stock markets instead became an increasingly popular choice. As of 1999 their global value exceeded $23 trillion.

The capitalization of U.S. stock markets has always been significantly greater than that of any other nation. Overall, capital values have increased

2. International Monetary Fund, *International Capital Markets* (Washington, DC: International Monetary Fund, 1988), Table A5.6.
3. Ibid.
4. InterSec Research as cited in *The Economist*, May 20, 2000, 127.
5. It appears that the Muscovy Company of London issued the first equity shares in 1553.

Table 8-2. *Private and Public Net Capital Flows to Developing Countries*

Flow Source	1990	1991	1992	1993	1994	1995	1996	1997
Private flows								
Foreign direct investment	17.6	31.3	37.2	60.6	84.3	96.0	114.9	138.2
Portfolio investment	17.1	37.3	59.9	103.5	87.8	23.5	49.7	42.9
Other	−3.7	58.4	23.8	0.7	−11.7	72.5	76.2	−7.3
Total private	31.0	127.0	120.9	164.8	160.4	192.0	240.8	173.8
Public flows								
External borrowing	22.2	25.7	17.6	18.7	−2.5	34.9	−9.7	29.0
Overall total	53.2	152.7	138.5	183.5	157.9	226.9	231.1	202.8

Source: International Monetary Fund, *International Capital Markets, 1998.*

at a 12.2-percent annual rate, the stock markets of developed countries at an 11.8-percent annual rate, and those of middle-income countries by 15.9 percent. Stock market values in the poorest countries have increased the most – by 27.7 percent annually – because of the lower base. The U.S. stock market, by far the largest, has increased at an annual rate of 17.8 percent. In 1990, capitalization of the U.S. and Japanese stock markets was quite close, but by 1998 the U.S. markets had grown to a value of $11.3 trillion whereas the Japanese stock market was valued at $2.2 trillion – less than in 1990.

Despite their rapid growth, stock markets, at least until now, have played an extremely small role in international finance. In the flow of capital from public and private sources to developing countries, public capital has declined relative to private capital. Thus in 1990, public flow to developing countries represented 22.2 billion U.S. dollars and in 1997 29 billion, but private flow rose from 31 billion in 1990 to 173.8 billion in 1997 (see Tables 8-2 and 8-3). Table 8-3 gives a comprehensive picture of gross

Table 8-3. *International Financial Flows*

Finance Method	1987	1990	1994	1997
Bank loans	91.7	124.5	202.8	n.a.[a]
Euronotes	102.2	73.2	279.8	n.a.
Bonds	180.8	229.9	426.9	388.1
International equity offerings	20.4	14.2	58.1	57.8
TOTAL	395.1	441.8	967.6	n.a.

[a] n.a. signifies "not applicable."
Source: International Monetary Fund, *International Capital Markets, 1995.*

capital flows in billions of U.S. dollars and how they have changed since 1987. It illustrates that, despite rapid growth of stock markets, they, at least until now, have played an extremely small role in international financings.

Until the 1980s, stock brokers served as the primary agents for the buying and selling of stocks. After that, mutual funds took over. They are popular because mutual funds are paid on assets managed rather than on a buying and selling transactional basis and because, in as much as they invest in many stocks, the risk is reduced. By the end of 1998, U.S. mutual fund investments exceeded $5.5 trillion or approximately 50 percent of all U.S. stock exchange assets. U.S. investment banks, which developed as part of commercial banks but were split off in the 1930s when their activities seemed too risky for commercial banks, now primarily help organizations, both public and private, raise money in bond or stock markets or through private placements. Their strengths lie in their extensive networks for raising money.

Investment Management Companies. Insurance companies, pension funds, and mutual funds generate large money pools that have to be invested, and with few exceptions these organizations put all of their efforts into marketing their products and pay others to manage their money. The result has been development of an independent investment management industry. Typically an insurance company or pension fund will invest through several of these organizations and let them compete on a rate-of-return basis. One leading company in this industry, the Frank Russell Company, which is headquartered in Washington State, operates in more than 30 countries and advises more than 600 international clients with assets in excess of $1 trillion. It both manages money for institutions and offers a rating service on other investment management companies to organizations that have financial assets to be managed.

Venture Capital Firms. Venture capital firms, which started in the United States and are now centered in the Silicon Valley in California and Boston, Massachusetts, near top universities that have spawned numerous hi-tech startup companies, are also growing extremely rapidly. This growth, too, is expected to continue. Their key role is in the commercialization of research ideas – more specifically, in finding promising startup companies in hi-tech industries such as medicine and telecommunications. They offer these firms management expertise and financing, and, in return, negotiate for equity shares in the companies. Although their high-risk investments have a failure rate of 80 percent or more, their successes yield very high returns. It is estimated that investments made by U.S. venture capital companies grew in a single year from \$19.2 billion in 1998 to \$48.3 billion distributed among 3,649 companies in 1999. Venture capital firms have now spread to Europe and Asia.

Hedge Funds. Hedge funds were originally investors who saw a market discrepancy that could be taken advantage of to make money. The capital source for hedge funds was and is wealthy individual investors or institutions that are willing to take larger risks for higher returns. If the U.S. dollar were trading at a different rate against the French franc in Paris than in New York, the hedge fund would buy in one location and sell in the other. Such arbitrage remains a major part of hedge fund activities, but they are also now known for taking highly leveraged positions. The Hedge Fund Association estimates that hedge fund assets are between \$200 billion and \$300 billion and that they are growing at an annual rate of 20 percent. The World Bank has invested its own pension money in hedge funds for the past 20 years. According to the World Bank's 1998 annual report, the rate of return on hedge funds has fluctuated dramatically: 7 percent in 1992; 70 percent in 1993. Hedge funds lost money in the next 2 years; they gained 30.9 percent in 1996 and 64 percent in 1997. In 1999, Long-Term Capital Management, one of the largest hedge funds, had to be rescued by its banks.

For every new financial activity, a new set of institutions has emerged. However, with deregulation of the financial services industry in Western nations, the distinctions between commercial banks, investment banks, pension funds, mutual funds, venture capital firms, and insurance companies are breaking down. The enlightened are trying to become future supermarkets of financial services similar to the pattern in the information industry, where telephone companies, TV cable companies, TV satellite companies, TV networks, Internet providers, and computer hardware and software companies are trying to become the single provider of information to individuals and institutions.

The information revolution has opened up many possibilities for the financial services industry. There is, for example, no technological reason why there cannot be a single, global, stock exchange open all the time with purchase and sales prices determined by buy and sell orders managed by computers. The standards now required by different regulatory bodies could be monitored by private rating services such as Standard & Poor's and Moodys. Thus, a stock in full compliance with U.S. Securities and Exchange Commission accounting and information disclosure standards could receive the highest information disclosure rating, whereas a stock that trades on, for example, the Turkish stock exchange would get a lower rating.

Table 8-4. *Various Risk-Adjustment Contracts Outstanding (in U.S. $billions)*

Contract Type	1986[a]	1990	1994	1998[b]
Interest rate futures	370	1,455	5,778	7,702
Interest rate options	147	600	2,624	4,603
Interest rate swaps	388	1,264	6,241	17,067
Currency futures	10	17	40	38
Currency options	39	57	56	19
Currency swaps	173	426	759	2,271
Stock market index futures	15	69	128	321
Stock market index options	38	94	238	866
TOTAL	1,179	3,980	15,863	32,887

[a] The figures for swaps in this column are for 1987.
[b] The figures for swaps in this column are for 1997.
Source: Bank for International Settlements.

2. The Risk-Adjustment Industry[6]

One of the most striking revolutions in the financial services industry has been the emergence of "risk adjusters" – those who change the risk profile of any investment. Perhaps the best-known forms of risk adjustment are insurance and pensions. The client pays the risk adjuster a commission to reduce risk. Institutions and individuals also pay risk adjusters to increase potential return and consequent risk – for example, hedge funds. There has been a dramatic increase in risk adjustment activities over the last 15 years, and much of it has been related to stock market investments, foreign exchange, or interest rates. To get some perspective on the magnitude of the risk adjustment business, consider the following: only $3 trillion in currency trading is needed to finance the world's imports and exports of goods and services annually. There is $1.3 trillion in currency trading daily, and much of this involves risk adjustment.

In early 1995, the combined value of bonds, equities, and bank assets for North America, Japan, and European Common Market countries was $68 trillion. Although a significant part of this activity (see Tables 8-4 and 8-5) has been undertaken by speculators trying to earn income, well over half of this activity probably involved risk adjustment. But what is driving all these transactions?

It works this way. Lufthansa buys a plane from Boeing for delivery in 5 years. Lufthansa earns euros but must pay for the plane in dollars. For a

6. For an account of humanity's increasing ability to manage risk, see Peter L. Bernstein, *Against the Gods: The Remarkable Story of Risk* (New York: John Wiley & Sons, 1998).

Table 8-5. *Contract Turnover (in millions)*

Contract Type	1986	1990	1994	1998
Interest rate futures	91	219	629	760
Interest rate options	22	52	117	130
Currency futures	20	30	70	55
Currency options	13	19	21	12
Stock market index futures	28	39	109	178
Stock market index options	140	119	198	195
TOTAL	315	478	1,143	1,329

Source: Bank of International Settlements.

fee, Lufthansa can find a risk adjuster to guarantee today's euro-to-dollar exchange rate 5 years hence. Or suppose a firm has borrowed money with both interest and principal payments due in dollars. A firm that primarily earns nondollar income might want a risk adjuster to guarantee the borrower against interest and principal fluctuations resulting from changes in the dollar exchange rate. On a more general level of the risk-adjustment business are markets for puts and calls, commodity futures, and derivatives.

In the last 20 years, U.S. bank regulators, fearful that U.S. commercial banks would not be able to predict the movement in mortgage interest rates, took two steps to protect banks from unexpected changes. First, they created a secondary market that banks could sell their mortgages into, thereby eliminating the risk that bankers would guess wrong on interest rates. Secondly, they allowed banks to issue adjustable rate mortgages. So, too, individuals and institutions are willing to pay fees to have their returns and risks increased. Instead of paying $10,000 and a small commission to ensure they will get a specified amount of Hong Kong dollars next year, they might pay $10,000 in commission to buy a much larger amount of Hong Kong dollars next year. This means they have leveraged the $10,000 into a much larger gain or loss. It is possible to get a macroestimate of the change in leverage by comparing the equity capital of banks with their derivatives exposure. For the 25 largest U.S. banks, the leverage ratio increased from 70 in 1996 to 91 by the third quarter of 1998.[7] The increasing risks that banks and other institutions are paying risk adjusters for are becoming of great concern to global financial policy makers, and, as a result, several working committees are considering whether additional safeguards are needed. With the development of secondary markets for a wide array of financial

---

7. International Monetary Fund, *International Capital Markets*, Table A5.6.

instruments, risk-adjustment activities have emerged as the leading business in the financial services sector, surpassing the mobilization of savings for investment opportunities.

3. Changing Money Mechanisms

The role of paper money, coins, and checks is declining. Credit card use is rapidly expanding with the greatest impact in the United States, but it is increasing in Europe, Asia, and Latin America as well. So, too, it is common in a several countries across Europe to arrange for banking institutions to pay regularly recurring bills such as utility charges by wire transfer. The tremendous consumer debt that has been generated via credit cards is not controlled by central banks or other government agencies.

E-Money, or sending money by wire, which was started in 1972 by the Federal Reserve Bank in San Francisco with a transfer of $2 billion, today exceeds $800 billion daily. Online finance itself is off to a slow start in maintaining aggregate demand at desired levels, but, with the growth of the Internet, it is quite likely to become the dominant payment mechanism of Western nations in less than a decade.[8] The purchase of goods over the Internet is in its infancy, but its expanded use will contribute further to the demise of paper money as a payment mechanism.

These changes in payment mechanisms have weakened existing monetary policy tools. This is because controlling the rate of increase in the money supply is believed to be effective in maintaining aggregate demand at a satisfactory level. With changing payment mechanisms, the question is to determine how the money supply is defined. In the early part of the twentieth century, it was thought that defining it simply as money in circulation was adequate. With the expansion in the role of commercial banks, the money supply definition was changed to include money in circulation plus demand deposits. The increasing breadth and flexibility in money mechanisms in use is causing traditional monetary policy tools to lose their effectiveness.[9] In recent years, money supplies, however defined, have increased rapidly in China and in the United States. Traditional economic theory holds that a rapid increase in the money supply at a time of full capacity utilization should result in inflation. However, in China, despite a rapid increase in the money supply, there has been no inflation because significant excess

---

8. A good survey of online banking appears in "Online Finance: The Virtual Threat," *The Economist*, May 20, 2000.

9. For an extended discussion of the weakening of traditional monetary policy tools, see Benjamin Friedman, "The Future of Monetary Policy," *International Finance*, November 1999.

capacity and disguised unemployment have meant that demand could increase without supply bottlenecks and consequent inflation.

The U.S. case is different. Until recently, the economy had been operating for some years at very close to full-employment and full-capacity utilization with no increase in prices as traditionally measured. In somewhat different terms, the wholesale and consumer price indices had not increased appreciably. But these indices only measure price increases in goods and services. What appears to have happened in the United States is that the increase in purchasing power resulting from growth in the money supply went into stock market purchases, real estate purchases, and imports. There was a significant "inflation" in stock prices and in real estate. By the same token, U.S. imports are at a record level. In short, the increase in U.S. purchasing power resulting from a rapid increase in the money supply has not resulted in an increased demand for U.S. goods and services and a consequent inflation in goods and service prices. Instead, the increase in purchasing power has been used to buy stocks, real estate, and imports.

Traditional statistics indicate that the U.S. savings rate is extremely low, but disposable personal income, from which savings rates are calculated, does not include capital gains – realized or unrealized. By starting with the U.S. stock market's value of $11.309 trillion at the end of 1997 and multiplying this by the percent change in the Standard & Poor's 500 index for 1998 and 1999, we can estimate capital gains of $1.945 trillion and $1.749 trillion in 1998 and 1999, respectively. Personal savings rates in the United States were 2.22 percent in 1998 and 1.97 percent in 1999 when calculated in the traditional manner (see Table 8-6). However, when capital gains income is added to the traditional measure of disposible income, and when savings is defined as disposable income minus personal consumption, the savings rates jump to 25.32 and 22.41 percent in 1998 and 1999, respectively.

Table 8-6. *U.S. Savings Rates with and without Capital Gains Income*

Item	1998	1999
Personal consumption	5,849	6,255
Savings	140	131
Disposable personal income	6,286	6,639
Savings rate	2.22%	1.97%
Savings (including capital gains)	2,085	1,880
Income (including capital gains)	8,231	8,388
Savings rate (including capital gains)	25.32%	22.41%

4. Changing Criteria for What Constitutes a Good Investment and a Strong Currency

Until recently, commercial banks determined whether to make a loan to a firm on the basis of the its short-term earnings potential and whether it had assets the bank could seize in the event the firm could not make its debt service payments. So too, with the exception of "bubble" periods, equity valuations were based on short-term earning estimates, which accounts for the popularity of such statistics as the price to earnings ratio. Today, short-term earnings potential seems less important than what sort of hi-tech story can be told about a company. For example, Cisco Systems paid $6.9 billion for Cerent, a small networking startup company with an annual turnover of $10 million that had not made a profit in its 30 months of operation.[10] Moreover, banks no longer worry about the long-term viability of their loans; instead, they earn a commission by selling them off into some secondary market.

Several factors seem to be causing this new orientation to value. The first is the tremendous asset value increase that can be realized by getting a private company listed on a stock exchange. The experts who write the "stories" for such initial public offerings (IPOs) have come to realize how important telling an exciting story is relative to earnings projections: the corporate "concept" and how it fits into a technological revolution is what now sells. The second is that, with the broadening and deepening of capital markets, one can promote a company and then sell it off immediately. In other words, the expansion of secondary markets means that few have to worry about the long-term prospects for an investment. Of course, this is something of an overstatement. Sophisticated investors are reading carefully whatever is being written about companies, and without a believable long-term strategic plan there would be few takers. However, with increasing numbers of individuals investing in stocks, more can be easily fooled by a good story.

Some argued at the end of the last century that there had not been a fundamental change in how assets are valued and that instead we were experiencing a massive speculative bubble.[11] According to historical standards, prices on the U.S. stock exchanges are far higher than they should be. For example, the U.S. stock market value to net worth is 48 percent higher than

---

10. *The Economist*, August 28, 1999, 5.
11. For example, see Richard A. Oppel, Jr., "A Tiger Fights to Reclaim His Old Roar," *New York Times*, December 19, 1999.

its historical average, the price-to-earnings ratio 54 percent higher than the historical average, and the dividend-to-price ratio 63 percent higher than the historical average. But against this, some say that historical valuations are no longer relevant: the massive transfer of assets into stock markets is causing prices to jump as the demand for stocks increases far more rapidly than the supply of stocks to purchase. Supporters of this view claim higher stock valuations will be permanent because of the new demand–supply imbalance.

A derivative of the phenomenon just described was that borrowing was out while the purchase of ownership was in. How quickly things turn around! The 1997 Asian economic crisis was really a story of banks making bad loans. By the end of the last century, the focus was almost entirely on purchasing equity such that, if China did not place restrictions on foreign ownership, large foreign pools of money would quickly purchase ownership control in the best Chinese companies.

5. Changing Criteria for a Strong Currency

In former times, the strength of a currency was determined by its trade balance and domestic rate of inflation. A trade deficit, inflation, or both would weaken a currency. The capital account was viewed as an "adjustment item" with long-term credits regarded as somewhat better than short-term credits. In 1999, the United States was running an annual trade deficit in excess of $200 billion; despite this, the dollar remained a strong currency. What accounted for this change? In part, it was attributable to international financial flows. U.S. government securities and stock markets had been a magnet for foreigners for the previous few years. For example, net purchases of U.S. stocks by foreigners in 1998 were $115 billion, which by itself was more than half of the trade deficit. Another international demand for U.S. dollars stems from its role as the primary international medium of exchange, and its use in this manner continues to increase with the growth in international trade. If enthusiasm over the U.S. stock markets ebbs, or some other currency becomes more acceptable as an international medium of exchange, the demand for dollars will weaken, causing the value of dollars relative to other currencies to fall.

For the last two decades of the 20th century, Germany was second only to the United States as an international trader measured by either imports or exports. This might suggest that the deutsche mark would rival the U.S. dollar as an international currency. However, this did not happen, and the deutsche mark has now been replaced by the euro.

Over the past 25 years, the yen has played a small role in international markets. (Far fewer commercial contracts, bonds, bank loans, and official reserves are denominated in yen than in U.S. dollars or deutsche marks, in spite of the size and performance of the Japanese economy.) Because of large and persistent Japanese current account surpluses, the yen appreciated 250 percent against the U.S. dollar from 1970 to 1994 – an appreciation that should have made the yen popular among international traders and foreign exchange traders. However, the trade surpluses coupled with a Japanese government policy to keep the yen from becoming an international currency have meant there are very few yen available to foreigners for international transactions.

The euro could become a competitor to the U.S. dollar as an international currency. The combined exports and imports of the countries using the euro exceed U.S. imports and exports. When the euro was launched at the start of 1999, it lost value against the U.S. dollar and other major currencies, but this could all change as confidence in the euro grows.

THE TWENTY-FIRST CENTURY: EXPECTATIONS AND SPECULATIONS

As we look ahead into the first decade of the 21st century, we ask how these financial revolutions will evolve, what new changes can be expected, and what are the implications of these changes for MNCs and the global economy? Our own primary speculations for the future are as follows:

1. Financial services, now the largest global industry, will continue to grow in importance as it escapes national boundaries and regulations and is marketed into the emerging nations of Asia and Latin America. The gap between the financial services industry in developed and developing countries will be reduced as the multinational financial services companies market their products globally just as Gillette, Coke, Unilever, and Toyota did in the past. Pensions, insurance, and mutual funds will grow dramatically in the emerging countries just as they did earlier in developed nations. It is likely that by the end of this decade companies offering these services will determine how more than 50 percent of the world's financial assets are invested.

2. Commercial banks, formerly the most important player in financial services, lost their dominant position to the other, less regulated financial institutions: insurance companies, pension funds, mutual funds, investment banks, investment managers, hedge funds, and derivative providers. Competition within the industry now focuses on who can become the "full-service" or "supermarket provider" of financial services. Although banks have slowly begun to offer insurance products, stock brokerage, and securities underwriting, much of the change taking place results from mergers and acquisitions as regulations within the financial services industry are reduced. The merger of Citibank

and Travelers is an excellent example of this trend. The resulting new entity, Citigroup, sells Travelers' insurance and other products through Citicorp's vast global retail network.

Behind the scenes, a new industry of investment managers has emerged. They are hired to find places to invest the large pools of money generated by the institutions discussed above. The business is highly competitive, and these managers are judged on quarterly to 6-month rates of returns.

3. In the past, trade balances and the rate of domestic inflation largely determined exchange rates, whereas capital flows were primarily adjustment items. With the rapid expansion of global borrowing, equity markets, and risk adjustment activities, however, international capital flows are becoming a primary determinant of exchange rates. International economic theory has focused primarily on commodity flows and has had little to say about the growing importance of capital flows. Without coherent economic theory for guidance, policy makers will use various outdated or hit-or-miss actions to deal with instability.

Consider the International Monetary Fund (IMF). It was established at the end of the Second World War to mitigate major fluctuations in exchange rates at a time when the primary cause of exchange fluctuations was rapid increases in a country's money supply in periods of full employment. In such circumstances, the increased aggregate demand resulting from the money supply increases domestic inflation and imports. The IMF would then lend the country money provided it would agree to take certain actions to reduce aggregate demand such as reducing the rate of increase in the money supply.

The 1997 Asian economic crisis, for example, was not the result of excessive aggregate demand (there was excess capacity and significant unemployment in many Asian countries) but of massive short-term capital inflows that resulted from the liberalization of financial and capital markets. Despite wholly different causes and symptoms, the IMF offered the same medicine it provides when a country had been fiscally irresponsible.[12]

4. With the expansion of risk adjustment services, the ability to control financial risks is greater than at any other time in history. On the other hand, the growing importance of international capital flows introduces the potential for financial instability.
5. The venture capital industry has grown rapidly over the last decade in the United States. Venture capital services are extremely valuable because they provide a means by which good ideas can be converted into commercially viable businesses. For venture capital to be successful, it must have direct access to innovative ideas that can be made commercially viable. It must also have

---

12. For an excellent critique of the Fund's role in the Asian Crisis, see Joseph Stieglitz, "What I Learned at the World Economic Crisis," *The New Republic*, April 17, 2000.

access to stock markets where the commercially viable firms can be taken public. One can expect that venture capital will expand to other countries as this venture capital "infrastructure" is established.

6. As economic activity becomes increasingly global, there will be a growing rationale for a global currency. Indeed, most of the foreign exchange contracts are ensuring exchange rates between currencies will remain fixed in a way somewhat analogous to their actually being a global currency. For all intents and purposes, the U.S. dollar serves as a global currency. And so long as foreign exchange users are satisfied with this state of affairs, there is little likelihood that a true global currency will emerge.

In addition to the broad structural changes outlined above, several important changes can be anticipated in response to technological advances.

- It is likely that within the next 10 years there will be a single, computer-driven global stock market that will be open 24 hours daily. The function of government stock market regulatory bodies will be taken over by private information and rating services.
- Payments will increasingly be made by wire with decreasing portions carried out via coins, currencies, and credit cards. This will make monetary policy more difficult to implement as the relative importance of payments mechanisms continues to change.
- As companies worldwide take steps to increase their e-business capabilities, they are realizing it cannot be done without effective credit and financing processes. On-line financing services are being developed to fill these needs. In 1998, 1,200 U.S. banks offered online banking. It is estimated that by 2003, 16,000 banks will offer online services.

These financial revolutions need to be understood if one wants to comprehend how MNCs will evolve and globalization will proceed in the twenty-first century. Our thumbnail sketches of the changes raise questions that need to be answered. Among these questions are the following:

- With the growing importance of international capital flows, should new global regulations be adopted to restrict flows that appear to be destabilizing?
- With the growth in risk adjustment activities, is more research needed to determine whether they should be more closely regulated?
- Should the mandates of the IMF and other international organizations be revised in light of the dramatic changes taking place in the financial services industry?
- As the world moves financially to a global economy, what monetary policy role is left for individual nations? And are we approaching a time when we need a global central bank that could perhaps have different policies for different geographic regions?

9

Multinational Corporations, the Protest Movement, and the Future of Global Governance[1]

STEPHEN J. KOBRIN

Globalization is difficult to define precisely. It certainly transcends economic relations, including social, cultural, and political processes that are enmeshed in a larger "global" order – forms of social, political, and economic organization beyond the pale of the state.[2] Globalization is a transition from a world ordered geographically, in which the basis for economic and political organization was sovereign territoriality, to an aterritorial, networked mode of organization whose present and evolving form is not yet clear. Control over space, national markets, and nation-states is no longer sufficient to ensure control over economic and political activities.[3] The new forms of governance just beginning to emerge lack legitimacy and are poorly understood. Old and familiar modes of governance are becoming problematic, and new institutions more suited to a global age are just beginning to evolve.[4]

THE ISSUES AND PREMISES OF THE ANTIGLOBALIZATION MOVEMENT

Much of the opposition to globalization today is itself a function of globalization led by individuals and groups from disparate geographic locations tied together through electronic networks and common objectives. A sign held by antiglobalization protesters at Davos in 2001 read "Our resistance is as global as your oppression." The emergence of an aterritorial, networked global system is at the root of the problem of legitimacy and power of international institutions and inexorably links both multinational corporations

---

1. The paper on which this chapter is based was presented at the meeting of the International Studies Association in Chicago, Illinois, in February 2001. Lorraine Eden, Virginia Haufler, and Robert Wolfe provided helpful comments on an earlier version.
2. See Martin Albrow, *The Global Age* (Stanford: Stanford University Press, 1997).
3. See Stephen D. Krasner, "Westphalia and All That," in *Ideas and Foreign Policy*, ed. Judith Goldstein and Robert O. Keohane (Ithaca, NY: Cornell University Press, 1993).
4. James Rosenau, *Along the Domestic-Foreign Frontier* (Cambridge: Cambridge University Press, 1997).

(MNCs) and the anticorporate movement in interwoven, global electronic webs.

The relative importance of MNCs in the world economy has increased dramatically since the 1970s. The number of MNCs with headquarters in the 15 advanced countries responsible for most foreign direct investment (FDI) increased from about 7,000 in the late 1960s to 40,000 in the late 1990s. The ratio of FDI to gross domestic capital formation increased from 2 percent around 1980 to 14 percent in 1999; the ratio of the world's stock of FDI to world GDP increased from 5 to 16 percent over the same period.

In the dramatic expansion of MNCs during the 1950s and 1960s, the number of subsidiaries of American MNCs, for example, more than tripled from 1950 to 1967, and the average size of subsidiaries grew by 50 percent. This growth produced a first wave of response about the political, social, and economic impact of the MNC. By the year 2000, 63,000 transnational corporations with more than 690,000 foreign affiliates accounted for about 25 percent of global output. Roughly half of world trade now takes place between units of multinational firms; MNCs coordinate international economic flows and allocate activities and resources worldwide.

The antiglobalization movement of the end of the century and the first years of the next is itself made up of many disparate groups; no one speaks for it. The opposition to the Multilateral Agreement on Investment (MAI) negotiated at the Organization for Economic Cooperation and Development (OECD), for example, included more than 600 organizations in 70 countries – many linked electronically through e-mail and the Internet.[5] Diverse in its concerns and inchoate, the movement nonetheless emphasizes certain broad themes: the growth of poverty and inequality, abuse of human and worker rights, consumerism, and environmental degradation. Inequality – both across and within nations – has increased over the past decade, and the number of people living in extreme poverty (less than $US 1 per day) has declined only marginally in those 10 years.[6] Both might, however, exist independently of MNCs. What is at issue is whether a temporal correlation with globalization, for instance of environmental degradation, implies causality. Though the movement is diverse, it has common targets in international economic institutions such as the World Trade Organization (WTO), the World Bank, and the International Monetary Fund (IMF). "Defund the Fund" and "Break the Bank" have become frequently repeated mantras of the protesting marchers' raucous efforts to disrupt meetings by widespread

5. Stephen J. Kobrin, "The MAI and the Clash of Globalizations," *Foreign Policy* 112 (1988): 97–109.
6. UNCTAD, *World Investment Report: 2000* (New York and Geneva: United Nations, 2000), xvii.

mass marches that block the streets in cities where these global conferences occur.

The power and dominance of multinational corporations inform the underlying and unifying theme of the antiglobalization movement. In Ralph Nader's words, globalization represents an institutionalized "global economic and political structure that makes every government increasingly hostage to a global financial and commerce system engineered through an autocratic system of international governance that favors corporate interests."

Four interrelated and interwoven premises characterize the present criticisms of globalization and the MNC:

1. That there has been a dramatic increase in the power of multinational corporations relative to national governments and civil society. As a result, globalization and its institutions are dominated by corporations: the international economic system is structured to protect and enhance the profitability and power of the MNC;
2. That the global system and international institutions are neither transparent nor democratic; a marked loss of accountability and democratic control has resulted from the shift of power from national governments to the market and international institutions;
3. That deregulation and neoliberalism have extended the scope and power of the market to envelop all aspects of social, cultural, and political life and that nonmarket values no longer matter; and
4. That globalization involves a Western or American consumerist mentality overwashing all – a mentality that has markedly reduced diversity and the availability of local products and a force for homogenization: the "McDonaldization" of the world.

A RELATIONAL GLOBAL NETWORK

The Peace of Westphalia, which ended the Thirty Years War in 1648 and is generally accepted as the end of medieval universalism and the origin of the modern state system, was a transition that entailed the *territorialization* of politics and the replacement of overlapping and interlaced feudal hierarchies by geographically defined, territorially sovereign states. But the globalization of the present world is corrosive of territoriality and of the organization of economic, political, and social life by clearly defined geographic territory. Globalization renders the traditional boundaries between the domestic and international diffuse and permeable, requiring a dramatic reconceptualization of what is meant by "political space."

Globalization entails both deep integration and interconnectedness: networks of relationships among numerous heterogeneous social, cultural, political, and economic organizations. MNCs are the primary vehicles of deep integration. Deep integration reflects the internationalization of production – a shift from trade to investment – and thus a shift from political concerns about border regulations to the domestic regulatory framework at large; it is a major impetus for the blurring of the line that has long separated the domestic from the international.

The emerging world economy – and more generally the global system – is thus relational rather than hierarchical. A networked world economy entails, in turn, a complex web of numerous transactions rather than the more traditional series of bi- or trilateral arrangements between firms.

SYSTEMIC AND STRUCTURAL CRITIQUES

Concern about the impact of such international economic activity predates the term "multinational corporation" first used by David Lilienthal at a conference at Carnegie Mellon University in 1960. Marx and Engels themselves argued that globalization (or at least the bourgeoisie being chased over the "whole surface of the globe") was a consequence of capitalism's need for constantly expanding markets. To Marx and Engels, the internationalization of capital was simultaneously destructive ("all that is solid melts into the air, all that is holy is profaned. . . .") and progressive – a necessary step in the eventual evolution of socialism. The elimination of national industries and universal interdependence is *structural*; it is a property of the system – that is, individual capitalist firms and individual capitalists cannot act in any other way.

Hobson, a liberal not a Marxist, writing just after the turn of the twentieth century, called the international expansion of capitalism through economic imperialism a malfunctioning of the system. The "taproot" of imperialism was the maldistribution of income in the advanced countries, which forced a struggle for overseas markets. The remedy was also systemic: an increase in the purchasing power of the mass of workers. Similarly, Lenin saw imperialism (and by extension the First World War) in systemic terms as a function of uneven and "spasmodic development inevitable under the capitalist system." His briefest possible definition of imperialism was "the monopoly stage of capitalism" with imperialism involving the export of capital rather than goods.

Much of the mainstream criticism of the MNC has dealt with the impact of global firms on states and the state system,[7] the distribution of costs

7. Stephen J. Kobrin, "Soverignty@Bay: Globalization, Multinational Enterprise and the International Political System," in *Oxford Handbook of International Business*, ed. Thomas Brewer and Allan Rugman (Oxford: Oxford University Press, 2001).

and benefits, jurisdictional conflict, and problems of control resulting from asymmetry between an interstate system grounded in territorial jurisdiction and the international network of the multinational firm. The earlier critique was structural and systemic; it did not assign culpability to firms or their managers but to the asymmetry between the scope and organization of international firms and local, territorial nation-states. Solutions proposed often involved increased international cooperation.[8]

A more radical critique of the MNC during the 1960s and 1970s, based on a charge of neoimperialism, was rooted in a Marxist view of the international economy. It identified structural problems implicit in international capital in general, and in MNCs more specifically, as within a global capitalist system.[9]

Theories of neoimperialism assume that dependence and poverty in the developing countries are structural and systemic. Neoimperialism sees national economies and nation-states as subsystems within global capitalism. "Development and underdevelopment, in this view," Osvaldo Sunkel writes, "are simultaneous processes: the two faces of the historical evolution of the capitalist system."[10] The mechanism of control differs from classical theories, in which control of the periphery by the center is established directly through colonialism, and neoimperialism, in which control is exercised though international organizations rather than by a physical presence in economic imperialism through MNCs.

The Report of the Group of Eminent Persons (to the United Nations) concludes that "fundamental new problems have arisen as a direct result of the growing internationalization of production as carried out by multinational corporations." The new problems are seen as structural: "multinational corporations in their present form and dimension are products of the international economic system in which they operate."[11]

Thomas J. Biersteker, however, sees the impact as negative: denationalization of existing industries through acquisition and competition, a detrimental impact on indigenous production, displacement of the indigenous entrepreneurial class and co-option of local nationals as managers of the MNC, transfer of technology that increases dependence on the center and inhibits indigenous technological development,

8. D. K. Fieldhouse, "The Multinational: A Critique of a Concept." In *Multinational Enterprise in Historical Perspective*, ed. Alice Teichova, Maurice Levy-LeBoyer, and Helga Nussbaum (Cambridge: Cambridge University Press, 1986).

9. See Department of Economic and Social Affairs, *Multinational Corporations in World Development* (New York: United Nations, 1973).

10. Osvaldo Sunkel, "Big Business and 'Dependencia': A Latin American View," *Foreign Affairs* 50: 519–20.

11. Report of the Group of Eminent Persons (to the United Nations) 1979, 310, 318.

and displacement of local products by artificially induced patterns of consumption.[12]

The essence of dependency is a shift from the developing to the advanced industrial countries. The dependent developing countries have little, if any, control over critical decisions affecting their economies and their societies. Nor are concerns about dependence limited to developing countries. In his introduction to Kari Levitt's *Silent Surrender*, referring to Canada as a satellite of the United States, Watkins writes of a probable "insidious tendency for foreign direct investment to result in the shift of the locus of decision-making from Canada as host county to the United States as imperium."[13] "The new colonialism," Levitt says, which is "carried by the ideology of materialism, liberalism, and antinationalism," seeks "to disarm the resistance of national communities to alien consumption patterns and the presence of alien power."[14] She argues forcefully that power must be restored to national governments.

Short of revolution, alternative futures – counterfactual scenarios – are far from clear in the literature of the critics. Biersteker believes that the critics assume that state corporations, "an indigenous private sector, or some combination of both," are "feasible alternatives to the multinational corporation."[15]

Richard J. Barnet and Ronald E. Muller's critique in *Global Reach* is in many ways closer to the current wave of protest. Barnet and Muller sees the global corporation as "the first institution in human history dedicated to central planning on a world scale." *Global Reach* argues that managers of global corporations are demanding "the right to transcend the nation-state, and in the process, to transform it." Barnet and Muller see the power of MNCs and their managers as excessive and illegitimate and the solution as a combination of empowerment of national governments and effective international regulation.[16]

These authors see those who run the global corporations as "the first in history with the organization, technology, money, and ideology to make a credible try at managing the world as an integrated unit." Their underlying assumption is that MNCs manage the world to reflect their interests at the expense of everyone else's. "By what right," the critics add, "do a

---

12. Thomas J. Biersteker, *Distortion or Development? Contending Perspectives on the Multinational Corporation* (Cambridge, MA: MIT Press, 1978).
13. Mel Watkins, in Kari Levitt, *Silent Surrender: The Multinational Corporation in Canada* (New York: St. Martin's Press, 1970), xiv.
14. Levitt, *Silent Surrender*, 98.   15. Bierstaker, *Distortion or Development?* 2.
16. Richard J. Barnet and Ronald E. Muller, *Global Reach: The Power of the Multinational Corporations* (New York: Simon and Schuster, 1974), 14, 15.

self-selected group of druggists, biscuit makers, and computer designers become the architects of the new world?"[17] *Global Reach* is concerned with increasing concentration – global oligopolies, central control, the separation of production from territory (the global factory), and the imposition of developed-country consumption patterns on the world (the global shopping center). To MNC managers, any local law or regulation that inhibits the free flow of capital, goods, technology, and so on is an "irrational nationalism" that blocks efficient world economy.

Barnet and Muller argue that neither organized labor nor the nation-state has the power now to oppose the MNCs' own. Neither elected nor subject to popular scrutiny, the MNC managers "in the course of their daily business . . . make decisions with more impact on the lives of ordinary people than most generals and politicians."[18] Among the consequences are dependence, uneven development and thus exacerbation of poverty and inequality, the deterioration of living standards and employment rights, stimulation of inappropriate consumption patterns in poor countries, and promotion of capital flight from LDCs that compound world hunger.

Echoing Lenin's famous phrase, Barnet and Muller ask "What then, can be done?" Their answer is that because the challenge is systemic, so must the responses be: First, compelling MNCs to disclose information to allow national governments to understand the real nature of their transactions; second, "the restoration of certain powers to national governments and local communities to manage their own territory"; and third, on the grounds that the free market is an "historical relic" and MNCs public actors, regulation of MNCs "to restore sovereignty to government."[19]

Barnet and Muller foreshadow arguments of the current protest against "corporate globalization." They focus clearly on MNCs as the problem, citing the decline of countervailing power of national governments and labor; they target firms and managers as individually culpable and assume that the genie can be put back in the bottle – that power can be given back to national governments and that this would be a solution to the problem.

There is, however, much disagreement about the extent to which state power has eroded, and, conversely, how difficult it would be to restore the authority of national governments. Those who may be described as globalization romantics assume that, because globalization is socially constructed, reversing it by restoring full power and authority to national governments is

---

17. Ibid., 13, 25. 18. Ibid., 214.
19. Ibid., 372, 375.

a matter of political will. Global realists believe, on the other hand, that there is a material basis to globalization and that it is irreversible; therefore, control requires reforming international governance and shifting powers back to states where this is possible, thus increasing the benefits of globalization.

The Declaration of the United Nations Millennium Summit takes a similar view, that "... the central challenge we face today is to ensure that globalization becomes a positive force for all the world's people. For while globalization offers great opportunities, at present its benefits are very unevenly shared while its costs are unevenly distributed."[20] Realists ask, Who makes the rules, how are they made, and who benefits from them?

"Corporate globalization" assumes it is corporations that are the dominant political actors of our time, that economic and to some extent political decision making has shifted from national governments to international institutions controlled by corporate interests through international institutions such as the WTO or the IMF, and decision making has shifted from national governments to the corporations themselves through private sector domination of international politics. Lori Wallach and Michelle Sforza claim that "The Uruguay Round Agreements ... create a system of global commerce best suited to large multinational corporations...."[21] Agreements such as the North American Free Trade Agreement (NAFTA) and organizations such as the WTO are seen as a means to institutionalize ever-more extensive charters of rights and freedoms for corporations.

The International Forum on Globalization (ITG) argues that international trade and investment agreements, the WTO, and regional agreements such as Maastricht and NAFTA combined with the structural adjustment polices of the IMF and the World Bank result in weakened democracy and "a world order that is under the control of transnational corporations."[22] Tony Clarke, a Canadian activist in the anti-MAI effort, argues that there has been a silent coup, that "what seems to be emerging is a corporate state that is primarily designed to create the conditions necessary for profitable transnational investment and competition."[23] He believes that corporations and their managers have taken political and economic power from the state and other segments of society to restructure the system to their benefit.

---

20. United Nations, *The Declaration of the United Nations Millennium Summit* (New York: United Nations, 2000), 2.
21. Lori Wallach and Michelle Sforza, *Whose Trade Organization* (Washington, DC: Public Citizen, 1999), 173.
22. ITG, *Beyond the WFO: Alternatives to Economic Globalization* (2001). <http://www.ifg.org/beyondwto.html>. Accessed January 12, 2001.
23. Tony Clarke, *Silent Coup: Confronting the Big Business Takeover of Canada*, <http://www3.sympatico.ca/tryegrowth/MAI_can.html>. Accessed January 12, 2001.

PUBLIC OPINION ON GLOBALIZATION AND ANTIGLOBALIZATION

The large, disparate and, at times, violent protests against globalization in Seattle, Washington and London – "N30," "A16," and "J18" – take their names from their dates. The extent of popular support for these protests is far from clear, though they may reflect widespread angst about the direction that globalization has taken, a sense of a loss of democratic control over outcomes, and a lack of faith in the legitimacy of international institutions.

A *Businessweek*–Harris poll conducted in the United States just after the "Battle of Seattle" found that a majority of those responding (56%) were either very or somewhat familiar with the events surrounding the WTO summit, 52 percent felt sympathetic toward the protesters, and 22 percent viewed globalization less favorably as a result.[24] Americans tend to see globalization (or trade) as "good" for consumers, companies, or the American economy, but "bad" for creation of jobs at home and for the environment. In the *Businessweek*–Harris poll, 64/65 percent said they believe that trade/globalization is good for consumers, 59/65 percent for American companies, and 60/61 percent for the U.S. economy; 57/45 percent considered it bad for domestic jobs and 43/44 percent for the environment.

Other data indicate a similar ambivalence about globalization, multinationals, and free trade. Americans view globalization as a mixed bag of positive and negative elements with 53 percent of respondents in a national poll conducted for the Program on International Policy Attitudes "rating" globalization as positive and 30 percent rating it as equally positive and negative. Although 61 percent believed that the United States should either actively promote globalization or simply allow it to continue, a significant minority (34 percent) believe that it should be slowed down or even reversed.[25] Fifty-four percent said U.S. officials give too much consideration to the concerns of multinational corporations; overwhelming majorities said too little consideration was given to the concerns of the general public (68%), to working Americans (72%), and to "people like you" (73%).[26] In a Pew Research Center Poll in April of 1999, 52 percent stated that globalization

---

24. *Businessweek Online*, December 22, 1999. As Matthew Mendelsohn and Robert Wolfe observe in "Probing the Aftermath of Seattle: Canadian Public Opinion on International Trade, 1980–2000" (Working Paper, School of Policy Studies, Queens University, Kingston, ON, Canada, December 2000), the public often does not have a great deal of information about international affairs in general and trade in particular. Mendelsohn and Wolfe argue that opinion is more latent than real and that "a survey question about 'trade,' therefore, may be asking citizens about something they neither think about nor understand" (p. 13).
25. Program on International Policy Attitudes (PIPA), *Americans on Globalization* (2000). <http://www.pipa.org/OnlineReports/Globalization>. Accessed January 12, 2001.
26. Ibid.

would hurt the average American because of competition from cheap labor overseas and consequent job losses at home. Sixty-nine percent believed that increasing globalization would have considerable or some impact on them "personally." All of the polls just cited were conducted when the U.S. economy was strong and when most respondents were, no doubt, experiencing unparalleled prosperity. A serious economic downturn could, and in the event did, boost the average American's anxiety about the effects of globalization.

ANTIGLOBALIZATION PROTESTS AGAINST THE POWER OF MNCs

Protests against international business and multinational corporations are not new and in fact go back to at least the middle of the nineteenth century, but current protests differ significantly from past protests in several ways. In the past, MNCs have been taken individually to task for specific reasons for "doing something wrong;" thus, worldwide protests were launched against Nestlé for marketing baby formula in poor countries and Shell's actions in Nigeria. However, though criticism of individual multinationals persists (e.g., the protest against Nike's labor practices), much of the concern of the early 2000s has been more general: MNCs are under fire for being MNCs and for their role as primary integrative forces in the world economy. Yet, MNCs and their managers are still seen as individually culpable – if not for individual actions, then for their power – and not as agents of a global capitalism. The perceived demon now is the power of MNCs themselves. Naomi Klein, an articulate and thoughtful anticorporate campaigner, puts it well, noting that it is not now specific injustices but the power and prevalence of MNCs that are under attack.

During the years of apartheid, companies [in South Africa] such as the Royal Bank of Canada, Barclays Bank in England and General Motors were generally regarded as morally neutral forces that happened to be entangled with an aberrantly racist government. Today, more and more campaigners are treating multinationals, and the policies that give them free reign, as the root cause of political injustices around the globe.[27]

So, too, earlier protests against MNCs and globalization were generally academic in origin, for their ammunition consisted more of essays than street dramas. The movement has become more visible and physical. In 1999, 40,000 people took to the streets in Seattle with millions more involved through the Internet and the World Wide Web. The information

27. Naomi Klein, *No Logo* (New York: Picador, 2001), 338.

revolution has made it possible to link geographically dispersed individuals who are concerned about globalization and MNCs. In many ways, the protest movement is now as global and technologically dependent as the firms it opposes; international civil society and the antiglobalization movement are both products of the information revolution. One of the principal reasons for the extent of the antiglobalization movement to date has been the ability to link geographically dispersed groups and individuals with common interests electronically through e-mail and Web sites. The movement is thus inherently electronic. All of the major demonstrations – including the ones in Seattle, Washington, DC, and Davos – were planned and coordinated over the Internet. This may well be a significant reason why the current protest movement stirs a larger constituency than similar protests of the past.

Popular demonstrations against globalization a decade ago were specific: 25,000 European farmers marched in Brussels in 1990 to oppose possible cuts in agricultural subsidies during the Uruguay Round of trade talks.[28] The farmers had direct material interests at stake. But, although the majority on the streets in Seattle were U.S. and Canadian union members worried about the impact of trade negotiations on their jobs, a considerable minority were concerned with broader, more theoretical concerns – with what Jeffrey Berry calls "postmaterial" interests such as the environment, cultural homogenization, and human rights.[29] The present opposition to globalization focuses on social and cultural rather than issues alone.

As a consequence, the new wave of protest may resonate more broadly than those of the past. It may serve as a canary in a mine, warning of widespread, if less than explicit, concern about the process of globalization and the role of MNCs.

ACCOUNTABILITY AND DEMOCRATIC CONTROL

Despite the focus of many critics on returning power to nation-states, the world now faces serious problems that are inherently international, not national, in scope: global warming, acid rain, AIDS, drug trafficking, nuclear proliferation, and world peace. Each requires international cooperation through multilateral agreements, international institutions, or both; none can be dealt with successfully at the national level. Many in the antiglobalization movement accept this reality. Lori Wallach, for example, writes that

---

28. Peter Torday and David Usborne, "Farmers Riot as World Trade Talks Head for Collapse," *Independent* (London), December 4, 1990, 22. (Retrieved electronically.)
29. Jeffrey M. Berry, *The New Liberalism: The Rising Power of Citizen Groups* (Washington, DC: The Brookings Institution, 1999).

"there need to be international rules, no doubt – again, we're not calling for autarky . . ."[30]

The perceived loss of accountability and democratic control as the decision-making process shifts from national governments to international institutions like the WTO, the World Bank, and the IMF is an overriding concern of many in the movement. As the New Economics Foundation asserts, "None of the problems thrown-up by globalization . . . can be effectively tackled without accountable and representative institutions for global governance." Decision making is perceived as having shifted from open and democratic national governments to a murky and much less democratic set of poorly understood international institutions. Thus, The Public Eye on Davos, a joint effort of several nongovernmental organizations (NGOs) to challenge the 2001 Annual Meeting of the World Economic Forum, described a cabal of the world's elite at Davos that "shape opinions and take decisions affecting the whole world in an environment de-linked from the earthly constraints of democracy, transparency and accountability."

The controversy surrounding globalization has spawned a renewal of interest in the work of Karl Polanyi – particularly his *The Great Transformation*[31] – which maintains that history indicates that self-regulating markets are not sustainable and that markets must be embedded in the social and political order to survive. In a postmodern world system, however, the appropriate social and political order in which markets are to be reembedded is problematic.

GLOBALIZATION, CONSUMERISM, AND HOMOGENIZATION

During the trial of Jose Bove, the French farmer and antiglobalization activist who smashed McDonald's, protesters carried banners that proclaimed "The World Is Not for Sale." Globalization has become synonymous with neoliberalism, deregulation, and the extension of the market to virtually all areas of social life: health care, education, and consumer protection, among others; the antiglobalization and anti-MNC movement is as much a protest against neoliberalism and commoditization of social life as against globalization itself. The argument from commoditization is that most aspects of society and social life would be more effective and efficient if they were subject to the discipline of the market – that, to paraphrase Robert Kuttner, all life should be taken as economic life and organized as a pure

---

30. Quoted in Moses Naim, "Lori's War," *Foreign Policy* 118 (2000): 28–57.
31. Karl Polanyi, *The Great Transformation* (Boston: Beacon Press, 1977).

market.[32] Neoliberalism is seen as support for the removal of barriers to free movement of goods and capital around the globe. But whether open borders with unrestricted flows of goods (free trade) and capital (both short term and long term) bring benefits is far from clear. Critics point to markedly negative effects on workers, the environment, and disadvantaged groups in both poor and rich countries. William Greider sees it as a race to the bottom – as a flow of manufacturing and jobs to the poorest countries, where the wages are lowest and working conditions the worst. In an argument parallel to Hobson's, he asks if the system is sustainable if jobs are transferred to workers who do not make enough to buy the products they produce.[33]

Globalization and multinational corporations are much more visible than they were in the past. Telecommunications link the world instantaneously, and images are an immediate and universal currency. Globalization, no longer intangible, is the McDonald's restaurant, the Benetton store, the Nike shoes. One of the world's largest advertising agencies has gone so far as to declare that belief in consumer brands has replaced religious faith as the thing that gives meaning to people's lives.[34] Global brands, intended to be visible and unforgettable, are obvious symbols of the spread of consumerism and the market and are seen as threats to local cultures and ways of life. Global brands, which contribute to "global culture," reinforce concerns about homogenization and make who the "they" are very clear. Seemingly innocuous intrusions of foreign culture can serve as larger symbols such as when Valentine cards were burned in Bombay on Valentine's Day 2001 as a protest led by the Hindu Shiv Sena party against a Western tradition seen as a violation of Indian culture.[35]

To many, globalization is an expansion of American consumerism throughout the world resulting in increased homogenization of goods and with replacement of local products and local ways of life by mass-produced and mass-advertised consumer goods. Jose Bove gave as a reason for trashing McDonald's that it is such a symbol: "In each McDonald's in the world, you eat the same thing. It is exactly the same kind of standardization of food in France and Asia and America and Africa. It is always the same."[36]

---

32. Robert Kuttner, *Everything for Sale: The Virtues and Limits of Markets* (Chicago: University of Chicago Press, 1999).
33. William Greider, *One World, Ready or Not: The Manic Logic of Global Capitalism* (New York: Simon & Schuster, 1997).
34. Richard Tomkins, "Brands Are the New Religion Says Ad Agency," *Financial Times*, March 1, 2001, 4.
35. "Valentine's Day Massacre, London," *Financial Times*, February 14, 2001, 1.
36. Quoted on *Nightline*, "A New French Revolution," New York, ABC News, August 29, 2000. <http://abcnews.go.com/onair/nightline/transcripts/n100829_trans.html>.

Globalization, deregulation, and homogenization of products, life styles, and culture are interlinked. In *No Logo*, Klein relates globalization and global branding to "another kind of global village, where the economic divide is widening and cultural choices narrowing." She argues that multinational corporations and global branding are transforming culture into "little more than a collection of brand extensions-in-waiting . . . and that in turn, is a function of deregulation. . . . At the heart of this convergence of anticorporate activism and research," Klein writes, "is the recognition that corporations are much more than purveyors of the products we all want; they are also the most powerful political forces of our time."[37]

COUNTERVAILING POWER OR ALTERNATIVE APPROACHES?

From the end of the Second World War perhaps through the 1970s, national governments and labor unions provided effective countervailing power to the power of the private sector, but, since the 1970s, both have lost power whereas that of the MNC has grown.

Labor union membership in the United States declined precipitously from a peak of 35 percent of workers in the 1950s to 13.5 percent in 2000.[38] Meanwhile, internationalization of production, mobility of capital, formation of alliances that allow rapid shifting of business functions, and international outsourcing have compromised labor's bargaining clout.

Similarly, the mobility or potential mobility of capital has compromised the bargaining power of national governments. Corporate tax revenue as a proportion of total revenues has fallen in the United States and has declined relative to the share of corporate profits in all of the OECD countries. Further, given the scale and complexity of technology and the trend toward research and development alliances, national governments have become increasingly dependent on MNCs' international operations to sustain their technological competitiveness.

In the ordered and predictable Cold War era in which the overriding issue was security, the international system was structured around the two strongest nations: the United States and the U.S.S.R. The current world order, evolving as a complex network, is much less ordered and predictable. There is increasing awareness that we live in a complex world with no one in charge, leading to an increase of angst and uncertainty expressed,

37. Klein, *No Logo*, xvii, 330.
38. Steven Greenhouse, "Unions Hit Lowest Point in Six Decades," *New York Times*, January 21, 2001.

for example, in the accelerating protests against globalization and its most visible actors – the MNCs.

Although the end of the Cold War was not the "end of history," it markedly loosened the grip and explanatory power of Marxist and Socialist megatheory and all macrostructural explanations for events and for solutions to megainternational crises like the environment. There are marked disagreements about the form capitalism should take and about the limits of the market, and as yet there are no serious contenders for a new model of the organization of economic activity. When we are all inside the tent, it becomes difficult to see clearly. It is easier to ascribe negative outcomes – the dark side of globalization – to the motives and actions of individual actors such as MNCs and their managers than to prescribe positive remedies.

Globalization entails a systemic transformation of the organization of politics and economics from the modern state system grounded in sovereign territoriality to a still unclear mode of organization that will entail nonterritorial, transnational governance structures. It is a period characterized by what James Rosenau calls "governance without government."[39] Although many of the international institutions themselves, such as the WTO, are representatives of democratically elected governments, this fact is not well understood and often not transparent.

A good part of the angst felt by many about globalization may be explained by an increased sense of dependence and by a loss of control over events that affect one's life directly or indirectly. It is difficult to see how the democratic process and, particularly, participatory democracy can function at the international level. Although civil society groups in the antiglobalization protest movement, including several NGOs, can serve as a countervailing force to MNCs, there is no reason to assume that they are any more broadly based or accountable to national publics than are the MNCs themselves. Nor is there any assurance that such protest groups would make the process more effective, fairer, or more democratic. The future of participatory democracy in a global system is far from obvious or assured. Indeed, there is a real danger that international governance will come to replicate the control of American interest group politics over public policy in an National Rifle Association of global governance.

Charles Kindleberger, the economic historian, once said that nation-states may be about the right size politically but are too small to be meaningful economically and too large to be meaningful culturally. Yet, it is very clear

39. James Rosenau, *Turbulence in World Politics* (Princeton: Princeton University Press, 1990).

that existing institutions of global governance are not yet meaningful to most people and lack political legitimacy, although a large and growing number of significant problems can only be dealt with internationally. The task is to resolve the negative consequences of globalization through a governance structure responsive to a wide range of needs and concerns and consistent with effective participatory democracy. Both globalization and the antiglobalization protests have to be taken seriously.

Although any phenomenon is socially constructed – at least in part, there is a very real material base to the global world system. The dramatic increases in the scale of technology, the internationalization and integration of production, and, especially, the digital revolution and the emergence of an electronically networked world economy will be impossible to reverse. National governments have lost power because they have lost the capability to deal unilaterally with many of the critical problems of our time. Turmoil and uncertainty are to be expected well into the future, for globalization will certainly not take a linear or smooth trajectory. Its genie cannot be put back into the bottle.

The reasons why globalization has come about matter. Is globalization a function of material conditions – of underlying technical and economic change – or is it socially constructed, an artifact of the way we have chosen to organize political and economic activity? Should one agree with Marx that " . . . neither legal relations nor political forms could be comprehended whether by themselves or on the basis of a so called general development of the human mind, but that on the contrary they originate in the material conditions of life . . ."[40] or with Mark Lichbach and Paul Almeida that "Globalization . . . involves a conscious process of restructuring and reconstituting the global political economy – molding international, regional, national, and local institutions to serve the increasing economic integration of the world"?[41]

Although there is marked disagreement among antiglobalizers about the nature of globalization and feasible solutions to its problems, they are likely to agree that poverty, inequality, and abuse of the environment are caused, at least in part, by "corporate-dominated" globalization. At best, there is an assumption that the cost-to-benefit ratio can be redressed through social

40. Karl Marx, *A Contribution to the Critique of Political Economy* (New York: International Publishers, 1970), 20.
41. Mark I. Lichbach and Paul Almeida, "Global Order and Local Resistance: The Neoliberal Institutional Trilemma and the Battle of Seattle," Working Paper, University of California, Riverside, February 26, 2001, 5.

control of the process and at worst that the new liberal paradigm and globalization itself are inherently flawed and must be stopped or even reversed.[42]

Poverty, inequality, and the environment are critical issues of our time. The question of their causal relation to globalization and MNCs is complex and contentious and will not be dealt with here. My objective is to compare the current opposition to the MNC to earlier efforts and to try to understand whether, and why, the anti–MNC and antiglobalization movement resonates more widely now than in the past. Those objectives will best be served by dealing with objections to globalization and MNCs at a somewhat more abstract and less specific level of analysis.

42. Stephen Buckley, "Foes Take Moderate Tack on Globalization; Rhetoric Restrained at Brazil Meeting," *Washington Post*, January 27, 2001.

Conclusion

A long stretch of time exists between the first of what may be called multi-national enterprises, such as the East India Co. and the Hudson Bay Co. of the seventeenth century, and the multinational corporations (MNCs) of today that we are calling the new Leviathans. In the case, for example, of the East India Co., it was a government unto itself, exercising state functions as well as economic ones in the course of its existence. Such enterprises have changed shape, grown enormously in number, and shifted from monopoly concerns to market-driven entities.

What is constant is the presence of change whose pace has rapidly increased in the last half century or more. It is not only the MNCs that have changed ceaselessly but the context in which they now operate. That context is a process of globalization that has taken on dimensions hitherto unknown. One such dimension is consciousness. The coining of the term "globalization" in the 1960s and 1970s is itself testimony to the newness of the new globalization.

We have tried, in the Introduction to this volume, to give some idea of how this new globalization can be studied. That is what New Global History is about. It is made up of many parts that must be brought into conjunction with one another. The MNC, we have argued, is one such part. It plays a major role in the developing process of globalization and can best be studied in the larger context it has helped create. Such an approach, we recognize, may dismay those who wish for a strict interpretation of the subject that limits it to economic or business analysis; we can only disagree, or rather point out that our interest is in the MNC not only in itself but especially as it plays its larger role in the emerging global society.

There are other ways of aiming at the same goal. The anthropologist Arjun Appadurai arranges the context of globalization in terms of relationships among five dimensions of global cultural flows. He identifies ethnoscapes, mediascapes, technoscapes, financescapes, and ideoscapes. As he remarks, "The suffix *-scape* allows us to point to the fluid, irregular shapes of these landscapes, shapes that characterize international capital as deeply as they do international clothing shapes."[1] Some view this description as fanciful, but it effectively calls our attention to interrelations among the diverse dimensions. The techno- and the financescapes are closest to our own focus on the MNCs.

A more familiar way of talking about today's globalization is pursued by the sociologist Manuel Castells. The subtitle of his three-volume work devoted to the Information Age, "Economy, Society and Culture," reflects his view that these three are intrinsically related — both to one another and also to the overall phenomenon of globalization. The key words in his analysis of globalization are information revolution and the network society. He, too, talks about flows, but they are principally flows of information. Needless to say, all parts of his analysis can be applied to the subject of the multinational corporations.

We have focused intently in this book on the MNCs, and in its chapters attention is given to the economy, society, and culture, as in Castells' formulation, and to certain common themes and pivotal questions. Many more could be imagined, and further research, we hope, will be devoted to expanding and exploring such themes and questions.

Almost at random, we indicate several significant inquiries that should be pursued. What is the effect of the MNCs, for example, on the quality of life? Obviously, this question must be dealt with on many levels, ranging from the local to the global, and must involve a consideration of industrial ecology and issues of North and South. Attention must be given, too, to the differential effects on various segments of society; the effects on the worker, for example, as Neva Goodwin points out, have been seriously neglected.

A closely related concern is the normative one. As we would phrase it, how much good and how much harm has resulted from the MNCs? This answer, too, must be provided in nuanced and segmented form. In general terms, we must inquire into the relation of MNCs to matters of poverty, inequality, the environment, and so forth. More specifically, one might engage in sustained discussion about the effect, for instance, of Nike

---

1. Arjun Appadurai, *Modernity at Large. Cultural Dimensions of Globalization* (Minneapolis: University of Minnesota Press, 1996), 33.

in Vietnam: exploiting depressed workers or giving them and their country a chance to improve their condition marginally.

One might inquire further whether MNCs create or replace trade, export or create jobs, or distort or direct exchange. Are they truly multinational or merely extensions of a national corporation? Are they capable of taking on more citizenship-like roles and in what ways? What are the directions in which they are headed, and is the shift to finances and services and the attendant risk adjustment, as announced here by Zhu and Morss, the last word in regard to MNCs' role in the process of globalization? And is that process itself accelerating or on the edge of a decline similar to that which followed the late-19th-century wave of economic globalization?

Merely to raise such questions is to indicate the importance of further research. It also reveals that our authors have not come to common conclusions but have offered diverse points of view on related diverse themes. Nevertheless, this book will have partly succeeded if it helps set up certain significant signposts pointing to promising directions for future work. It will truly have succeeded if it orients future work on MNCs in terms of the New Global History perspective that has inspired this book. In that case, both subjects – MNCs and globalization – will take on new dimensions in which each enhances our understanding of the other.

No one doubts that multinational enterprises have played a central role in creating today's global economy. That economy first appeared and flourished in the last two decades of the 19th century and the first 30 years of the twentieth century. Then, with the onslaught of the world's first global economic depression, the global economy began to disintegrate. It was further shattered by the world's first modern global war. A second global economy only began to emerge in the 1970s some four decades later.

Many students of the MNCs, as well as of globalization, wish to stop there with the economic factor. Thus, they sometimes conflate the fact that, by certain measures, global trade and investment were greater from the 1870s through 1890s with the assertion that there is, therefore, nothing new about globalization today. This is to mistake a part for a whole. It is to focus solely on the global economy and not on the emerging global society. In that global society – and here is the grain of truth in the Cyclopean vision of economists and their confreres – the economic is indeed extremely powerful. And as part of that power we must recognize the centrality of the MNCs themselves.

As the Introduction indicates, our inquiry is directed both at attaining greater understanding of the MNCs by placing them in the larger context of present-day globalization, as we have defined it, and at achieving a greater comprehension of the globalization process by acquiring better knowledge of one of its essential components, the MNCs. This is an initial attempt – a foray into certain parts of this extensive topic – with the hope of indicating places where further exploration is needed. Others, of course, have been to many of these places before us and have staked out claims and raised their flags but not necessarily with the concerns we have primarily in mind. For our part, we are trying to bring together the perspective of New Global History and the work already done on MNCs, recognizing that we are mostly raising questions rather than providing answers – definitive or otherwise.

Work of this sort, as befitting its subject, must be interdisciplinary (to invoke that overused but essential term). The new body politic of our Leviathans must be viewed as a multidimensional phenomenon. It is made up of economic, managerial, political, social, cultural, and other parts – all of which need to be examined separately and as they interact. These parts arouse the interest of those who work in economic history, business history, political economy, international relations, anthropology, politics, and many more disciplinary areas as well as those who try to bring these interests together in the sphere of globalization. Those concerned with the interdisciplinary reach face a problem of rhetoric because each discipline has its own specialized language and perspective. Thus, there is also a need for translation across discipline lines as we seek to reconcile particular approaches with the "global" one of globalization itself.

Our task is made easier by identifying common themes and recognizing pivotal questions, some of which are systematically addressed in the individual chapters and others merely suggested. One major theme is the relation of MNCs to the state system. In the eyes of many scholars, MNCs and the globalization they foster can, and perhaps will, lead to the withering away of the state. The MNCs, of course, are not alone in transcending national boundaries and thus calling into question the sovereignty of the nation-state: all the other factors we cite as part of the globalization process tend in the same direction. Yet, to leap to this conclusion – the disappearance of the state – is to tackle the question in the wrong way. Abjuring such a black-white decision, we must ask rather, What actual effect does the MNC have on the state, both supporting and undermining its sovereignty, and what role does the state play in the expansion of MNCs? Research must revolve around questions of more or less and in what ways.

For example, through specific government policies, national markets have been opened and the forces of globalization have been allowed relatively free play. It is as a result of competition and collusion between national and global elites that decisions have been made. It is the state, as well as nongovernmental organizations and other institutions, that raises the question whether, and how, MNCs should be regulated globally and domestically. These are hardly the tasks of a withering state. They are the actions of a changing state operating in an increasingly global society.

Other themes and questions relate to governance within the MNCs. How do MNCs handle their responsibilities both to society and to their shareholders? How do they exercise corporate citizenship, and what are the possibilities for a better fulfillment of this exercise? How do they reconcile short- and long-term consequences of their pursuit of profit? Can they and should they be affected by investors like pensions and insurance companies whose time horizons may differ from that of the CEO and his or her personnel? And how can these other constituencies get into the act of corporate governance?

Behind such questions may be disagreements on the nature of the MNC itself. Disagreement, in turn, may relate to different interpretations of history and hopes for the direction in which it will go. It may relate also to the weight given to workers and other groups in society – and not management alone – in setting the goals of the corporation. A related theme involves the global and the local, the question of hierarchy and social structure, and, at a slightly further remove, the issue of whether the corporation is fostering homogenization or heterogeneity (a moment's reflection suggests both, not one or the other).

The chapters of this book perforce reflect a skewing of material and viewpoint – that is, an emphasis on the MNC in the context of the United States along with a significant look at Japan – that further work will need to transcend. In the debate over whether globalization is merely a synonym for Americanization (or at best Westernization), we do not accept this equation of the MNC and the United States, but we do recognize our vulnerability to a charge that our own emphasis here on MNCs in the American mode betrays our larger conclusion. We can only plead for future work with an even more global outlook.

The authors of the chapters in this book offer a rich and wide-ranging view of the rise and provenance of the new Leviathans of our time. They contribute to a discourse with a new tone: looking at MNCs in a broad and interdisciplinary fashion that is infrequently encountered. The discourse takes place in the frame constructed from the very process of globalization and stretches that frame even farther as we view it historically, systemically, and analytically. In sum, though there are other important actors that still need to be explored, we have entered the scene of the new globalization in a very special way: through the persona of one of its preeminent actors, the multinational corporations of our past and present times.

Index